Seduced and Abandoned

Related titles in the Cassell Sexual Politics list are:

Broadcasting It: An Encyclopedia of Homosexuality on Film, Radio and TV
Keith Howes

Male Impersonators: Men Performing Masculinity
Mark Simpson

Out in Culture: Gay, Lesbian and Queer Essays in Popular Culture
Edited by Corey K. Creekmur and Alexander Doty

Queer Noises: Male and Female Homosexuality in 20th Century Music
John Gill

What Are You Looking At? Queer Sex, Style and Cinema
Paul Burston

Seduced and Abandoned

Essays on gay men and popular music

Richard Smith

CASSELL

> For a catalogue of related titles in our
> Sexual Politics/Global Issues list
> please write to us at the address below:

Cassell plc
Wellington House   215 Park Avenue South
125 Strand   New York
London WC2R 0BB   NY 10003

First published 1995

British Library Cataloguing-in-Publication Data
A catalogue record for this book is available from the British Library.

ISBN 0–304–33343–3 (hardback)
      0–304–33347–6 (paperback)

Typeset by York House Typographic Ltd, London
Printed and bound in Great Britain

Contents

For Peter Newton,
thanks for seducing me

About the Author

Richard Smith is a freelance writer and cultural enigma. Born in Oxford in 1968, he was 'educated' at Dr Challoner's Grammar School in Amersham, and Sussex University – he left after two years, becoming its most noted drop out since Billy Idol. After a long spell claiming unemployment benefit (which *you* paid for with *your* taxes) he began working as a freelance journalist.

He has been a regular contributor to *Gay Times* since 1990. *The Observer* last year praised his music writing for the magazine as 'some of the sharpest pop critiques today'. Richard is held in a similarly high regard by *Gay Times* readers who have called him 'a prat', 'a wanker' and 'the sort of person oxygen is wasted on'.

His work has also appeared in *Melody Maker, MixMag, Muzik, The Guardian, Time Out, Deadline,* Australia's *Outrage,* America's *Out,* and *Capital Gay.* He has also written for the Health Education Authority, Release, Project LSD and *The Guinness Encyclopedia of Popular Music.* His career in broadcasting began in 1993 when he was part of the team behind BBC Radio One's lesbian and gay series, *Loud and Proud,* and may well have ended when his 1994 documentary on drugs and pop, *Lost in Music,* was disowned by Radio One. They thought it 'disgraceful' and that it 'glamourized drugs' and promised the nation that 'nothing similar would be allowed to happen again'.

His essay on cross dressing in popular music appears in *Drag: A History of Female Impersonation in the Performing Arts,* and he is now writing a history of homosexuality and pop: *We Have Come for Your Children,* to be published by Cassell. Essentially a sad and lonely man, Richard collects Bart Simpson dolls and in 1993 achieved his ambition of appearing on *The ITV Chart Show* (dressed as a policeman) in the video for Huggy Bear's 'Pansy Twist'. He is currently trying to find a pop group stupid enough to let him appear on *Top of the Pops* with them.

Acknowledgements

The biggest thank you goes to Peter Burton for his encouragement and friendship over the last five years. Especially over the last six months. Hugely big thank yous are also sent spinning out to Sebastian Beaumont, Steve Cook at Cassell, Alex Gerry, Andy Medhurst, my mum and my sisters; Idris Moudi, Mark Ovenden, Tom Sargant, Michael Tomkins and Seb Wright. And to Special Bart, Ben, Joe and Ruby.

Thanks to everyone who agreed to be interviewed, but especially to Jon Ginoli, James Horrocks, Mixmaster Morris, Nick Raphael and Jon Savage.

The following have all given me information, opinions, addresses, phone numbers, records, books, unsubstantiated gossip, encouragement or help, or had conversations with me that helped to shape these essays: David Alderson, Martin Aston, Jeremy J. Beadle, Dave Bennun, Boy George, Steven J. Carter, Murray Chalmers, Rose Collis, Jayne County, Dave Davies, Fred Dellar, Jonathan Dollimore, Drako, Malcolm Duffy, Elvina Flower, Matthew Glamorre, Ed Heath, Warren Heighway, Stewart Home, Robert How, Inger, Julian Hyde, Jeremy Joseph, Chris Kelly, Martin Kelly, Graham Knight, Wolfgang Kuhle, Matthew R. Lewis, Little Mick, Simon Lovat, Judy Lyons, Jay McLaren, James Maker, Joe Mills, Richard Norris, Peter Paphides, Simon Price, Colin Richardson, Damon Rochefort, Johnny Rogan, Nicholas Saunders, Phil Savidge, Eileen Schembri, Bill Short, Alan Sinfield, David Smith, Greg Smith, Ben from The Stud Brothers, Peter Tatchell, David Toop, Miss Nicky Trax, Tony Warren and Hayden Wayne.

Thanks also to the late Kris Kirk, Denis Lemon and Little Dazzle. I miss you.

'Back in the YMCA' is based on an original joke I once made in *Time Out*. The version of 'Bad?' that appears here is an updated version of the piece that ran in *Gay Times*. The piece on Queercore is adapted from 'Queer, There and Everywhere' (*Melody Maker*, 23 October 1993). 'Little Town

xii: *Acknowledgements*

Flirt' is based around 'The Great Maker Sex Debate' (*Melody Maker,* 12 December 1992) which was co-chaired by Simon Price, The Stud Brothers and Cathi Unsworth. 'Ambisexuality' appears here with a final section that was cut from the piece that ran in *Melody Maker* by a very busy sub-editor.

He hit me . . .
And it felt like a kiss.

The Crystals

Foreword

THERE are many books on the market which, quite rightly, pay pop music the compliment of taking it seriously. But, too often, 'seriously' becomes 'solemnly', or, worse still, 'pompously', and the end result is unavoidably reminiscent of those 1970s progressive rock 'concept' albums, where pop music congratulated itself on the fact that it had grown up. This book is not 'grown up'. It pouts and it flounces and it sulks when it doesn't get its own way. It is reckless, spiteful, delirious and magnificently obsessed. It is not an Emerson, Lake and Palmer album of a book, but a jukebox stuffed with Motown singles. It is a scrapbook of love letters, a catalogue of depravity, a case study in devotion, a settling of scores and an autobiography you can dance to. If Roland Barthes had ever made a record with Little Richard, this book is what it would sound like.

There are many books on the market about homosexuality which, quite properly, are fuelled by fury and indignation at the excessive oppressions visited upon us by heterosexual society, and which advocate programmes of campaigning, education and direct action in order to try and change that state of affairs. This book is not that logical or rational; it has no overt political platform, but that does not prevent it being radical in its own way, since every page is a manifesto for the fabulousness of queerness. It has no time for the liberal delusion that straight and gay people are only different when they are actually 'at it', insisting instead that to be queer is to see the world utterly and irrevocably otherwise from those not so fortunately equipped. It is a book about the aesthetics of sexuality and the sexual politics of aesthetics; about what happens when you realize the intoxicating, life-changing, society-transforming possibilities of putting Che Guevara and Debussy to a disco beat.

xvi: *Seduced and Abandoned*

If you're looking for a linear history of homosexuality and pop, then you will not find it here. *Seduced and Abandoned* is not the story of who is and who isn't. It won't give you a map of where to find gay-relevant lyrics, and, mercifully, it is indifferent to the social-worker simplifications of 'positive images'. Its primary concern is to convey passion – to celebrate those moments where pop can reach out and touch, and where that touch is as queer as queer can be. Even then, it has no pretensions towards comprehensiveness, it does not identify every record that has ever turned a queen's heart to jelly, so there's no mention of The Elgins' 'Heaven Must Have Sent You', Helen Shapiro's 'You Don't Know', Ce Ce Peniston's 'Finally' or Fairport Convention's 'Who Knows Where The Time Goes?'. But then there wouldn't be, because they're on *my* 'desert island' compilation tape, not Richard Smith's, and if this book tells us anything, it is that our taste in pop is one of the most personal things about ourselves, one of the key ways in which we send signals to each other and the world at large about who we are.

And when we're queer, that can be crucial. Sharing a taste for music is one of the main glues of gay culture, whether it's nervy nancies in the 50s swooning along to Judy, twirling disco bunnies in 70s clubs shrieking when they recognize the first bars of a Sylvester record or cocky post-modern 90s queerboys playing guessing games about Take That. Even before we reach that stage of sub-cultural intercourse, music is a lifeline that points a way out of the smothering constrictions of straight culture – a promise that being different might also mean being special. For Richard Smith, skulking misunderstood in his bedroom, Morrissey's lyrics were both a haven and a weapon. For me, in the decade before, it was David Bowie and Patti Smith, but the principle is the same: lone teenage queers finding ecstatic consolation in the shimmering perversities of pop.

Hence, we are grateful. We remember; we over-invest furiously, and we share those feelings when we find others like us. Then comes a new twist when we discover (confirming all our cherished suspicions) just how indebted pop music is to queers' contributions. At the risk of being only slightly fanciful, one could argue that without us there would be no good British pop music at all – once you think of the queer Svengali managers of the 1950s, listen to the other-worldly records produced by Joe Meek, imagine how far The

Beatles would have got without the igniting fuel of Brian Epstein's lust for John Lennon, try to envisage Mick Jagger's persona without the queening, consider the fate of the 1970s without the impact of Glam, note the gay input into punk and (ahem) New Romanticism, and recognize that heterosexual dance music is virtually a contradiction in terms. If you try to construct a list of British pop acts utterly untouched by homosexuality, without a single trace of camp, who do you get? Phil Collins? Deacon Blue? The Wedding Present? I rest my only slightly fanciful case.

So pop is pretty much ours, and this book will help you to understand why. It doesn't do so through laborious theorizing. It prefers instead to take snapshots and send postcards, making its case through the accumulation of besotted fragments. That, after all, is how pop works, triggering our deepest feelings with its lacerating revelations. Richard Smith knows this better than most, which is why, with the aid of a great record collection, an enviably incisive turn of phrase, and a sure, queer grasp of the fundamental importance of the apparently trivial, he has written a book which thrills as much as it matters, and matters as much as it thrills.

Andy Medhurst
University of Sussex
June 1995

Chapter one

Introduction

POP music's a bit like boys. I mean, I just really, really love it.
Let me tell you some stuff that I love.

The chorus of Psychic TV's 'Godstar'. Robert Wyatt singing
'I love you still, Caroline'. Elvis's smile. Elvis's dick. Listening to
Definitely Maybe or *Nirvana Unplugged in New York* when I'm
feeling depressed, or, if I want to snap out of it, Red Sovine's 'Teddy
Bear' or 'Harper Valley PTA'. Laughing out loud at the video for
Take That's 'Could It Be Magic'. The guitar sound on Yeah Yeah
Noh's 'Prick Up Your Ears'. Evie Sands singing 'I Can't Let Go'. *In
Bed With Madonna* – my favourite film ever (after *Freaks*). The day
I found a copy of DAF's reunion album in a junk shop. Nancy
Sinatra's make-up. 'How does that grab you darling?' The time I
started rushing on my first E at Shame. The picture of Phil Spector at
school in *Rock Dreams*. Spending whole afternoons playing 'Waterloo Sunset' over and over again. Meeting Ray Davies and all I could
think was *'Fuck me! You wrote "Waterloo sunset"! And "Wonder-
boy". And "Shangri-la"!'* The very existence of Pansy Division. The
time Granny Smith told me her favourite record was Gloria Gay-
nor's 'I Will Survive'. Klaus Nomi's voice. The way I can't think of
anything else when I play his records but how many of my friends
are still gonna be around in ten years' time. And then I think: 'will I
be?' The sleeve of the Hoodoo Guru's *Stoneage Romeos*. The
Poohsticks' 'Indie Pop Ain't Noise Pollution'. Seeing Primal Scream
when they first started and they were just like the sweetest little boys
in the world. *Screamadelica*. Ten a.m. at Trade, dancing with Tom,
and I can't stop smiling cause that gorgeous boy who's always here
is dancing right behind us. He's just perfect, *just so perfect*. Thinking

about Kurt Cobain. 'Streets Of Your Town' and 'Part Company' and 'Apology Accepted' and 'Bachelor Kisses' by the Go-betweens. Me being 15 and putting on 'Smalltown Boy' and just crying and crying. Me being 18 and liking George Michael's 'A Different Corner' so much I went and bought it from Woolies – I was too embarrassed to get it from the place I usually bought records. '1 – 2 Crush On You' by The Clash. The first records I bought again on CD because the vinyl was worn right through; *London Calling, Behaviour, Music for Airports, The Red Bird Story,* a Kinks compilation, everything by Robert Wyatt, *The Supremes Anthology,* loads of Elvis, *Dare,* and, already, *Automatic for the People.* That night at The Astoria, Elvis is singing 'Love Me Tender' over the PA, I'm chatting with Damon from Blur, then just as we kiss goodbye, Gene comes on stage. And I'm thinking 'I love my life'. Hearing that 110 decibel scream, scream, *screeeeaaamm* when Take That came on stage at Wembley Arena. Thinking Nick Heyward was the most beautiful man in the world when I was a kid. The Pet Shop Boys' 'Go West' video. That really cute boy in the one for 'Domino Dancing'. That time at Pleasure Zone when the DJ played 'Let's Rock' and we all went bananas and then realized how old we all were getting. Or when I play 'A Deeper Love' these days and I just feel like crying. RuPaul at Heaven. Pet Shop Boys at Heaven. *Dusty in Memphis. From Elvis in Memphis.* My Nick Kamen picture disc. Playing Tom Waits' 'The Heart of Saturday Night' when I'm staying in on a Saturday night. Being twenty-fucking-seven and still having a poster of Madonna over my bed. Seeing The Fall for the fifteenth time. Seeing *Grease* five times when I was ten, just 'cause I thought John Travolta looked so fucking horny. Feeling really embarrassed about it when I was 13. Being allowed to admit that I love it again now I'm a queen. Finding a note an old boyfriend had left for me which he'd written when he was pissed, a few lines from 'Always On My Mind', and just bursting into tears. Mark driving me home one time and 'There Is A Light That Never Goes Out' comes on. And Mark guessing why I'd suddenly started giggling. *The Simpsons Sing the Blues.* One day one summer when I'd just shagged this boy that I'd fancied for ages, couldn't believe that he fancied me too, so happy, that afterglow you get, we were sitting out in the sun the next morning on this queen's boat on Brighton Marina and playing in the background was that version of 'I Feel Love' that mixes into 'Our Love'. So beautiful. That line in Blondie's 'Picture This': 'I will give you my finest hour, the one I spent watching you shower'. When someone's really fucked me off playing the first side of Easterhouse's *In Our Own Hands* EP. Kevin Rowland's songs – from 'There, There My Dear' to 'This Is What She's Like'. Having in-depth discussions with my friends about which members of Take That we think are gay and which ones we want to shag the most. Me saying Jason's the best 'cause he's the only one who looks like he could give you a really good seeing to. The way that Robbie's turned into such a sexy dog in the last year. The record that most reminds me of Seb – Claudia Brücken's *Love: And A Million Other Things*. Or the way I always think of Michael whenever I hear 'Tired Of Waiting For You'. They're such sweet boys. Writing a live review for *Melody Maker* which was just a thinly disguised love letter to this boy that did the band's press. Best review that band ever had. That bit exactly five and a half minutes into The Blue Nile's 'The Downtown Lights'. Me singing Elvis songs to Idris on Elvis's birthday this year. Buying *Ziggy Stardust* when I was 12 and just staring at the cover, totally fucking entranced. The Jam's last album. My almost complete run of *Smash Hits*. The way I still organize my Thursdays around *Top of the Pops*. The way I still can't walk past a record shop without going in. Getting high on caffeine and dancing round the house to The Grid's 'A Beat Called Love' or Jam & Spoon's 'Right In The Night' or Baby Doc's 'Eurotic' or *Reactivate 9*. The Gang of Four's 'Call Me Up'. The way I still put on the Buzzcocks' 'Get On Our Own' when I'm sweet on some boy I've just met. And the way I still play 'What Do I Get?' and 'You Say You Don't Love Me' when I realize he's not sweet on me. Michael Jackson singing 'My Girl' in that beautiful unbroken voice and sounding like he's absolutely suicidal. The first time I heard 'Back For Good'. So happy for them. Patrick Prins. *Patrick fucking Prins!* The opening bars of The Rubettes' 'Sugar Baby Love'. Being 16 and getting stoned with Phil and Mark and Bez and Hugh and listening to *Beggars Banquet*. All The Chiffons' singles – the best songs about boys ever made. Diana Ross's *I'm Still Waiting* – the faggiest album ever made. The way I used to feel this warm glow whenever Madonna came on TV because I loved her so much. And, after that great 'fuck you' of an album *Bedtime Stories*, realizing that I still do. Lou Reed singing 'Pale Blue Eyes' or 'Crazy Feeling'. The agony and the ecstasy. *Songs For Drella*. The Band's second album. The first side of Prince's *Controversy*. I could go on. I could go on forever.

But pop's also a bit like boys 'cause sometimes I really hate it too. You know how you start going 'ooh you're fab, you're really fab!' then you get a little bit closer and you end up going 'ooh, you're fucking vile, you are'? And sometimes you get closer and you realize that they really are fab. *Really fab*. And that's what makes it all worthwhile.

This book is basically about me – it's me trying to figure out why I love and hate this thing called pop. What it means to me, but also what it means to us. The ways that gay men use pop and the ways that pop uses gay men. How pop thrills us and how it keeps letting us down, leaving us feeling seduced and abandoned once more.

Like I said, pop music's a bit like boys.

April 1995

Chapter two

The Acid Queen: Mixmaster Morris

WHEN I was a boy I was desperate in that way little gay boys are for anything that looked a little like me. I was about twelve and it was about 1980 and the only homos I could name were Oscar Wilde, Tom Robinson and Quentin Crisp. Then I read this piece about Tchaikovsky. Really sad. Said he was in love with this boy. A love that could not be. Broken heart. That kind of thing. He wrote this piece called *Pathétique* then died a broken man. 'That's me!' I thought and tried to get a copy. I found one in a charity shop. Sadly it was crap. As indeed all classical music is.

Seven years later I first heard Brian Eno's *Music for Airports*. It sounded the way I thought *Pathétique* should sound. Made me feel how I thought Tchaikovsky felt. And this, apparently, was Ambient music. Totally electronic and yet totally human.

These days Ambient's the fastest growing form of music on the planet. And its main ambassador is Mixmaster Morris. A camp Jewish queen, a 200-gig-a-year DJ and, as The Irresistible Force, the creator of two astonishingly beautiful albums; *Flying High* and *Global Chillage*. And it's all Aldous Huxley and Timothy Leary's fault.

'I wouldn't be sitting here today if it hadn't been for reading them when I was 14. That was the first thing that diverted me from normality – the idea that LSD was the most powerful de-programming tool on the planet. I was interested in acid before I realized I was queer – though I wondered why I kept getting beaten up all the time and knew I hated football and didn't want pictures of Jane Fonda on my wall. Acid House began in this country when the papers put the words "Acid" and "House" together, and every acid head thought "that sounds interesting!" I was one of them. I'd been waiting years for an electronic psychedelic music.'

Electronics, psychedelics and music are Morris's big three passions. He says he's 'been glued to the Internet for the last year. It's going to change the world as we know it. People feel a lot more freedom to speak out on the Net. When you're in cyberspace you have no colour, no gender, no sexual orientation. You can assume any identity you want which is completely liberating. If you live in Shitsville, Ohio and you're 14 and queer, there's probably not a lot of people you can talk to. But you can go onto a gay teen forum on the Net and find out exactly what you need to know. It brings people together from all over the planet.'

Acid can also dissolve boundaries and it shares the same attitude as Ambient music: 'open your mind'. Hallucinogens have enthralled queens from Rimbaud to Foucault and informed gay culture from Pop Art to Acid House, from Ziggy Stardust to Leigh Bowery and from Howl to ff. There's a good deal of overlap between the trippy and the camp – think of *The Wizard of Oz* and *Pink Narcissus* or of Funkadelic and The Grid – they share much the same aesthetic; rejoicing in the ridiculous, seeing the ordinary as strange and vice versa. When I ask Morris if he agrees that tripping's camp he thinks for a bit and then goes 'ha ha ha ha' for ten minutes. Which I think I'll take as a yes.

'You can certainly have camp hallucinations. People's hallucinations are totally informed not just by set and setting but by their experiences through life. The higher designer hallucinogenics like DMT are even more camp because they take you into a complete Disneyland.

'But all these things – computers, drugs, Ambient, being queer – are about being prepared to experiment and explore. I've always been interested in experimental music that's more way out than what has gone previously. When I was 14 I started to hear early Pink Floyd, Soft Machine and all the Canterbury Music and getting into the British psychedelic musical heritage. Then punk happened so it was a bit schizophrenic for me – all that stuff was automatically untouchable – but I always had both in my head. I was convinced that sampling was the future of music even before I had my hands on one and was obsessed with the idea that it could make any sound into music. It's like Burrough's cut up technique – snatch and scratch, mix and match. I got my hands on one in 1984 and started campaigning to get people to use them.

'Things started to happen in England before House music was even mentioned. The beginning of the modern age was the first Cold Cut record – they were the first English DJs to go off and make a record that was all made of just other peoples' music. They kicked off the DIY dance music revolution. It's the ultimate heresy to say that. The official history is that it all came from America and Ibiza. But there was a massive explosion of underground activity in England in 1986 and the industry has swept it under the carpet.'

Morris gripes a lot about the music industry and 'corporate music'. He's part of a grand tradition of gay independent electronic mavericks from Joe Meek through Walter Carlos to Mark Moore of S'Express. But there's one thing he hates even more than the music business.

'Normality. Who needs it? Who wants to be normal? Even when I'm playing Techno I play completely different records from everybody else. I like to play the riskiest and the weirdest and the strangest.'

Even though his name is almost synonymous with Ambient, Morris uses the word 'Techno' to embrace 'all electronic music that uses technology inventively and intelligently. I like extremes so I love the harder and faster Techno too. It's all about pride. Just like you have Gay Pride I think you should have Techno pride. They've created a movement that's changed the world.'

So just what is this thing called Ambient?

'Ambient is an openness, an openness to lots of possibilities. You only have to go to London's Ambient clubs to see that people are eager to hear whatever people have got to bring them. People come up after I play and say "that was brilliant 'cause I could do whatever I wanted" – you just express yourself. I wouldn't be interested if it wasn't. All the Ambient parties I've been to have black, white, gay, straight, old and young all enjoying the party together without any segregation. As opposed to most clubs which have become just a lot of boys on bad drugs competing to be the hardest, the fastest and the stupidest. Ambient is restating the feminine in Techno. Using technology but giving it a human edge, an emotional content instead of something just visceral.'

Unsurprisingly, Ambient has attracted other gay musicians, like Vapor Space's Mark Hage and Australia's Paul Schutze who has just released his ninth album, *Apart*. Morris likes Schutze's *More Beautiful Human Life* LP (released last year under the pseudonym Uzect Plaush), as indeed did rather a lot of people.

'It's the same reason why I've always liked Robert Wyatt,' explains Morris, a man who thinks Wyatt's 'O Caroline' is the most beautiful record ever made. Which, of course, it is. 'Because it was very much anti-aggression, anti-rock. Very English. Twee almost. And all of that is there in what I do now. Robert's made some of the most personal music ever made. Heart-wrenchingly so. A perfect combination of the personal and the political. Left wing and left field.'

Morris is a bit of an old leftie too. His first involvement with music was back in the days of Rock Against Racism and his first record, 1988's 'I Want To'/'Guns', was a double A-side single celebrating the joys of both cocksucking and of shooting the ruling class. Many see Ambient as apolitical music, but not Morris.

'Just to play Techno is a political statement. Read the Criminal Justice Act! There's a subtext to everything you play. Ambient is saying this music has roots, there is a continuum. It's all about progress and change. I'm a neophyte. I like the new. I get bored very quickly. I'm always looking for something better, pushing the conception of what music is. Ambient is a collective desire of people not to conform. To stand up in the face of ridicule. A maverick spirit – opting out of the way music was going, turning it round and showing there was another way.

'But there has to be an edge to the music. A lot of Ambient is just shit. It's a real challenge to create music that's radical and experimental but still beautiful. When pushed to describe Ambient I always say it's radically beautiful music. It's not enough to just play pretty melodies. You have to do something new with sound.'

How sound affects people, how it makes us feel, is often overlooked. Ambient sounds unmasculine. But it's also unphysical –

9: *The Acid Queen: Mixmaster Morris*

mind not body music. Unrock but uncock too. Ambient floats instead of thrusts. So is it a gay sound?

'Ambient comes from everybody and it belongs to everybody. But I really want to take it into the gay scene. I just played an Ambient cruise bar on the Castro. What a great idea! My friend Jonah Sharpe played a backroom in a gay club in the US and everyone was shagging. A lot of people have told me they've had really good sex to my records and that's such a compliment. When you're having great sex you lose track of time and start floating in another universe and ambient music helps. I always wanted to write music for porn movies. I was watching one from the Seventies the other day and the music was just like modern electronic music. The natural format for porno shorts is a really good format for ambient music – just pulsing for a long time and then coming to a climax.'

But your records are a series of pulses and climaxes?

'Come again.'

Oh. Right.

Gay Times, April 1995

Chapter three

Ambisexuality

'All rock 'n' roll is homosexual.'

Richey James, Manic Street Preachers

CLOSE Richey, but no cigar . . .

True, if you want to know what rock 'n' roll would sound like without any gay input, imagine a Michael Bolton record playing for *ever*. Gay men have been instrumental in shaping the direction pop music has taken over the years. But although their position has been central, it's also been extremely fraught. Because gay men can be, have to be, or are made invisible, theirs has been a secret history. All rock 'n' roll isn't homosexual, it's ambiguous, ambivalent – *ambisexual*.

It has made people ask questions ('Is he or isn't he?' or 'Is he a she?'), but has rarely seen those questions answered. It hints and denies, but rarely specifies. The grand total of out gay men who have performed on *Top of the Pops* (as good a yardstick as any) barely scrapes into double figures. Yet that programme, like pop itself, has been absolutely riddled with camp, androgyny, male effeminacy and moral outrage.

Much of the shock of the new wave of ambisexual acts (Suede, Manic Street Preachers, Fabulous, Army Of Lovers, Right Said Fred) comes because things have been disturbingly quiet on this front since the Gender Bender explosion of the early Eighties. But the ambisextrous have always shown this alarming tendency to radiate and fade away. Their secret history makes it seem as if they've come out of nowhere, and so dooms them to going straight back there. Gay men are in the unique position of being central yet marginalized; informing mainstream culture, but rarely making any real in-roads into it.

Each time something that they've fostered crosses over, they're left standing in the shadows unloved. With their roots denied, they then cease to have any meaning beyond being a mere fashion and are thus doomed to rapidly fall out of favour and out of sight in the way that fashions always do.

You can't talk about or trace a 'gay music' in the same way as you can 'black music'. Usually gay men have been allowed the stuff that no one else wants. Because the rock snobs of the Seventies despised Disco, it could be dismissed as 'faggot music' (hence 'Disco Sucks'), yet the gay origins of its more fondly regarded modern counterpart, House, which are if anything more distinct, are often denied.

Early punks were more than happy to take their inspiration from ambisextrous Americans like Lou Reed, Patti Smith and The New York Dolls, and to take refuge in gay clubs. But when Punk got properly under way over here, gay men were only allowed to ride in on its coat tails, attaching themselves to an aspect of its outlook that would afford them a voice – either through outrage (Jayne County) or political comment (Tom Robinson).

'I think the world is ready for a true fairy.'
Jobriath, 1973

The ambisexuals act as shock troops, testing and contesting the climate for the out gay acts that follow in their wake. In the Seventies, the world could cope with the fey campery of Marc Bolan and David Bowie but, despite the gay glam rocker Jobriath's assertion to the contrary, it still wasn't ready for a true fairy.

The first mass breakthrough wasn't to come until ten years later, when the Gender Benders were swiftly followed by Erasure, Bronski Beat, Frankie Goes To Hollywood *et al.* Even Boy George, whose image had previously been more asexual than ambisexual, later found the courage to come out fully.

'I wouldn't have missed that fucking bender for anything.'
Anonymous fan after Erasure concert.

12: *Seduced and Abandoned*

Gay stars can be liked in spite of their sexuality, or because of a reading of it that perpetuates the myths that fans most need to believe. The position for these stars is problematic and they're guaranteed a hard time, no more so than if they've politicized their homosexuality. Few artists have been so persistently vilified and ridiculed as Jimmy Somerville, as if audiences are happy to be entertained by him but don't want to hear about the problems he articulates. It's a very English attitude – no one really minds what you do, as long as you're discreet about it, as long as you don't frighten the proverbial horses.

Little wonder then that, for many, the ambisextrous star is even better than the real thing, nor that they arouse such suspicion and contempt from gay men – who view them as either gay cowards or straight thieves. The former are dismissed as traitors, taking an easier option than fully coming out. The straight thieves steal from gay culture and appropriate its imagery to embellish their act with a little of the erotic exotic. This is a form of aural voyeurism; posing as a sodomite, wearing the dresses, but without having to suffer the consequences.

Of course, pop's always been about plunder, but what grates is that this particular debt is rarely acknowledged. And when such things are taken up by those who aren't fully immersed in the culture from which they've sprung, they never get it quite right. Camp goes from being something specific but indefinable, to something meaningless.

Content to only touch the surface, everything they do rests not on conviction but artifice. Is there really any difference between what Brett from Suede is doing and what The Black and White Minstrels did? If it's only an act, are audiences allowed the luxury of laughing along with it before they go merrily queer-bashing into the night?

At its worst, ambisexuality is a mask for both straights and closets to wear. Used and abused like this, much of the time this particular gay man will be left screaming 'Come out or fuck off!'

'Confusion is a very useful tool, for it is only when we are confused that we are sometimes obliged to think.'
Lana Pellay

13: *Ambisexuality*

I want music that speaks my name, that talks to me directly. But – and here's the rub – the ambisextrous acts often thrill and fascinate me just as much. Sometimes more. I'd much rather listen to a Buzzcocks' album than one of Tom Robinson's. And give me Morrissey over Andy Bell any day of the century. If they're driven by dishonesty they can still provide an honest representation of how things are for many, if not for most, people. Sex, sexuality and gender aren't always clear-cut issues, but ones that try, trouble and torment. Perhaps pop has a duty to mirror this confusion – where nothing is certain, where it's all just one big blur – *ambisexual*.

I guess what I'm really trying to say is, I'm just not really sure.

Melody Maker, 12 December 1992

Chapter four

Baby Don't Apologize: Nirvana

Kurt Cobain and River Phoenix are two of my favourite people. I think the only people that have the right to be gay positive in that kind of simplistic way are straight people, straight men who are ... 'trying to get in touch with their feminine side' (laughs). They were both trying to go the distance. I think they're the new Judy Garlands – martyrs to the cause.

Bruce La Bruce

FRANCES Bean Cobain, I just wanted to tell you a few things about your daddy ...

When he was a teenager in the late Seventies, Kurt Cobain used to graffiti the words 'GOD IS GAY' all over his home town of Aberdeen in Seattle. God wasn't alone. 'I thought I was gay,' Kurt said later. 'I thought that might be the solution to my problem at one time during my childhood.' Kurt's best friend definitely was gay and Kurt was frequently fagbashed for his friendship.

In 1986, Kurt started this band called Nirvana. Five years later the massive success of their single 'Smells Like Teen Spirit' seemed to signal the end of the Reagan–Bush 'go get 'em' era, and the song became an anthem for those who were never going to get anywhere. Suddenly everyone started going grunge, slackers, Generation X, blah, blah, blah. Kurt became the reluctant leader of the beaten generation, and one of the biggest rock stars in the world. But he'd always championed the outsider and the failure, and was never at ease with his success. 'I'm anaemic royalty,' he once sang, like a leper messiah.

'I definitely have a problem with the average macho man,' Kurt told *Rolling Stone*, 'because they have always been a threat to me, I've had to deal with them most of my life – being taunted and beaten up by them in school, just having to be around them and be expected to be that kind of person when you grow up. I definitely feel closer to the feminine side of the human being than I do to the male – or the American idea of what a male is supposed to be.'

When fame came, Kurt found that many of his fans were 'that kind of person'. He kept sticking his neck out. I don't think you could call it being principled; it was more of a passion. He wrote on the sleeve of *Incesticide*: 'I have a request for our fans. If any of you in any way hate homosexuals, people of different colour, or women, please do this one favour for us – leave us the fuck alone! Don't come to our shows and don't buy our records.'

Was Kurt gay? 'In spirit'. Bisexual? 'Probably'. Nirvana dragged up for their 'In Bloom' video ('Cross dressing is cool'). They kissed each other on *Saturday Night Live*. On the ruddy lips! The band goaded lumpen metalheads Guns 'n' Roses at the MTV Awards. Nirvana played gay benefits. Frocks and flirtation may be part and parcel of Britpop, but for an American rock group these were still real acts of defiance. In the States, kids in Nirvana t-shirts started getting queerbashed. When the world's press was dying to talk to him about their new album, *In Utero*, Kurt gave an interview to *The Advocate*.

Kurt wrote my favourite song of last year, 'All Apologies': 'What else should I say? Everyone is gay.' My favourite band of last year, Pansy Division, recorded 'Smells Like *Queer* Spirit' – 'With kisses to Nirvana: No superstar rock band has ever before had the guts to take such an overtly pro-gay stance. Right on!' Kurt appeared on the cover of *The Face* in a nice frock. Kurt made a record with his hero William Burroughs. Kurt killed himself. The night he died I played Nirvana records over and over. I noticed for the first time that on the fade out of 'Stay Away' you can hear him screaming 'GOD IS GAY!' Kurt stuck by his friends to the end.

Frances Bean, I just wanted you to know that your daddy was one of life's good guys.

16: *Seduced and Abandoned*

I wrote those notes the night I heard Kurt Cobain died. I should point out that I don't normally do that sort of thing, but sometimes it helps to write stuff down. I remember the newsflashes coming through on Radio One's *Pete Tong Show* that Friday evening. First they said that a body had been found at his house and I was going up the wall and saying to myself: 'don't let it be you Kurt, don't let it be you, let someone I've never heard of die'. 'Cause that's how your mind works, isn't it? They kept on bringing in the latest update every 20 minutes or so. Then finally they confirmed it. Kurt Cobain was dead.

I realized then how much I loved Kurt, how much he meant to me, and how much we needed him. Usually when someone kills themselves you catch yourself thinking: 'I just don't understand it'. But the real tragedy about Kurt's death was feeling you could see exactly why he did it.

Nirvana's *Unplugged In New York* album is proof of how knowledge of an artist's biography completely changes the way we hear their music. Now Kurt's gone, that album sounds like his suicide note – even though he sounds so happy when he's speaking between the songs; laughing and joking with everyone, putting himself down just to make everyone smile and muttering before every other number: 'I bet I screw this one up'. He knew which mask to wear. But in the songs there is no mask. You can see right through him.

Now *Unplugged* sounds like Kurt might have meant it as his epitaph. A tertiary scream. All that hurt and all that stuff about dying. Kurt had said he wanted the next Nirvana album to be like *Automatic for the People*. Maybe he knew *Unplugged* would be his last gasp. All the way through, he howls like his heart's been caught in a snare. The closing tracks, 'All Apologies' and 'Where Did You Sleep Last Night?' are almost too painful to listen to. Like he's got inner demons he can't exorcize.

Back to death. Many tried to dismiss Kurt's suicide by blaming it all on smack. The news reports and the obituaries described him as 'a drug addict' almost as often as they called him 'a rock star'. But heroin was a solution to his problems not the cause. Using heroin regularly usually means your life's nothing but pain and you'll do anything to make that pain stop. The vast majority of addicts are young men, and heroin addiction is often seen as a male equivalent of anorexia – a retreat from adult responsibilities, adult sexuality and adulthood itself, as well as a way of taking control over one's own life, a cry for help, a silent scream, and, sometimes, a death wish. The slowest kind of suicide. Tough Love is no way to deal with someone with suicidal tendencies. At the end of March 1994, Kurt's wife, Courtney Love, threatened to leave him, and Pat Smear and Krist Novoselic told him they'd break up the band if he didn't check himself into rehab. Less than two weeks later Kurt killed himself. When the heroin stopped, Kurt stopped his life. In his suicide note he wrote: 'I'm too sensitive. I need to be slightly numb in order to regain the enthusiasm I had as a child'. Which means, I guess, that Kurt just wanted to stop feeling.

I once had this theory that part of the reason smack became so attractive to some people in our time is because so many women are now given opiates during childbirth. Life begins just after the stuff seeps into us through the umbilical cord and then we pour out into this new world. Then they cut the cord. And that's when the trouble starts. Here we are now. Entertain us. Like the baby on the cover of *Nevermind* swimming innocently towards that pretty little green thing. Little does he know. Kurt saw death as a chance to return to the pacifics of the womb: 'Throw down your umbilical noose so I can climb right back' ('Heart Shaped Box'). The last album was even called *In Utero*. And there's babies on the sleeve again, this time looking grotesque, like foetal carnage or something off an anti-abortion propaganda leaflet. On the front there's an anatomical model of a woman – womb exposed – that someone's added the wings of an angel to.

Back to life. A troubled youth, Kurt didn't like his dad and his mum didn't seem to like Kurt much. He told Jon Savage that at school he 'felt so different and so crazy that people just left me alone. They were afraid. I always felt that they would vote me Most Likely To Kill Everyone at a High School Dance. I could definitely see how a person's mental state could deteriorate to the point where they could do that. I've got to the point where I've fantasized about it, but I'd have always opted for killing myself first ...

'I thought I was gay. I thought that might be the solution to my problem at one time during my school years. Although I never experimented, I had a gay friend, and that was the time I experienced real confrontation with people. I got beaten up. Then my mother wouldn't allow me to be friends with him any more, because she's homophobic. It was devastating, because finally I'd found a male friend who I actually hugged and was affectionate to. I was putting the pieces of the puzzle together, and he was playing a big role.'

It's that Genet thing – the fuckers give you a bad name and if you're smart you just think 'yeah, sure am!' Kurt sure did. He told *The Advocate* he used to 'pretend I was gay just to fuck with people. Once I got the gay tag it gave me the freedom to be a freak'. Kurt got arrested when he was 18 for spraying 'Homosexual sex rules!' on the side of a bank. Another favourite was painting 'Queer' on the side of rednecks' trucks. He was once asked by *Melody Maker* how he felt about Nirvana fans getting branded 'fags'.

'I love it,' Kurt cooed. 'Knowing that gives me as much pleasure as when I used to dress up as a punk at high school and rednecks driving by in trucks would yell "Devo!" at me. It's good to have a nice, healthy battle going on in high school between the Guns 'n' Roses jocks and the Nirvana fans. It vibes up the kids who are more intelligent, and at least it brings the whole subject of homosexuality into debate. It's very flattering our fans are thought of as fags. Actually I've heard a lot of stories about kids being beaten up for wearing Nirvana t-shirts.'

Kurt had been seeing a lot of Michael Stipe just before he died. Apparently the only thing he could get excited about was a possible collaboration. Stipe said he wrote 'Let Me In' about Kurt and River Phoenix's deaths. Faith No More's Roddy Bottum flew out to look after Kurt at the start of 1994. Queens liked Kurt. Kurt liked queens. Kurt was cool.

Kurt Cobain was the first to bring sexual politics into the arena of American stadium rock. Of course they'd always been there – just like they've always been everywhere – but Kurt was the first to discuss the issues, to talk it like he walked it. He did as much for us as Madonna. And he got just as much shit. Maybe more. In our society good men tend to get crucified.

'What else should I be? All apologies. What else should I say? Everyone is gay.' What else could anyone say? Now Kurt's gone 'All Apologies' is the saddest song I know. He sounds like someone who's had all the fight knocked out of them. 'I wish I was like you, easily amused.' Just trying to explain himself, just trying to be good, and all he gets is trouble. I always thought he screamed out 'Mary! Mary!' at the end of the song, but the lyric sheet reveals he's actually wailing 'I'm married! – buried!' Christ, Kurt ...

In Utero was to have been called *I Hate Myself and I Want to Die*. But Kurt thought people wouldn't get the joke and changed it, even taking off the song itself at the last moment. That joke isn't funny any more. Kurt's death brought home to me why music is so important to so many people. Sometimes we listen when we can't talk to other people and records can say what we daren't say: 'I hate myself and I want to die'. 'Hold on, everybody hurts, you're not alone.' Pop music means there's a whole lot of trouble in the world. Here we are now, atomized and alienated, unable to communicate our pain. We look to pop stars to give us something that we're not getting from real people. Do you understand?

Kurt, I'm glad you did all you did, just like I'm sorry you couldn't go on. I'm trying to think of a better word for you than 'fag-friendly'. 'Cause you were much more than a friend. You were so beautiful and you were so very special, you were a fucking sister. It's like you said one time: 'if there's a glimmer of hope in anything you should support it'. And you were much more than a glimmer. The light poured out of you. Kurt, don't worry, you didn't screw up. Your suicide was a quite understandable response to living in the late Twentieth Century.

Suicide is painless. It's life that hurts.

Oh well, whatever, never mind ...

March 1995

Chapter five

Back in the YMCA: Village People

AT their late Seventies peak the Village People meant all things to all people. Such was their appeal with kids that the Walt Disney Corporation released an all quacking tribute record, 'Macho Duck'. Anita 'Save Our Children' Bryant was more than happy to appear with them on *The Johnny Carson Show*. The YMCA considered filing suit against the Village People for bringing the association into disrepute. And the US Navy wanted to use 'In The Navy' in a TV recruitment ad. 'I've heard it on the radio, it's great!' gushed a spokesman. 'The words are very positive, they talk about adventure and technology. My kids love it!'

Which is not to say the group were without their uses. To some kid who thought he was the only lonely little gay boy in Straightsville, Arizona, their three biggest hits offered some pretty good advice. One – go to the YMCA. Two – join the Navy. Or three – move to San Francisco.

Though they were savaged at the time by many gay men for being closeted and apolitical, their songs were joyous – if oblique – celebrations of the then emergent gay subculture. Numbers like 'Ready For The Eighties' and 'Liberation' were defiant and curiously moving, and they – like the in/out group that made them – were deeply redolent of a time long ago when things seemed to be moving inexorably forward for many gay men.

They were the creation of one Jacques Morali. Born in France in 1947, he moved to America in the Sixties and swiftly made a name for himself as a record producer. Together with his partner, Henri

Belolo, he used the cream of Philadelphia's session musicians to make records that emulated the then popular Philly Disco sound – clocking up a number of dance-floor hits under the name of The Ritchie Family.

After their biggest single, 'The Best Disco In Town', the pair moved to Casablanca Records, where president Neil Bogart agreed to put up the money for Morali to create his dream band, Village People. The Ritchie Family had been part of an older gay tradition in music – songs about boys sung by women but aimed at gay men (their record sleeves invariably depicted the girls draped over some muscled hunks). But Bogart – the man who'd signed Donna Summer – and Morali felt the time was now right for a group featuring gay men who sang about men.

The idea for the Village People came to Morali one night in 1977 when he wandered into a gay bar in Greenwich Village and saw one Felipé Rose. He was wearing 'Red Indian' costume and dancing with a group of men in various kinds of 'butch drag': 'I say to myself "this is fantastic". To see the cowboy, the Indian and the construction worker with other men around, and also I think to myself that gay people have no group, nobody to personalize the gay people, you know? I'm gay and I wanted to make a top star gay group.'

With Belolo, Morali wrote and recorded an album of four songs celebrating America's gay meccas: San Francisco, West Hollywood, Fire Island and Greenwich Village. As yet there was no band. They used session players, and the group shown on the cover was, in fact, Felipé Rose surrounded by good looking models from Colt Studios. But when the record took off, clubs began to demand PAs and a touring outfit was hastily assembled comprising of 'gay singers and dancers, very good looking and with moustaches'.

The image Morali wanted to project tied in with the new masculinist gay culture then sweeping the States ('you've got to be a mucho, macho man'). As gay men's visibility increased many sought to break the old stereotypes of effeminacy they felt had dogged them. The clone look was very American (no one has ever found English policemen or building site workers a turn on) and extremely problematic – many gay men refused to embrace such an endorsement of how men had been traditionally taught to look and act.

22: *Seduced and Abandoned*

What price coming out of the closet if you just walk into the wardrobe of your oppressors?

Morali's slightly dubious casting methods ('Every time I see someone good looking I say "do you sing?"') led to a rapid turnover in their line up, but by the time 'Macho Man' made it into the mainstream charts he'd already found a permanent cast of cop, GI, leatherman, hardhat, cowboy and Indian. At the end of 1978 – the year of *Saturday Night Fever* – they won the *Billboard* award for best disco group.

Morali said he 'never expected them to go over', and once the mainstream began to embrace the Village People they began to walk a precarious path of campy ambiguity. Their dress codes and points of reference may have made them screamingly obvious to other gay men, but this was still surprisingly lost on many straights, who, like the US Navy spokesman, could display a quite breathtaking capacity for self deception.

As the big time beckoned, the group retreated further into the closet – 'I'll tell the gay press I'm gay. If the straight press asks, we tell them it's none of their business. Or "none of their fucking business!" depending on how they ask,' Rose explained. 'I don't know why people think we're blatantly gay because it's never been presented that way. The people who live in the rest of the US, Middle America, these people still don't know.'

Some of the problems lay in the fact that both the lead singers – Victor Willis and his replacement Ray Simpson (the brother of Motown songwriter Valeri Simpson) – were both heterosexual, and if asked could put their hand on their heart and declare their straight credentials quite honestly. Though a little confusingly.

By never declaring their sexuality absolutely Village People allowed people to reach whatever conclusions they found it easiest to live with. And in so doing they ruptured their parody of masculinity and became a mere cartoon – Randy (the cowboy) felt that '13-year-old girls buy our records more than anybody else'. In their prime the Village People could sell out Las Vegas – complete with a spectacular stage show involving cranes, tee-pees, jeeps and horses.

In 1979 they reached their commercial peak with 'YMCA', a British number one that sold nine million copies worldwide, but this was also the start of their decline. The record-buying public had taken them to their hearts as a novelty act and, as such, would only allow them the briefest of shelf lives. The world was tiring of Disco too. In America the blatantly homophobic 'Disco Sucks' campaign ('Disco Sucks Cock' if you have to have it spelt out to you) was well under way. At a concert in Chicago the band were pelted with pink marshmallows.

Their record sales went into a swift downward spiral and their 1980 movie *Can't Stop The Music* was an unmitigated disaster. The film, produced by Alan Carr, flush from the success of *Grease*, was meant to be a homage to one of those 'let's do the show right here!' movies of the Thirties, but the plot was somewhat less than inspiring: agent needs group for milk commercial, agent finds group for milk commercial (as luck would have it, Village People), group makes milk commercial. Any hints of homosexuality in this re-write of the Village People story were excised ('You can't spend $13 million making a minority movie,' Carr explained helpfully). Put bluntly, the movie stank and died a death. Soon after, Casablanca Records dropped the group; the money lost on the movie was one of the main reasons for the collapse of the company soon afterwards.

A number of comebacks were tried. First they went New Romantic for the *Renaissance* LP (somewhat unwisely just as everyone else had stopped) and there was the almost hit of 'Sex Over The Phone' in 1985. Arguably the first pop song to deal in the realities of safer sex, it received the dubious honour of being banned by the BBC. The cover showed them hedging their bets as usual – a hardly dressed dolly bird on the front, whilst a 'tached piece of beefcake was relegated to the back.

Morali gave up his association with the group soon afterwards, though they continued to tour and were as likely to be playing some of Britain's less glamorous gay discos as they were the Kentucky fried-chicken-in-a-basket circuit in the States. But same as it ever was.

Morali had tried to add other strings to his bow. He took the pretty-boy French singer, Patrick Juvet, under his wing in 1979. They had a minor hit with 'I Love America', but his career failed to take off. He and Belolo collaborated on Eartha Kitt's highly amusing, high camp 1984 comeback album *I Love Men,* and were also behind Break Machine, the band at the forefront of the all-too-brief break dance craze. But after 'Sex Over The Phone' proved rather limp, Morali returned to his native France and went into retirement. He died of an AIDS-related illness in November 1991.

It's hardly surprising that the Seventies revival should also see a revival in the fortunes of the Village People. They appeal because they are rooted in some mythic 'golden age of the homosexual'. 'The words have become very sad,' said Neil Tennant of the Pet Shop Boys' decision to cover 'Go West', 'because it's a pre-AIDS gay ideal, the idea of moving to San Francisco and everything will be fabulous. Now it has a kind of elegiac quality.' For all their talk of liberation, the group became an embodiment of limitations and the high price that must be paid by minorities for assimilation into the mainstream.

This time round Village People are being repackaged as pure camp, something Susan Sontag once defined as 'a seriousness that fails...when the theme is important, and contemporary, the failure of a work of art may make us indignant. Time can change that. Time liberates the work of art from moral relevance. Thus things are campy, not when they become old – but when we become less involved in them, and can enjoy, instead of be frustrated by, the failure of the attempt.'

Jacques Morali's dream of creating a 'top star gay group' may have failed. But as a metaphor for gay men's position in society they remain without equal. In the Village People's world the best of times weren't here, they were always just around the corner, the rainbow just out of reach.

December 1993

Chapter six

Bad?: Michael Jackson

I figured out at an early age that if someone said something about me that wasn't true, it was a lie. But if someone said something about my image that wasn't true, then it was okay. Because then it wasn't a lie, it was public relations.

Michael Jackson

AND so it was. Michael Jackson was 12 years old when his father got the Jackson 5 an audition with Motown. When Berry Gordy signed them up he told Michael to knock two years off his age and to tell reporters this fairy tale he'd concocted about how Diana Ross had discovered the Jackson 5.

He never forgot that first lesson in showbusiness. There's the man, and there's his image. Lies and 'public relations'. A walking identity crisis, no one knew who Michael Jackson really was. The only problem was, Michael didn't seem to know either.

His story reads like a race through the history of black music. When Motown was in its heyday he was learning the ropes from James Brown at the Apollo Theatre. The Jackson 5 signed to Motown just as Philadelphia International had become *the* label. The Jacksons recorded two albums with Philly's Gamble & Huff just as the world was going Disco crazy. Michael's first solo album, *Off The Wall*, was that genre's last great moment. And then came *Thriller*. Big enough to warrant a new musical genre, Crossover, Michael had finally caught up and cleaned up.

It would be a little too easy and far too patronizing to write off *Thriller*'s 40 million sales as just some kind of mass hysteria. Michael Jackson touched something in a hell of a lot of people. He offered them something they couldn't get from the other Eighties megastars. Prince was the Stones to his Beatles, cooler and making explicit questions Jackson only hinted at ('Am I black or white? Am I straight or gay?' 'Controversy'). Madonna was every bit as open as Jackson was shut. Bruce Springsteen was a real man, blue collar and down to earth, to Jackson's androgyne glamour from another planet. Compared to them Michael Jackson was 'something else' – if only less certain. And whereas other stars demanded of the public 'love me', or at the very least 'respect me', Michael just fluttered his big doe eyes and said 'like me'.

James Baldwin once argued that white people would only allow a black man to be 'either saint or danger'. Until last year Michael Jackson was firmly on the side of the saints – like so many black singers, from Little Richard to RuPaul, he sanctified himself by emasculating himself. His falsetto voice wasn't recognizably adult or male. And neither was Michael.

He was careful to love all the things we were told we had to love in the Eighties. He may have said a book about P.T. Barnum was his Bible ('I want my whole career to be the greatest show on earth') but he was more revered as the man who put the *business* back into showbusiness. His rags to riches story – equal parts Monkees, *Sound of Music* and that old Motown magic – was, he regularly reminded us, all thanks to God and his family.

In the Seventies, the Jacksons became black America's first family, though the reality was that they were as dysfunctional as hell. On the one hand there was his mother, a devout Jehovah's Witness, constantly sermonizing against sex. On the other, his father, who had a string of affairs and one-night stands behind his wife's back, but often in full view of Michael. All his brothers carried on with female fans, both before and after they married young, as if to assert their own manhood and defy their father. Served with such ghastly role models it's perhaps not that surprising that Michael would later take refuge in his Peter Pan fantasies. Although the fabled 'boy who never grew up' was, in fact, forced to grow up pretty damn quick.

Estranged sister LaToyah apart, Michael's family have all stood by him (though this might only be because they don't want to speed the axe that kills their golden goose) but some change in their relationship took place in the late Eighties. After a series of run-ins with Jehovah's Witness leaders, Michael left the church at the end of 1987. The following spring he moved out of the shared family home to live alone in Neverland Ranch. One reporter claims to have been present during a final row between Michael and his father, who allegedly accused him of being gay after he'd brought a male guest to a family gathering.

Michael's is a life that's been lived in the shadow of such rumours. The first was that a voice as good as his had to come from the mouth of a midget, not a child. Then they said his father was injecting him with female hormones to stop his voice from breaking. By 1977 Michael was supposed to be planning a sex change so he could marry the actor Clifton Davis. A year later he would tell a reporter: 'No, I am not gay. I am not a homo. Not at all...I'm not going to have a nervous breakdown because people think I like having sex with men. I don't and that's that.'

But that wasn't that, and as the rumours refused to fade with time, his consternation grew. In September 1984 he called a press conference 'to once and for all set the record straight'. Going against advice from his management that to address any speculation over his sexuality would only fan the flames, he told reporters in a printed statement: 'No! I've never taken hormones to maintain my high voice. No! I've never had my cheekbones altered in any way. No! I've never had cosmetic surgery on my eyes. Yes! One day in the future I plan to get married and have a family. Any statement to the contrary is simply untrue...we all know that kids are very impressionable and therefore susceptible to such stories. I'm certain that some have already been hurt by this horrible slander. In addition to their admiration, I would like to keep their respect.'

The *L. A. Times* were not alone in noticing that 'there does not appear to be any precedent for a celebrity going to such lengths to proclaim his heterosexuality', though he didn't actually say 'No! I am not gay', just as he didn't say 'No! I haven't had plastic surgery' (he admitted to the nose jobs later). Perhaps this was the difference between public relations and a lie.

Despite his desire to carefully control his public image, Michael Jackson has always had an extremely playful attitude towards the press. Like Charles and Diana and God knows who else,

Michael's planted stories about himself (it was him and his ex-manager Frank Dileo who fed the oxygen chamber and Elephant Man fictions to *The National Enquirer*). And like Di he cries when it all backfires, unable to grasp why the press has suddenly dubbed him 'Wacko Jacko'.

The video for 'Leave Me Alone' (including shots of Michael dancing with the Elephant Man's bones) may show an ability to laugh at himself and laugh off some of the rumours, but like so many of his songs ('Wanna Be Startin' Something', 'Beat It', 'Will You Be There?', 'Who Is It?') the lyrics suggest an incredible level of paranoia. This is a man whose most famous record is not about love or loss, but an accusation; the paternity suit he sang about on 'Billie Jean' was another fiction (though such is the nature of fandom a number of women have subsequently claimed to be Billie Jean) and showed a fear of the female that runs through his work.

Pop music is obsessed with sex. Michael has run from it. Once describing himself as being like 'a haemophiliac who can't afford to be scratched in any way', only Cliff Richard and Morrissey have made quite so much out of being chaste. Last summer, in answer to Oprah Winfrey asking if he was still a virgin, he giggled like a schoolgirl and told her: 'I'm a gentleman'. He's claimed romances with Tatum O'Neal and Brooke Shields. They've both denied there was anything between them.

Others have claimed (even more improbably) that he's had romances with David Geffen and Boy George. His biographer, J. Randy Taraborelli, has argued that 'Michael would never allow himself to have homosexual relationships, even if he did have feelings for other men. He is much too puritanical as a result of his religious background...When it comes to child raising, Jehovah's Witnesses are encouraged to withhold affection from any child who disobeys the rules of the church or parent. Even as a teenager, Michael didn't want his father's affection any more. But he needed his mother's and would probably have done anything to keep it, even bury his true identity and feelings.'

Jackson may not be a sexual actor, but he's definitely a kind of voyeur. He knows sex is the currency a pop star has to deal in, and is apparently always probing friends. He's learnt to act sexy too (he's said the crotch grabbing is 'subliminal') and there's some bizarre moments in his music: 'Muscles' ('I don't know whether it's supposed to be Michael's fantasy or mine,' Diana Ross quipped, a little mischievously) and 'In The Closet' (intended as a duet with Madonna, who said after meeting Michael: 'He needs to come out more...I'd love to turn (my dancers) José and Luis on him for a week'), both reveal a certain amount of knowingness. Or else, an astonishing naivety.

'Ben', along with Elton John's 'Daniel', is one of the few male to male love songs to chart (though we were constantly reminded they were written about a rat and a brother respectively), and in the middle of 'The Girl Is Mine' Michael and Paul McCartney begin cooing sweet nothings seemingly to each other. Michael suddenly screaming out 'I'm melting' (the Wicked Witch of the West's last words in *The Wizard of Oz*) in 'Don't Stop 'Til You Get Enough' is one of Disco's campest moments. In *Moon Walk,* his autobiography, he wrote how people keep asking about the words to both 'Muscles' and 'Human Nature' ('Why does he do me that way? I like loving this way'), and pointed out that 'people often think the lyrics you're singing have some special personal significance for you, which often isn't true. It's important to reach people'. In pop such sexual tourism is commonplace, but Michael was someone who didn't seem to have anywhere to call home.

Many pop stars have cloaked their true sexuality (hetero as much as homo), but a colour closet of sorts also exists. It was something Motown excelled at – from the missing word in its slogan 'The sound of young America' – to its policy of keeping photos of its acts off early album sleeves. And as with sexuality or gender, many in the public eye find it convenient not to make an issue of their race and to pretend that everything in the ghetto's rosy. Michael Jackson was no Public Enemy, and no public enemy either. His breaking of MTV's policy of musical apartheid was the only occasion on record when Jackson refused to sit at the back of the bus.

But Michael wasn't just downplaying his colour. His lightened skin, straightened hair, and thinned nose and lips seemed to be a denial of it. Over the last ten years he's come across like some black Dorian Gray. Some blame his family's taunts to the kid they nicknamed 'Big nose' and 'Liver lips', others have speculated that his prime motive is not to look as white as possible, but simply to look as unlike his father as possible. Others still have said he wanted to look as beautiful as Diana Ross. Everybody from brother Jermaine to black muslim leader Louis Farrakhan have questioned the price he's had to pay for his 'crossover' appeal.

But Michael's real crime wasn't not wanting to be black, or not wanting to be gay. It was that he didn't appear to want to be anything. He didn't want to be black. Or white. He didn't want to be gay. Or straight. And this is a world where you have to be something.

Michael Jackson treated those binary divisions we're told we have to live by – adult/child, man/woman, black/white, straight/gay – as a playground not a prison. But when he sang 'It don't matter if you're black or white' (and by implication if you're straight or gay) he showed a complete failure to understand how important these identities are to people. Sure, it *shouldn't* matter, but right now it *does*.

The glimpse of the future he provided was immensely frustrating to those of us still trapped in the present. Ambiguity is, after all, to evasion as 'public relations' is to lies.

'Fame,' wrote John Lahr, 'is America's Faustian bargain . . . the public relishes each fall of a star as a sacrifice.' Each story – those of the real stars – must have a beginning, a middle, and, most importantly, an end as dramatic as that of Elvis or Lennon or Monroe or Garland. So, what would befit the biggest star better than a big scandal, where the last star is accused of breaking the last taboo, and, like a leper messiah, 'The Peter Pan of pop' is shown to have been its J. M. Barrie all along?

Nothing makes us as happy as the sound of the mighty falling. The Jackson scandal is the Wilde Trial of our age. Speeding towards the end of the century we can kid ourselves that, by making an example of one man, we eradicate all our fears about some 'new perversion'. The analogies go further still; the Wilde and Jackson stories are almost the same. The man who is the talk of the town has been the subject of a whispering campaign for some time. Rumours have been circulating about the nature of his relationship with a series of young male friends. One boy's father had once been pleased about their friendship, but now he confronts the man and threatens to drag him through the courts. All know the court case will be the man's downfall. Even his friends imagine he will flee the country. Concern for the 'victim' is all but forgotten as we lose ourselves in an orgy of hatred for the accused.

There the similarity ends. At the time of writing the civil action against Jackson has been dropped. A perfect ending could be provided by this scandal having no real ending. Michael Jackson leaves us all in limbo once more; the Great Not is also both *not* guilty and *not* not guilty.

But the talk continues that a criminal prosecution may yet be brought. We want the certainty of a verdict. Michael Jackson may still get to replay the Wilde trial right through to its sorry conclusion. If he does, I'd rather be an Ada Leverson than one of the whores who danced on the steps of the Old Bailey when the guilty verdict was announced, then kicked up their skirts with glee and shouted out ''e'll 'ave to get 'is 'air cut proper now!'

As Oscar said: 'a thing is not necessarily true because a man dies for it'. It could just be bad public relations.

February 1994

Chapter seven

Being Boring: Erasure

TWO questions for you first, dear reader. One: What do you already know about Andy Bell? Two: What do you want to know about Andy Bell?

Not much? Me neither. The only thing that's interesting about Andy Bell is that he's so uninteresting. He's a huge star. In terms of record sales he's the biggest unequivocally out gay pop star we've ever produced, and yet the man's a complete void. It's like when John Major comes on the news, and you ask yourself 'can this man really be Prime Minister?'

Is this man really a pop star? Is he loved? Is he adored? Are people desperate to know him? We're in a hotel room in London. When we leave, will the maid be fishing his pubes from the plughole for a souvenir? I doubt it somehow, don't you?

One last question for you? Do you remember at school how you'd always get double geography last thing on a Friday afternoon? There's you and all these kids who are only interested in the weekend and each other, and standing in front of them is some old guy with a beard and a CND badge wibbling on about water tables. Remember? Well interviewing Andy Bell feels just like that.

Let's talk about sex. Everybody else does. Andy's happily married to an American man called Paul. Has been for years. But straight journalists always ask Andy about shagging. Maybe they're just desperate for him to say something interesting.

'They find the whole thing fascinating,' Andy says. 'It's quite an eye-opener that they're not really interested in heterosexual foreplay or whatever they get up to. It's quite boring really. Everybody does it, but not many people talk about it. Madonna's my idol 'cause she does. I don't think sex is all that it's cracked up to be really. It's good fun but it's just a recreation.'

Andy Bell's favourite phrase is 'It's quite boring really'. Being a pop star is 'quite boring really'. Even being an out gay pop star is 'quite boring really'.

'It sounds so official – "coming out". It's almost like a document you have to sign. I don't like wearing a badge and I don't like being affiliated to anything . . . '

Zzzzzzz . . .

' . . . so I'll just be honest. If somebody asked what does your girlfriend do or what do you do in bed or anything like that I just tell them. But I don't feel it's like an issue. It has been before but I think it's quite old fashioned now. The Pet Shop Boys' last album was much more camp in a gay way than our last one. And with Elton John and people coming out I feel like I'm a bit of an old timer really. I've never been out in a strident way or chaining myself to the railings or anything. It's still been that laid back thing, you know?'

Is this a clone I see before me? Andy Bell's rather fond of such cosy but tired glay clichés. I point out that the world isn't yet exactly awash with out gay pop stars.

'Yeah, but I feel it's not a novelty any more – it's worn off.'

For you or for other people?

'For me. And I don't like apartheid, whatever it is.'

It's the policy of racial segregation they have in South Africa, but that's not important right now. Hang on, he's off again. . .

'People always call us a gay band because I sound gay. And people always think that a gay band has a gay audience but it's not true. Part of our longevity is because of the cross section that we attract. I think our fans are totally across the board.'

Neil Tennant once said the worst thing about going on tour was that he finally got to see what Pet Shop Boys' fans looked like. He'd been hoping for a gang of sexy rave kids but they looked 'like they could have been U2 fans'.

'I think it's very honest of Neil to say that. It does cross your mind, but I revel in that. If you have to categorize your audience or you cater towards one type of people you, umm, get into a corner.'

Erasure sell records. *Loads* of records, but it's the Simply Red syndrome – not many people give a flying bat's tit for them. But then, Andy Bell doesn't much either. He's said he's 'not particularly in love with our songs really' and that if Erasure never made another record he doubts anyone would notice.

'I think more people would notice now. I don't think it matters to them. I don't think it would be any great loss but I'd be quite sad.'

Happily for Andy, Erasure have got a new album out. And it's, umm, well, it's an Erasure album isn't it? It's called *I Say, I Say, I Say*. It's functional, quite beautiful in places, and it will sell by the bucketload. The music is often astounding, but the lyrics are like something the versificator at the Ministry of Truth's Music Department could have knocked out in its lunch break. At one point Andy claims to be 'filled with the joys of spring'. Whatever that means. He's also apparently 'waiting for a knight in shining armour'. For me, though, the album's greatest moment is the chorus that declares 'I want you back in my loving arms for eternity'. Three clichés for the price of one there. What a bargain!

Andy Bell sings on the record, but he's not really there. He says nothing and puts nothing of himself into the songs. And, unless I'm completely out of touch with the uniform scene, even 'waiting for a knight in shining armour' isn't gay – it's just guff. You see, Andy likes being anonymous.

'I can go everywhere and I pride myself on it. The whole star thing is a myth anyway. You use it to sell your records. But I've always been quite a loner and even now I just like to go out by myself to a club or a pub or anywhere. You might get hassled by people but part of the art is just talking to them for a while and making excuses or being genuinely involved in conversation.'

I almost add 'until they submit', but bite my tongue. Andy's said 'part of my job as an entertainer is to say "it's alright, don't get too upset or freaked out"'. Like pop's just one big baby blanket. He has a quietist view of queerdom. He troubles no one: don't get *too* upset or freaked out, it's only Andy Bell. Erasure are the absence of passion, of pride, of politics, of perversity, of pleasure, and the triumph of mustn't grumble-ism. His sexuality is stated but never discussed. There's no sense of there being any flesh on his gay bones.

As he's said, the Pet Shop Boys, for all their closetry, ultimately say more. The most high profile out gay artist has the lowest public profile and the most unassuming sexual identity. 'We give people good product,' Andy says. It's quite boring really. Has he ever thought Erasure might be popular *in spite* of the fact that they're fronted by a faggot?

'Yeah, the people you meet, they'll be very defensive about liking your music. There was one guy who was a trainee policeman and then he left the force, but he was an Erasure fan and there was always, whenever we met him, this, not antagonism but, sort of prickly sensation. I think part of his coming to terms with liking the group is when he left the police force. I really do think the two things were connected. We got a letter from some pupils in a class in Yorkshire and one of the guys, they were only like really young kids, wrote "I really like blah song but I don't like the song where you dress up like a woman". You know? And umm that's really the level of err that thing.'

Someone told me they went to see you live a while back. They saw this real lad there, he loved the show and told his mates: 'I wouldn't have missed that fucking bender for anything!'

'That's good. I like it. I think anything on a subconscious level is good.'

Does that sound like a typical reaction?

'It's really hard to say how much you infiltrate people's minds or change their lives. I had a letter from someone before, saying "my friend committed suicide and 'Hideaway' was on the record player". You can't take responsibility for that. But at the same time you can't take the praise or whatever either. It depends on them whether you have an effect or not and whether it's good or bad.'

I actually quite like Erasure. They've had some great moments. *Pop!* is a pretty damned good greatest hits album. They did a bollock-ticklingly good version of Cerrone's 'Supernature'. 'Sometimes' was one of the best records of the Eighties. And I'm grateful to Andy for singlehandedly masterminding the Abba revival. Though I'm still not sure whether their covering neither 'Gimme! Gimme! Gimme!' or 'Dancing Queen' was a good thing or not. He's also had a hand in the greatest Christmas number one that never was – the cover of 'Enough Is Enough' he did with k. d. lang.

Their performance at last year's Brit Awards was arguably the greatest four minutes of his career. The record sadly never got released (unless you call being tucked away on the soundtrack to *The Coneheads* a release).

'It was going to be a single. It was all packaged, but we left Sire. It was a record company thing. Our names were just bandied about because we were both gay, you know, ish.'

Andy Bell is gay-ish. Right.

It wasn't always thus. Erasure's first album *Wonderland*, was pure Boystown – just listen to a song like 'Pistol'. The first video for 'Who Needs Love (Like That)' had the two of them in drag and doing the Can Can. The video didn't get shown and the album sold about 12 copies. So the boys moved on. By the next album, *The Circus*, they'd turned into a chirpy Europop group. On record company advice Andy dressed down for *Top of the Pops* and for videos, in white t-shirt and blue jeans (arguably a gayer look than a frock but a more coded one).

Andy was still forthright about his homosexuality, and undoubtedly out. But they didn't want to bore everyone by going on and on and on about it. On record his sexuality skulked in the background, discreet enough not to trouble the listener. And Erasure got huge.

Live they were a whole different ballgown. Andy would dress up and camp it up in his own clumsy, almost embarrassing, way. But you expect to be entertained at a concert, don't you? It was panto – good clean fun. Only a laugh and 'all part of the campaign to get the ball rolling and make people interested. If you look stupid people are going to look at you.'

So that's alright then. They were back in drag for 1992's *Abba-esque* video. Have you found as you've got more successful you have more licence to be girlie?

'I think the live shows have always been girlie. They're more elaborate now but they were probably girlier before when we didn't have anything. But it's always good to dig when people are least expecting it. Or you can trundle along and do something like the Abba thing and just like drop ... err I don't know. Make a loud noise?'

You're on your own with this one Andy.

'Then let that happen. Then just go back and go gently along again. It's more effective really.'

So are you more of your own man now?

'I think so, yes. I don't really worry about it, not at all. It's funny you should say that. What's shocking, and I think it's true for any gay person, you kind of live with yourself and get on and you're happy and contented with your life and then all of a sudden someone says "you fucking poof" out of the blue, and you haven't had that for two years or a year. And you're devastated. And it takes a week or more to brush down and get ready again. And that hasn't happened to me for a long time. So it's always when you're most unaware that something happens. No matter how contented you feel it's always good to still have the little hairs on the back of your neck ... umm, I don't know. But it's always shocking when abuse happens, whatever it is.'

Andy lost me a bit back there, so I tactfully change the subject. Time for my big Erasure conspiracy theory: His musical other half Vince Clarke wasn't just searching for the perfect beat, but searching for the perfect pop group. Prior to pairing up with Andy, the wandering electro boffin had formed a pretty-boy-going-on-pervy synth band called Depeche Mode. Then during the great Gender Bender boom he ditched them to team up with an androgyne character called Alf. He packed her in to make classy white soul in The Assembly with Feargal Sharkey (and briefly with the man with the sexiest voice in Christendom, Paul Quinn). What next for our Vince? If you were forming a band in 1985 you'd probably want a faggot to front it. Dammit, it was practically compulsory.

Andy blows my theory by telling me he didn't tell Vince he was gay until after he'd got the gig. In fact, he didn't even tell Vince – 'it just dawned on him'. No plot. It just happened. But Vince was a vagabond before, why has he stuck with La Bell?

'I'm more persuasive,' Andy says before correcting himself. 'I'm more persuaded. 'Cause with Alison or Depeche Mode they're more forceful personalities than me. I think I'm more laid back and not as argumentative. It's a compromise. It's very boring.'

And for these reasons, the world, like Vince, has taken Andy to its heart. He's our first 'straight-acting, straight-looking' gay pop star. One of those people that homosexuality is wasted on. Quite boring really.

I take a last look at Andy and ask myself again – is this man really a star? And then it hits me – the real question is 'is Andy Bell really gay?'

The interview's over. The pop star clocks off. He likes his job. It's quite boring sometimes but the money's good. At least he's got it over with for another week. Soon be back with the wife and kids. They always have fish on Friday. He is happy because tomorrow is Saturday. He'll wash his car and then go to the match. The pop star yawns.

Ladies and gentlemen, a star is *bored*!

Gay Times, May 1994

Chapter eight

Blaming it on the Boogie: Stock, Aitken and Waterman

Elyot: Nasty insistent little tune.
Amanda: Extraordinary how potent cheap music is.

Noel Coward, *Private Lives*

IF you're a gay man who's had even so much as a nodding acquaintance with the scene in the late Eighties, or early Nineties, the songs of Stock, Aitken and indeed Waterman will have provided a sizeable chunk of the soundtrack for your life.

Just think, boys, in the years to come, when you're old and your hair is dyed, one day there you'll be in that little cottage you always dreamed of, after a hard day's cruising in your bathchair, you turn on the radio and that song, that song you thought you'd forgotten, but now, now it's all coming back and the tears start falling down your face. Him, you, then, there. That voice, singing, singing ' . . . you spin me right round baby right round like a record baby right round round round . . . ' Aah. And how you hate that song!

It's funny, I can more than understand boring little breeders getting all hot under their Burton collars about Stock, Aitken and Waterman, but I have to confess to being somewhat baffled at all the fags who are flustered by them. I mean, they try so hard to please us.

40: *Seduced and Abandoned*

The SAW boys are clever guys who know their market and who know that a pretty considerable chunk of it consists of gay men. They cater and even pander to this and as a consequence have given us lots of good faggotty pop – a perfect and beautiful hybrid of the two popular music forms that have been dearest to us in the past: Early Motown and Hi NRG.

It would seem that SAW have managed, as far as we're concerned, to hit that perfect beat again and again and again. Show me a gay pub that hasn't got a juke box blasting out a steady and constant diet of Bananarama, Kylie, Big Fun, Jason and the rest of them and I'll show you a load of naff queens sitting round a piano singing songs from *Showboat*. Probably.

So why do so many gay men profess to hate SAW so much? There are three main lines of argument: and all three of them stand up about as well as a baby giraffe.

'But all their songs sound the same,' goes the first and most-often-heard whinge. But so do most groups. If we like them we say they've got a distinctive sound. As my mum always used to tell me 'if it ain't broke – don't remix it'. Peter Waterman always answers this allegation with a withering *'And?'*

'And all their artists are puppets … ' the whinge usually continues. Once more one wonders how much this person knows about pop's torrid past. Motown and Stax, Phil Spector and Shadow Morton, The Sex Pistols and The Monkees are all living legendary examples of how the greatest records often have strings attached. Moreover, we should surely be grateful that SAW have decided not to inflict their ugly mugs and middle-aged spreads on us. Instead they get beautiful people to perform the songs … oh, and Cliff.

'And it's escapist,' the whinge delivers as its final puny blow. As if there was something intrinsically wrong with pop music being escapist! As if queens should feel guilty about wanting to go to a club every now and then to try to forget how rotten the world is outside. Yes, pop *is* a palliative, but it stops us from cracking up just as much as it calms us down. Similarly that other great glut of SAW fans – teenage girls – should not have to apologize for allowing themselves the inexpensive luxury of fleeing into fantasy and away from the frightening reality of compulsory and often brutal heterosexual relationships.

The staunchest critics of so-called 'escapist music' have always been middle class, white, straight men, who see the world through rose-tinted Raybans and for whom it is perhaps useful to do a bit of aural slumming now and again to find out how the other nine-tenths live.

The real reason that people hate SAW is because they feel they should. I strongly suspect that most of them are to some degree closet fans, hence the exaggerated and irrational hostility. They feel unable to admit to liking something they'd prefer to dismiss as the preserve of working class teenage girls. It was exactly this sort of ageist and misogynist snobbery that kept the likes of Emerson, Lake and Palmer in Lear jets during the Seventies.

Surely we shouldn't be playing the same sort of games as straights do? Most male hetero behaviour is just one big lie and it ultimately only brings them unhappiness – imagine having to pretend to like Phil Collins! When it comes to pop, the old adage rings true: the (straight) men don't know but the little girls understand.

Gay men understand, as we've thankfully got more in common with the little girls. We both like Sonia, Kylie and the 'Rams as they know what it's like to be continually crapped on by crappy men, or to have given your heart to someone who never asked for it. To the uninitiated it might seem like we never learn. But we don't, do we?

The men who sing for SAW are a whole different kettle of worms. Their women offer us comfort by singing of the real world where men are perfect beasts, but these boys are just plain perfect. No no-good, low-down, two-timing-cheats these guys; love junkies to a man and romantic to the point of idiocy, they are such stuff as dreams are made of. They're never gonna give you up, you'll be together forever, nothing can divide you – there's too many broken hearts in the world. Sweet, huh?

But it's the control exercised over the artists' visual imagery that gives the clearest indication that SAW know exactly who they're aiming at. And it's not just the pretty faces – but the way they've been dressed to thrill. Take our Jason for example, and compare the clothes and haircut from hell that haunted the poor boy in his *Neighbours* days with his post-SAW high-class, rent-boy chic of ripped jeans and white t-shirt. Big Fun, spookily enough, in their hooded tops and black 501s come across like three of your average provincial-scene queens. Whenever I see them on *Top of the Pops* I half expect them to start passing the poppers round at any moment.

The same sensibility also seeps into the videos, with none being complete without a handful of half naked men doing some formation dancing in the foreground. When one's confronted with these vast expanses of well-developed chest positively dripping with baby oil it's hard not to snatch a double take at the TV set, with much the same sense of joyous disbelief as when you first saw Nick Kamen taking his kecks off in his local launderette, and gasp out 'Huh?! Are you talking to me?'

Stock, Aitken and Waterman have consciously enriched British gay male culture. Thanks to them we can cry along with Kylie, swoon over Jason, laugh at Big Fun, or scream our proverbial tits off with Bananarama. Gay men who slag off SAW just don't know how lucky, lucky, lucky they are.

Gay Times, July 1990

Chapter nine

Cock Rock: The Secret History of the Penis in Pop

'Rock and roll bands go on stage for the same reason George Bush goes to war,' U2's Bono once claimed in a rare moment of insight, 'it's all about willies.' But the damned things remain one of rock's best kept secrets. In a world dominated by 7 inches, 12 inches and the CD's frankly unimpressive $4\frac{3}{4}$ inches, it's time to reveal some of the most noted penii in pop.

Chuck Berry

Chuck Berry had to wait until 1972 to get his first number one single both here and in the States with 'My Ding-a-ling', a piece of innuendo even George Formby might have thought twice about. The song became one of Mary Whitehouse's first *causes célèbres*, leading her to write to the then Minister of Posts and Telecommunications concerning 'the complaints we have received from young people as well as older ones, including two doctors, about the pop singer's obscene interpretation of lines like "I like to play with my ding-a-ling"'. After filing her complaint Mrs Whitehouse left for two weeks' holiday, 'returning just in time for Christmas where a huge pile of press cuttings, human excrement amongst my post and a Christmas card with "F... you" scrawled across it awaited me.' Merry Christmas Mary!

44: *Seduced and Abandoned*

David Bowie

Dame David commissioned rock artist Guy Peellaert to paint him for the cover of his *Diamond Dogs* album. And, for reasons best known to himself, Peellaert chose to depict Bowie painted gold and with the hind quarters of a whippet. RCA objected to the whippet's willy and had the offending member painted out. Bowie also adopted the penis-less look for *Aladdin Sane* and when he played Newton in Nic Roeg's *The Man Who Fell To Earth*. One can only presume his penis exploded on impact.

Wayne County

After a decade on the fringes of, first, the Warhol set, and then the burgeoning American and British punk scenes, Wayne County, rock 'n' roll's most famous transvestite, disappeared in 1980 only to emerge as Jayne County, rock 'n' roll's most famous transsexual. She's not the only pop star to have waved bye bye to his weenie – Amanda Lear, cover star of Roxy Music's *For Your Pleasure*, former girlfriend of Bryan Ferry and sometime Disco star, has also been snipped and tucked. And as for Katrin Quinol, singer with Black Box, well ... 'I'm interested in the rumours that she has been male,' commented Morrissey, 'it makes it more interesting. If you look at her from a certain angle you could possibly see her playing for Wigan.'

Dead Kennedys

In 1985 the parents of a 13-year-old school girl from San Fernando, California, discovered that their daughter had bought a copy of the Dead Kennedys' album *Frankenchrist*. As if that wasn't bad enough, they found the record contained a free copy of the aptly-named poster, 'Penis Landscape', by *Alien* set designer H. R. Giger. They complained to the State Attorney and Kennedys' singer Jello Biafra was busted and charged with 'distributing harmful matter to minors'. After Biafra won this important test case on music and censorship, members of the jury queued up to get their copies of the album signed.

45: Cock Rock: The Penis in Pop

The Doors

Miami. Florida, 2 March 1969. Whilst on stage a tired and clearly emotional Jim Morrison began berating the audience and – during 'Touch Me' appropriately enough – fiddling with his belt buckle. Ever the poet Jim began improvising lines such as 'do you wanna touch me?' and 'do you wanna see my cock?' Two days later the Florida police issued a warrant for the Lizard King's arrest on a charge that 'he did lewdly and lasciviously expose his penis and shake it'. Jimbo had always claimed to be 'an erotic politician', but English schoolboys have a far better word to describe people who put their hand on their penis and shake it. Joe Meek, Steadman Pearson of Five Star, Jimmy Somerville and Johnnie Ray have also been charged with getting their penises out in public, but in slightly different circumstances.

Led Zeppelin

Down through the ages wise men and poets have asked 'what is this thing called love?' For Zeppelin's Robert Plant it was simply something 'I want to give you every inch of'. Plant, known as 'Percy' to his friends, had clearly fought his way to the front of the queue when God was handing out Johnsons, and is living proof that there are some things that age cannot wither. Cod psychologists have made much of how rock stars use the neck of their guitar as a penis substitute. Absolute tosh. As anyone who's read the exposé of life on the road with Led Zeppelin, *Hammer of the Gods,* can tell you, rock stars use baby sharks as a penis substitute.

John Lennon

In 1971 John Lennon and Yoko Ono set up the suitably named Joko Productions with the aim of turning out a film a week. Following the success of their earlier collaboration, *Bottoms* – which Yoko assured us wasn't just 52 human butts, but hey! 'an aimless petition signed by people with their anuses' – came *Self Portrait.* 'My prick, that's all you saw,' Lennon recalled fondly, 'but it dribbled at the end. That was accidental. The idea was for it to slowly rise and fall but it didn't.' The short film was often confused for obvious reasons with the teasingly titled *Erection*, an Ono project that sped through 18 months in the life of a building site. John Lennon's John Thomas had previously been sighted on the full frontal sleeve of *Two Virgins*, and let's not forget that one of Beatles manager Brian Epstein's earliest, and arguably most important, decisions was to get the fab four out of leather trousers and into very, very *tight* trousers.

Madonna

On stage Madonna has appropriated the rap singers' habit of grabbing her crotch to reinforce a point. It's known in the trade as 'genderfuck' – she grabs her 'penis' and we are reminded that there is nothing there. See also Michael Jackson.

Marky Mark

More crotch grabbing. But Mark is the first male star who grabs his cock to centre it as an object of desire rather than to assert its mythic phallic power. Extremely popular with gay men; the well developed chest is always exposed, the kecks invariably fall floorwards but his Calvins stay put. Although American gay magazines are reputedly bidding very highly to get their hands on some outtakes from a recent photo session where the boy was allegedly seen in his full glory.

Milli Vanilli

The Dutch duo's first appearance on *Top of the Pops* – where they danced around in some skintight, religion revealing all-in-ones, with something visibly swinging around between their legs – caused Simon Mayo to raise his eyes skyward and to smirk in a Christian kind of way: 'Well, that's *Willy* Vanilli there'. The BBC switchboard was swiftly deluged with a record number of complaints. The band later fell from grace when it was discovered that they never sang on their own records, but the trouser snakes were clearly all their own work.

47: Cock Rock: The Penis in Pop

The Osmonds

Much has been made of the behind-the-scenes image makers who shape how we see the stars. But have there been any quite as fastidious as Donny Osmond's mum who ordered the lumpy bits to be airbrushed out of all photos of her son?

P. J. Proby

After scoring a huge hit with 'Hold Me', the American-born singer was forced to flee this country in 1965 when the press began hounding him over the alarming frequency with which his trousers would split on stage. Mind you, he was supporting Cilla Black at the time. 'Surprise,' as they say, 'surprise.'

PIL

How do you launch a solo career when you've just walked out of the most controversial group of all time? That's right, you put a picture of a bloody big cock on the sleeve of your first single. When Johnny Rotten left the Sex Pistols and became plain old John Lydon once more he wanted to put a fully engorged member on the fold out sleeve of 'Public Image'. Virgin Records would have none of it and a compromise of sorts was reached with a join-the-dots outline appearing. In 1986 King Kurt released their *Big Cock* album with a photograph of a big cock on the front cover. It had wings, lots of feathers and if it could speak, would undoubtedly have gone 'cluck cluck cluck'. Oh how we laughed.

Cynthia Plastercaster

No survey of peckers in pop would be complete without a mention of Cynthia Plastercaster. In the Chicago of the late Sixties, Cynthia made a name for herself by persuading more than a hundred of rock's biggest names to leave an impression on her dental moulds. The first was Jimi Hendrix: 'He was very large and very thick', the then novice Cynthia remembers, 'but I didn't know anything about lubing the pubes then. I didn't rip them all out. Maybe a fifth of them.' Ouch.

Elvis Presley

Don't believe the euphemisms! The real reason television stations would only film 'Elvis the Pelvis' from the waist up in the Fifties was that in the flickering shadow and light of the black and white screens something King-size was clearly visible trouserwards. Something that Elvis, a humble country boy at heart, referred to as 'Little Elvis'. Sadly it's now widely believed he'd sewn an iron bar into the lining of his strides. For me this was as distressing as finding out that there's no Santa Claus, but life goes on. Still if it wasn't the biggest, it was probably the cheesiest. Priscilla Presley had two extra heads fitted on the shower at Graceland, one at armpit level and one pointing crotchwards, because of Elvis's infamous aversion to good old soap and water.

Prince

The cover for Prince's 1989 LP, *Lovesexy*, had the imp of the perverse naked with only a carefully positioned (and nicely shaved) leg to cover his modesty. Except that is in prudish Dubai where all copies had a smart pair of blue trousers painted on. But though we couldn't see the purple one's purple one, the unfeasibly large lilies he sat amongst, and in particular their conversation inducingly shaped pistils, left little to the imagination.

The Rolling Stones

The greatest willy band of them all. From scoring a number one with the classic knob song 'Little Red Rooster', through the cocks-and-cops episode when Her Majesty's Constabulary caught the boys peeing against a garage wall, the raid at Keith Richards' Redlands home revealing the Mars Bar as penis substitute, the album cover todger on *Sticky Fingers* (when you pulled down the fly it was Joe Dallesandro's tool you saw outlined through the panties, not Jagger's), to the huge on-stage phallus during their Seventies tours. Seminal. There's no other word for it.

49: Cock Rock: The Penis in Pop

U2

Adam Clayton wopped out his wanger on the sleeve of *Achtung Baby*. He's now engaged to supermodel Naomi Campbell. You see, it pays to advertize.

The Velvet Underground

On original copies of the Andy Warhol designed sleeve for *The Velvet Underground & Nico*, next to the yellow banana was the invitation 'Peel it and see'. If you peeled it back (and who wouldn't?) you saw a pinkish sort of banana shaped thing.

And not forgetting...

Revolting Cocks, Rudimentary Penii, Throbbing Gristle, The Dicks, Buzzcocks, Big Black, Helmet, The Members, Stiff Records.

Gay Times, August 1993

Chapter ten

Dear Shaun: Happy Mondays

DEAR Shaun

Credit where credit's due I've got to hand it to you Shaun – you do make me laugh. Happy Mondays, like The Archies and The Ramones before you, are one of the great cartoon groups. A transparent parody of 'working-class man' that only a Tory Cabinet Minister could fail to see through. You are the Alf Garnett of rock and roll. Like I said, it's funny but, well, I've come to expect a little more from my rock stars.

You see Shaun, I always thought music was about challenging things, not submitting and presenting yourself as a grotesque caricature of a wilfully lumpen prole. In place of attitude you have a tired and brainless bigotry, centred on an unwritten philosophy: 'I am working class therefore I am thick therefore I hate poofs'. Surely one of the great things about pop, and about Punk in particular, is that it's provided a platform for working-class kids to show how articulate and intelligent they are. But all you can offer is a celebration of your own idiocy. Pop's been a place where people have rebelled against the dominant order and its values. Yet you seem content to endorse them, to offer only moral conformity masquerading as rebellion.

Just think of how the whole thing started: Little Richard's joyous camp squeal, Johnnie Ray bursting into tears or Elvis offering himself up as a sex object. They were the first in a great tradition of refuseniks – of men behaving in a way that went right against the grain of how 'real men' are supposed to behave. I don't know Shaun, maybe you think it's been downhill all the way from there. You certainly seem to, in place of intrigue and excitement you offer only reaction. The Mondays' public image is one of a couple of geezers down the pub talking about football and starting fights. I wouldn't even flatter you with that often-bandied-about comment that you're one of Thatcher's children. If you're a spokesperson for a generation then you're a spokesperson for my dad's.

Confirming and conforming to stereotypes is not the stuff great groups are made of. Your homophobia and your laddishness do not frighten me, they merely bore me. There's nothing 'hard' about being a 'real man' Shaun. Doing exactly what's expected of you is a piece of piss. Show me any queen, show me any dyke, and I'll show you someone that's a thousand times braver than you.

The funniest thing of all, though, was when you made that joke on MTV about how you used to be a rent boy. The thing that kills me is that if you *had* been hanging around Sackville Street trying to flog your arse in the early Eighties, you'd have been in one of the few places in Manchester back then that was playing the kind of music that everyone professes these days to have been into all along – dance. I've a feeling you're fully aware that dance music is, as much as anything, faggot's music. I know you make a big thing of pretending to be just a simple lad from North Manchester but I just don't think you're *that* thick. And maybe that's part of the problem – that it's all a big act, a spectacular attempt at disavowal: 'I might be making dance music but it doesn't mean I'm a poof, right?'

Or maybe I'm being too kind to you. Maybe you're for real. But if you are Shaun, then don't try and pass off your garbled homophobic twaddle as some representation of authentic working-class feeling. You know as well as I do that it's not.

I also know that if I called you a rock star you'd shrug your shoulders and say something like 'Naaah, I'm just an ordinary bloke that's made good and who's having a laugh with his mates'. But the thing is you are, and as a rock star there are far more interesting myths you could be spinning.

Whatever, I'm sure you despise me much more than I despise you. I have far more important things to focus my anger on than someone who, when it comes down to it, is just a rather dull and obnoxious little irritant. That said, for much the same reasons, I do find it pitiable that anyone could get excited about you or the Happy Mondays. Pop music matters to young people because it sneaks up on them and says 'dare'. All you've ever said is 'durr'.

Yours Richard

Melody Maker, 5 September 1992

Chapter eleven

Dragged into the Future: Trannies With Attitude

A MONDAY night in Manchester. I'm in the ladies loo in the basement of Paradise Factory. Opposite me Nick and Paul, the two Trannies With Attitude, are perched precariously on the sink. Nick Raphael, the one with the brown wig, blue mascara and the biggest eyes in showbusiness, is telling me his life story.

'I come from London and moved to Leeds when I was 18 to take up a career as a professional footballer ... '

Nick, stop it.

'I *was*! Bradford City offered me a contract as a professional footballer. Leeds asked me to trial. I played for Watford and Arsenal as a junior. I was Southern England's schools' captain ... anyway, after six months here I got bored and realized I wasn't suited. When we went out they'd all be shagging three girls a night by showing their football passes and I'd just be sitting there thinking "this isn't really for me". Eventually I realized I was more interested in going out with my friends to gay nightclubs. And that wasn't really the sort of lifestyle appropriate for a professional footballer. So I became a student because my parents wanted me to do a degree. And while I was a student I was so bored I started getting involved with running nightclubs.'

He first came across his partner to be, Paul Fryer, three years ago when he needed a flyer designed. Off he trotted to Paul's little DTP place, showed him a rough idea of what he wanted done and the pair got on famously.

'He turned round and said "that's a shit idea!" and I said "how fucking dare you?. I'm hiring *you!*" and he said "if that's your attitude you can fuck off!" ... and I'm thinking "I like this bloke". Paul was the first person to encourage me to go out in drag.'

So this is all quite new to you?

'Oh no. From nine years old it was fancy-dress parties. I was always the first person to say "Yeah! I'll be a woman". And at that stage your friends' mothers are always encouraging you. They think it's funny – this little boy who plays football and goes out and plays in the street and fights with his friends. "No problem, only a phase." At 13 it was like "C'mon Nick, there's another fancy dress you can wear. You can be a cowboy". At 15 it was "Nick, this has gone beyond a joke now. I know you've done acting for four years but this is not show make-up, this is your mother's make-up". And at 17 it's "you're playing football for a living – why are you going to clubs in drag?"'

Which rather begs the question: why are you going to clubs in drag?

'Nightclubs have always been shows. It's theatre, a visual as well as an audio experience.'

At long last Nick lets Paul get a word in edgeways. 'In a straight club the embodiment of everything queer is still a drag queen. When they see one it's "my God, the poofs are here!". It's the best way of fronting people out because you don't have to be ashamed. You can walk straight up to a straight man who's got his arse against the wall and say "what's your problem darling?" And he won't touch you 'cause they're so terrified.'

But you haven't gone for that RuPaul full-on glamour, total *total* type of look, have you boys?

'RuPaul's American. She's an absolutely brilliant trannie, but British queens have a far more down-to-earth persona. Especially the Northern ones. They're far more gutsy. They're far more ... Bet Lynch. None of this "Hi, I'm beautiful" stuff. We're just two rough girls going out for a night out in comparison.'

'Most people who look at RuPaul would think "What's the point?"' adds Paul. 'They look at us and think "I can do that!"'

When they first met, Paul was running Leeds' Kit Kat Club, 'a sort of proto mixed night', with his friend Suzie. 'It was started by default. We never intended to have a club. We just wanted some-where to go with our friends. And because we'd never structured it, it just got out of hand. People were pulling in all sorts of different directions and we were getting a bit of violence. It was great, though. We had an anti-DJ vibe. Me and Nick used to go to Flesh in drag and Suzie said we should start playing records in drag 'cause it would chase all the homophobic horrors out of the club.'

As David Bowie so nearly said 'I am the DJ, I am what I wear'. Trannies With Attitude see themselves as performers (at one point Nick tellingly refers to their punters as 'the audience'). They get out of the DJ box and dance if the fancy takes them. 'And the other thing,' says Nick, 'is that the microphone is not a dead implement as far as the DJ is concerned...'

'But the problem is you've got to have a personality to use a microphone ... '

' ... and how many DJs do you know who have got a personality?'

Before I have time to think, Nick's off again.

'We only started DJ-ing together the week before that. We played anything we liked. Very eclectic. Paul was always far more way-out than me. I always liked the funky side of things. I was into a lot of House but I wasn't going to play it as it wasn't appropriate. We had a policy of no House music as everybody else was playing it and Rave was in full effect then.'

But soon they discovered a kind of House they could call home. Originally, Nick explains, they called it Nineties Disco.

' ... until some young *fool* who was also a drag queen, called Tracey Techno, said to me [adopts simpering dim cow-type voice]: "I like Techno but I really like some of the Disco-y stuff you play 'cause it's Disno, innit?" and we said "*Disno!!!* You idiot! It's *Tesco!*"'

You can sample this warmer Techno, or Digifunk as its known in other quarters, on the compilation they've put together, *Let's Go Tesko* (React). The *k* came as a certain supermarket chain took offence. 'They were really keen until they found out we were a couple of trannies who run a gay club – then they sent us these legal letters telling us we couldn't use the name.' But Tesco weren't the only people to kick up a fuss over the album. The boys' single 'The

TWA Theme' appears on the album without its noted 'Vogue' pastiche rap: 'Barry Humphries, D. La Rue, fellas in the ladies loo ...', as Madonna's people refused clearance. Which is a little ironic if you think where she nicked Vogue-ing from.

Any road up. Paul, whither Tesko?

'I could never get into just pure House music or Techno, especially Trance which I found really boring. I just found it all too cold. But the stuff that started appearing with all the funky disco bits and all the girlies singing on, I just loved. So we played more and more.'

After they killed off the Kit Kat Club they opened Vague at the Leeds Warehouse in June. Their new Saturday nighter is already firmly stuck at the number one spot in *DJ* magazine's chart of the top ten clubs in the country. The secret of their successful formula seems to be mixing it, as with the music, so with the punters.

'We believe Vague to be the first purpose-built mixed gay night in the country. Something like Puscha has had a mixed gay crowd, but it's been mainly by default. Also they appeal to the upper end of the market which makes it a lot easier to police. We don't have any door policy in that way – we keep the admission charge artificially low. And everybody there is totally into the politics.

'We're making a stand not just for mixed clubbing but for a person's right to choose at any time in their life their sexual orientation, and for a person's right to be bisexual. To do whatever they want with their lives and not to be pigeonholed. Which means we come in for a lot of flak from both straights and gays. People are often suspicious of our motives when they first meet us.

'The idea for the mixed club was simply because we were in Leeds,' Nick illuminates. 'It's the North of England. We're not in London where there's 6.6 million people and a huge percentage of gay men. We're in a far more homophobic environment. There is no Soho. It's hush-hush up here. For straight people in the North to go to a gay club is a really big deal.'

'So we realized we couldn't do a gay club,' Paul adds. 'We had to stick our necks out and do a mixed gay night. Everyone told us it would never work, but we were committed to it and we thought "my God we're gonna make it work".'

The year 1993 will probably be remembered as the fag end of the great Ecstasy boom, but clubs like Vague show that E's effects will continue to be felt for some time yet. Ecstasy culture wasn't just about getting out of it, but about getting on with people; dancing with people who, in another time, and under the influence of another drug (alcohol), would most likely be kicking your head in. Paul agrees.

'We get straight men coming – real bruisers with broken teeth – and they're going "please make me a member. I'll come on me own, I won't bring me mates, oh please". One guy said – this sounds like bollocks but it's God's truth – "I used to be a hooligan but I'm not as insecure as I was and I want to be a member of this club because I love it so much here".'

'It's like Heaven having to accept women coming in,' Nick thinks. 'At the end of the day many gay men have straight girlfriends and they don't want to go to a bar and then say "bye, I'll go to my club now and you go to yours". It's bollocks! I can't turn round to female friends and say "oh I'm sorry I'm going to this club. Yes, I know I've borrowed your dress tonight but you can't come with me".'

Even the naffest of gay clubs will usually let you smuggle your fag hag in. Flesh at the Hacienda and Heaven's Fruit Machine have been the prime movers as far as dykes and fags dancing together goes, but what's so different about Vague is the straight male contingent. This isn't without its problems, but Vague prides itself on being a safe space.

A good doorman is the key, says Paul. Max at Vague asks for a snog from anyone he's not too sure about 'to prove they're not of a violent nature'. And as people are queuing up outside the words 'Homophobic? Kiss my ass!' and 'Bad attitude go home' are projected onto them. And unlike early pioneering mixed clubs like Most Excellent, Flying and Love Ranch, Vague prides itself on being gay first, mixed second. The straights are still in the minority.

'We've made announcements in the middle of the night,' remembers Paul, 'where we've stopped the music and gone "Hi to all the gay boys and dykes in the house". And everyone's like screaming. "Any straight men in?" "Waorghhh!" And I've gone "Right, well it's you I want to talk to actually".' Paul grows about four inches in stature while he's telling this story. '"If you've come here looking for a freak show you better not fucking come next week 'cause you won't get in. This is not about being gay or straight. This is about partying!" And we got a *ROAR!* All the gay people stood up and went "Yes-s! It's our club!"'

'Having a mixed club is the weirdest thing,' confesses Nick. 'But it's the most enjoyable thing too. At the end of the night you look through the audience and you get to the stage where you can't tell. The straight guys become more flamboyant. And it's really weird to see straight guys flirting with gay men . . . '

' . . . and experimenting with their own sexuality and realizing that it's not all black and white,' Paul continues. 'There's a whole lot of grey. It's nice to give people an environment where they can express a bit of that. It doesn't have to be sexual apartheid. We say this club is the future. The future is mixed and we're gonna make it happen now.'

Gay Times, November 1993

Chapter twelve

Getting Away with It: Right Said Fred

RICHARD Fairbrass is fortysomething but he told everyone he's 31. I don't mind. I think it's wonderful that he got away with it.

Richard and his brother Fred had spent years on the fringes of the music business watching and taking it all in, until three years ago when a mutual acquaintance introduced them to another failed pop star, Rob Manzoli. The three of them started to write songs together, and knowing this was their 'last fucking chance' they took it all very seriously, meeting three times a week for tea, biscuits and a jam. One afternoon in October that year they knocked out 'I'm Too Sexy'. Slowly, ever so slowly, Richard says that the song 'started to grow legs of its own. It's a bit like Frankenstein's monster. We invented it – two minutes and fifty-nine seconds of music which has changed our lives completely.'

A friend, Tamzin Aronowitz, just 20 years old, acting as their manager, managed to get 'a very influential record plugger' Guy Holmes to listen to a rough mix of 'Sexy'. After two listens, he decided it was 'brilliant' and gave them £2000 to record the song properly. Sadly, no record company seemed to share his high estimation of the track and so, two years ago this month, he spent a further £13,000 of his own money on making a video and pressing up five thousand singles. Radio One adored it and playlisted it – but then that's 'very influential record pluggers' for you. Just one month later it was at number two in the charts (only Bryan Adams was outselling it) and Frankenstein's little monster started to creak off the laboratory slab.

They've often admitted that they expected to be no more than one-hit-wonders, but Right Said Fred surprised us all by coming back with novelty hit after novelty hit after novelty hit. 'I'm pleased we've proved that you can come out with a silly record and it doesn't have to be your only silly record,' Richard has proudly boasted.

The boys presumed their first single would find an audience on the gay scene ('We thought it was very camp' – it was also an oblique but amusing swipe at attitude queens, specifically, Richard said, the male models who frequented the Putney gym which he co-ran with Fred), but the PAs they performed on the scene were only met with derision: 'they just thought we were taking the piss'. Well, you would, wouldn't you?

But world-beating pop groups aren't made in the gay clubs alone (especially when the gay clubs don't seem to want them) and a team was swiftly brought in to make Right Said Fred fit for more general public consumption.

A two-pronged attack was staged by designer Peter Hawker and make-up artist Peter Barton. Hawker worked on making them less 'masculine', and Barton tried to ensure that they didn't go too far the other way.

Any gay man who caught an early sighting of Right Said Fred would have automatically concluded: 'Uh-oh, over-enthusiastic gym queens!' Over the last decade, more gay-man hours may have been spent in the gym than the disco but, as yet, muscle still doesn't equal Mary in straight eyes.

But Barton realized they looked 'aggressive...frightening. We told them to get a bit less muscley. I wanted them to look softer, more glamorous and it's worked really well. They're far less threatening now. They're no threat at all.'

Fred already had a crop ('because I was going bald and I didn't want to do a Bobby Charlton') and Hawker sent Richard off to do the same (although he's now almost coot-like on top too). 'The single was outrageous, so I thought "Why not send up their image too?"' says Hawker, who describes the new look they achieved as 'a very masculine camp...they never look too feminine. They look outrageous, but straight people can cope with that. There's that thin line...you can't go too far.' You can hear the same conscious avoidance of the feminine in Richard's voice. Whereas the usual standby and signifier of poofery in pop is the falsetto, he has a big, deep throated croon. The effeminate homosexual may be a comforting stereotype for many straights, but simultaneously messing with gender is often what 'threatens' them most.

I've yet to meet anyone who dislikes Richard Fairbrass. He knows that much of the power of camp lies in its refusal to take anything seriously, most of all yourself. And although camp is the word most often, almost invariably, used to describe the Freds, what they're most symptomatic of is camp's imminent demise. What was once our secret (but by no means our exclusive preserve) has now passed over into an all-too-common parlance, and in the process it has turned from something almost indefinable to something meaningless. How can you hope to mock the dominant culture when the dominant culture is in on the act?

Straight journalists now throw the word 'camp' about as a synonym for the amusing and the silly, or worse still, for the whacky or zany – it's no small wonder then that the Freds were asked to write a song for this year's 'zany' Comic Relief Red Nose Day.

The Freds aren't that camp. They're more in the tradition of Sauce!, the latest in a long line that takes in Don McGill postcards, music hall and *Carry On* films. As English as it is straight, Sauce! tries to find the scatological in everything. Sauce! is an attempt by straight England to show it's at ease with sex which only proves the opposite.

Richard and Fred make a great double act. They give each other permission to talk dirty – Fred about women, Richard about men. Both are equally rare sights in the public arena; in these liberal times, post-Chippendale, straight men are the only sexual grouping who are embarrassed to talk publicly about what turns them on.

Richard Fairbrass even presented his own coming out as a kind of common sense. 'I don't believe it's particularly courageous to come out. If I hadn't said everything I did to the press they'd have just started following me around and looking in my dustbins anyway. I did it to give myself an easy life.' He came out to *The Sun* whilst the group were riding high with 'I'm Too Sexy'. Rob and Fred thought he'd gone mad. And when Richard realized what he'd done, so did he.

But there was no outcry. *The Sun* ran their story ('I'm bi-sexy too') and the world kept on turning. Thing was, Richard called himself bisexual, and knows that the likes of you and me would only doubt this. Indeed, what could we do but scoff when on the release of their second single rumours were fed to the press of the impending nuptials of Richard and Jocelyn Brown?

To his credit, though, over the last year he's clarified his position: 'There's a lot of misunderstanding about what a bisexual is. The most common is that you've got twice as many people to screw. The other is that you're bisexual all the time, and of course you're not. Sometimes you're gay and sometimes you're straight...I'm mostly gay at the moment, but I wouldn't like to think I'd never have another physical relationship with a woman.'

It would be quite a coup for us if Fairbrass was simply 'gay', but his popularity is intrinsically tied up with the 'fact' of his bisexuality. Bisexual stars – of which there are curiously many – are seen as not pervy but *kinky*, sex machines rather than sexual deviants. Like David Bowie before him, Richard's bisexuality is read as meaning he can sleep with women *and* men. It makes him more of a man rather than less of one.

'I'm Too Sexy' was the gayest song they've ever done – the rest of their lyrics are cautiously heterosexual ('You're my Lois Lane...', 'She was so fresh in that dress...'). Which is only to be expected – Fred writes them. And, of course, they're Saucy! 'Do you feel like taking 'em down?' Richard sings for no apparent reason on one track. Roping in the mighty Jocelyn Brown to sing backing vocals on 'Don't Talk Just Kiss' was camp, but having her sing 'Don't talk but kiss BIG BOY...' was Sauce! pure and simple.

Initially Richard's sexuality was simply stated as he was reluctant to politicize it, to ram it down people's throats. 'There are things I could rattle on about, but I don't want to end up like Jimmy Somerville and getting arrested on marches.' The public only really likes happy homos (they don't like to hear about our problems as they like to believe we don't have any) and Fairbrass knew all too well his band's place. 'In the middle of a recession people want to forget about their troubles and be entertained again – now is a good time for a group like us to appear.'

But to his credit, he *has* of late found things to rattle on about, lending his considerable weights to AIDS initiatives like Positive Discounts, and OutRage! campaigns.

If he carries on like this he could (just *could*) end up as one of our most effective public spokesmen. Like a Trojan Horse, he's crept into people's hearts and then WHAM! started to come out with all this radical stuff that he manages to make sound like just common sense. He's one of the few high-profile gay men, in or out, who smiles instead of scowls. 'I've got a theory about that,' he's said. 'I think you can get away with almost anything if you keep grinning...people will put up with all kinds of stuff if they like you.'

Laughter, the stuff that Sauce! produces, is a great leveller and the Great British Public like Richard Fairbrass immensely. He's an all-round family favourite, one of the good guys. Laugh, as the old saying goes, and the world laughs at you. *Err*, with you...

Problem is, the public tends to tire of jokes even quicker than they tire of pop groups. Ever since 'I'm Too Sexy' hit the charts, Right Said Fred have been living on borrowed time. The thin line Fairbrass walks is also a tightrope, and he could fall off at any moment. Yes, people will put up with all sorts of stuff if they like you, but getting them to like you usually involves not asking them to put up with too much 'stuff'.

Gay Times, May 1993

Chapter thirteen

The God that Failed?: Morrissey

IN the summer of 1983, I was 15 and in love for the first time. Naturally the object of my affections was a completely evil straight boy who despised my very bones. But this mattered little. For the first time, I encountered this thing called a heart and it hurt me so. All those attendant new feelings like love and lust and jealousy and fear and rejection led me into a hasty retreat into my bedroom and a compulsive addiction to the three Ms; music, misery and masturbation.

Looking back, it's a wonder I got through it at all. To be so young and so alone, wanting so desperately to escape – but not knowing where to start and where (if indeed there was anywhere) one could escape to.

It seemed I was only living for the three straight boys I loved: Andrew, then Ivan, and then Mark. And there was one person who told me all this was OK, that he'd been there too. No, still was there. Morrissey.

Sometimes it used to frighten me. I mean, how come he knew so much about me? Why did he understand me so well when most of the time I was so confused myself? And, equally, why on earth was he so massively popular (I was heartbroken when 'This Charming Man' charted)? Those songs were written for me alone – so what on earth could anyone else see in them? For just as only Morrissey understood me, only I understood Morrissey.

The over-riding theme seemed to be that all those things which had failed or frightened me – love, life, sex, school, work or whatever – were OK to despise because they were crap anyway. He inverted that old chestnut about how 'it's better to have loved and lost than never to have loved at all'. For love was a thing so awful that you're better off well out of it.

At the time, this seemed like pure genius to me, particularly as it was backed up by all the authority that only a bona fide pop star can wield over a teenager. There was something infinitely satisfying about shutting myself away in my room night after night and losing myself in those songs, as if his arms would come out of the speakers to comfort me. I was safe in the knowledge that my opinions and feelings were validated purely because *he* shared them. It wasn't me that was wrong after all, it was the rest of the world.

At the time it was undoubtedly a message I needed to hear but, oh, I don't know, these days I fear he allowed me to wallow in my own misery to the point where I became addicted to it. Now, just maybe, that was necessary, transforming my unhappiness into a virtue, and yet in his lyrics there was no real sense of there being a better life, an alternative. (This is a problem common to much pop music. It is, after all, a youthful genre and so almost inevitably will be wrapped up in the concerns of the present.)

It's just that I was so close so many times to ending it all, because I saw no alternative. Yet it is possible, against all the odds, to lead a good life, if you can just get away from all those dangerous people.

So many young lesbians and gay men are on the brink, and so to venerate gloom in the way that Morrissey does can only leave one, quite literally, with blood on your hands.

Morrissey inhabits a world of perpetual adolescence, and therein lies the danger. His closest contemporary, both in articulateness and in themes, Pete Shelley of the Buzzcocks, has a sense of progress over the body of his work: from that great paean to wanking, the Buzzcocks' first single, 'Orgasm Addict', through the infatuation of songs like 'Get On Our Own' and the resignation of 'You Say You Don't Love Me', leading up to the joyous sense of liberation and release on Shelley's first solo album *Homosapien*. With Morrissey there is none of this.

The only change is that, whilst the objects of his obsessions in his early songs were undoubtedly male ('Handsome Devil', 'This

Charming Man' *et al.*), they soon became more ambiguous. I've long suspected that the reasoning behind this was that, despite his assertions to the contrary, Morrissey never believed he'd be anywhere near as successful as he went on to become. Once it became clear that The Smiths were destined not for the originally intended indie cultdom, but for stardom, a large lyrical retreat and rethink was swiftly undertaken.

Nonetheless, whilst his songs then became non-gender specific to a man, they still only stood up to a homosexual reading. Which was extremely problematic – I *knew* what he was on about and he *knew* what he was on about but *they* didn't.

At times it seemed quite sweet to be in on the joke, and yet I wanted more than to feel 'You too!' I needed to be able to say to my peers 'Him too!' They certainly weren't going to take my word that someone they liked so much was gay. But it was all there and like anyone reasonably well-versed in gay culture I could pick up the references, allusions and signs; like that long line of 'cover stars' who graced The Smiths' record sleeves: a veritable who's who from the camp Hall of Fame. The message couldn't have been any clearer if he'd put Jeff Stryker or Judy Garland on them.

And yet in his interviews Morrissey has strenuously denied that he is 'gay'. Okay, so he's made it equally obvious that he's not straight, but that's lost on many people. So why all this talk? If he's just mucking about, I really don't like it one little bit. If the man is merely 'posing as a sodomite' then he is doing us a disservice. I don't want a straight man to rip off our culture and profit from it through cultivating a commercially 'naughty' image. To steal the things that are ours and throw them out into straight society, like so many pearls before swine, is divorcing these things from their meanings and is cultural imperialism of the very worst kind.

In the only interview he's deemed to give this year, with Nick Kent in *The Face*, Morrissey 'explained' the titles of his forthcoming album and single, *Bona Drag* and 'Piccadilly Palare'; 'Well ... "*bona*" is Latin for good and "drag" is ... well "drag". "Palare" is gypsy slang that was adopted by the theatre and in the Seventies I heard it being used by male prostitutes ... the song is about male prostitutes in Piccadilly.' Oh, *purr-leeez!*

67: *The God that Failed?:Morrissey*

Morrissey, if you're not gay, then get your hands off our history. You can't steal the very words from our lips just so you can embellish your songs with (pardon the pun) a bit of rough.

If you are gay then please, please, please wake up to the fact that it's 1990 and some sort of stand is expected. The words and labels you dismiss as 'limiting and restrictive' are empowering and necessary. You have to reclaim them and use them with pride. Outside your Never Neverland where homophobia doesn't exist and Stonewall never happened, adolescent lesbians and gays are, just as I once did, buying your records by the truckload and feeling far more miserable than you could feasibly fake as they think they're the only ones in the world.

Do we want Morrissey anyway? All those songs riddled with nothing but misery, loneliness, self-pity, failure, self-loathing and despair? Morrissey was brought up a Catholic, so can we expect anything better than such rampant erotophobia when he's got all those centuries of guilt and shame bearing down on him?

If he's straight, he should stop feeding off of us. Write about breeder culture: defaulting on the mortgage repayments, watching telly and going to football matches. If he's gay, then he really has to come out – he can't go on being the only fag in the world who doesn't despise with every last bone in his body the never-ending salvo of straight imagery and heterosexual propaganda that we have thrown at us. He should want to do something to redress the balance.

Oh, Steven, I used to think you were God and look at you now. But, after all I've said, I think of one of your songs: 'Rubber Ring'. I put it on and – oh, Christ Jesus – you're doing it all over again, cutting me to shreds just like I was 16 again. Its words shatter all my arguments and any hate that I had. It's that spooky stuff that used to trouble me. Almost like you've been watching me . . .

But don't forget the songs that made you cry
and the songs that saved your life
Yes, you're older now and you're a clever swine
but they were the only ones who ever stood by you.
And when you're dancing and laughing and finally living
hear my voice in your head and think of me kindly

68: *Seduced and Abandoned*

Do you love me like you used to?

Oh, forgive me. I do love you, I do, I do, I do. You were so important to me. Like Andrew, Ivan and Mark – those boys my heart used to race for – you'll haunt me 'till I die. If you taught me anything, it was never to expect perfection.

Nothing's changed ... I still love you. Sort of ...

Gay Times, August 1990

Chapter fourteen

Godfathers and Sugardaddies: Tom Watkins

ALTHOUGH one of the fun things about pop music is the way it keeps breaking its own rules, it is nonetheless a great respecter of its own traditions. And in this country one of the strongest of those traditions is that of the gay manager. It's one that's steeped in myth – the evil licentious Svengali, a gangster in the boardroom and a devil in the bedroom, wielding control over a gaggle of lads who worked their way up trousers down. There's a problem with myths though – they have this knack of just not being true. Anyone with the slightest knowledge of Larry Parnes or Brian Epstein will know that these men were not the 'Godfathers of British rock 'n' roll' but its Sugar Daddies.

Tom Watkins is the latest in this long line. A great big bear of a man, although understandably wary and suffering from the after effects of a minor operation the day before we met, he still managed to be friendly and forthcoming. Talking with the out ex-manager of Pet Shop Boys and Bros, I knew I might have to tread a little carefully. We began at the beginning.

'I got into full-time management in a very amateur way about six years ago when I wound up my design company, XL, and went off with a long-time friend called Michael Newton. He's a financial man and that's essentially what I was missing. I was always extremely creative and lacked the kind of business acumen that he provided. In a way he represents everything from the straight world and I represent everything from the gay world, and Massive Management is this kind of balance in-between.

'Neil Tennant was editing this book on Frankie Goes To Hollywood with Paul Morley who I worked very closely with at ZTT and he came along with his chum Chris Lowe and gave me this tape and asked me to manage them, which I was a bit iffy about. I was already managing one act.'

You're asked to manage the Pet Shop Boys and you're ... 'a bit iffy'? Tom makes it all seem terribly laid back and easy – particularly if you know that the band he wanted to concentrate on developing the career of were Giggles (Don't worry if you haven't heard of them, no one has). I asked why the boys had such faith in him, Tom Watkins, manager of Giggles.

'I think essentially what they needed was a third party who was a mouthpiece. They were far more ... reserved than I was. I had a lot of front and a lot of flair for drawing attention to acts and making sure they came to the right people's attention. It was really my job to supervise them and marshal them into getting a deal. Those guys were totally a unit. They needed no creativity, no direction from my end at all. If anything we learned a lot from those guys ... Neil did, and probably still does, know considerably more about the music industry than I do. And we were certainly very, very close. I had a five-year contract with them which expired at the end of 1989, which was really a good time for it to end for everyone. Though I can't say that I wasn't sad. But I think it was inevitable ... they saved a hell of a lot of money by not retaining me!'

And what, pray, did you see in them?

'Basically I was fascinated, like most queens, with Hi-NRG music and that whole Eurodisco thing was obviously quite obsessive if you were on the gay scene. That was the kind of music I gravitated towards, plus that very New York, Bobby Orlando thing which I didn't recognize by name but I recognized by sounds, which I liked very much ... and quite frankly they were really nice blokes. Neil and I have a friendship now that extends into our business: the antique shop we manage together. And Chris? Chris has always been an enigma really. He's the mystery man but he's fascinating and good fun to work with as well. So a relationship developed really early on between the three of us to forge ourselves ahead. And it was all a period of discovery based firmly on Neil's huge experience in the music industry, and both of their creative forces with me in this administrative-stroke-desk-banging role.'

But were you happy just banging your desk? Neil's said in interviews that at the start you tried to get them wearing ripped jeans. Didn't you hunger for a little more creative input?

'Ripped jeans? I think that's just artist's licence. I often encouraged them to be more animated on *Top of the Pops* but I learnt very early on with the guys, perhaps from the first photo shoot, that they knew exactly what they wanted to do. So it was ludicrous to think that a styling job could be done on them.'

Were you then so frustrated as a self-confessed 'extremely creative' person resigned to sitting at the desk all day and banging away from nine 'till five that you made a conscious decision to move to Bros – a band who could be moulded a little more easily?

'Oh no! The period between the Pet Shop Boys' initial success and when I took Bros on was a phenomenal period of time. It was over three years!'

Oh no indeed. My big Tom Watkins Theory has just been squashed. In desperation I try again. But Tom, I was under the impression that you'd plucked these poor Bros boys from obscurity . . .

'Well, I was approached by one of the ex-heads of A&R at CBS records – a guy called Nicky Graham – to look at this band with a view to managing them. I turned them down on two or three occasions 'cause I thought the material was incredibly weak. Though I thought the potential of having two pretty boys and a third . . . party . . . sort of like . . . complementing the two blond boys as being a totally unique idea for the pop market. When you met the two boys . . . and Craig, and saw the blind determination that they had, it was an obvious thing to get involved with them. But only when Nicky and I had come up with the material.'

I ask Tony what they (. . . and Craig) looked like when he first saw them – which sends him bounding across the room and digging out two photos. He comes back and says 'well first they looked like that', holding out a picture of these absolute loons who've run riot with the home perm kit and Top Shop gift vouchers.

' . . . And we persuaded them to look like that', and he shows me a photo of . . . well, Bros. I try to restrain myself from bouncing up and down on the chair with glee at sensing that my big Tom Watkins theory was correct after all. 'You say that you persuaded them to dress differently, and look it's those ripped jeans again. Very much a gay fashion item no?'

'It had nothing to do with being gay. The fact is . . . the jeans were really remnants of The Ramones if anything . . . '

And Dee Dee Ramone used to be a rent boy, and getting ripped jeans was pretty much par for the course if you spent a lot of time on your knees so we're talking about a gay fashion that originated with American hustlers and passed over into punk via The Ramones . . . Tom carries on oblivious to my fascinating history lesson.

'It may be a gay fashion now, but at the time I think you'll find it was very much a street vernacular. And it was something most kids could get into – having your arse and things ripped out of your jeans. But really and truly it was not really me coming along and saying "you've got to wear these" . . . '

But Tom you just said it was . . .

' . . . all that I'd show them was what the alternatives were. There was a whole team of people around that were ready to lend helpful hints to anybody that was unable to dress themselves or come up with a suitable look and I felt at the time there was a real need for a definite look. But they both (Matt and Luke Goss) certainly did have a particular flair. Matt was particularly clever in coming up with little designer things for his shoes.'

I take Tom's word for this as Matt's shoes are sadly out of shot in the first of the 'before and after' photos, but remain largely unconvinced. So it's completely untrue to say that, with Bros, you constructed your dream band?

'Certainly not a "dream band" of mine. I have no particular pursuit of youth sexually. Mine was moulded on exploiting a possible commercial venture in the right way. I felt it'd been a long time since Duran Duran had done anything, a long time since the Bay City Rollers were there. Those kind of teen bands have always done particularly well and all we did was take dance music which I was particularly obsessed with . . . '

Hi-NRG you mean?

'-ish! It was within that kind of mould. I mean there are some classics within the stuff that Nicky and I wrote for the first album, but at the time they were just built to suit the speed and the way that the fashions and the clubs were at.'

Thrilled at having at long last found someone who shares my high regard of Bros records, I ask if Tom shares my view of Bros as a camp band.

'Not at all no – *'cause they weren't camp!'*

Tom thinks I'm insinuating something and gets annoyed. I'm not though, in spite of his claims to the contrary I view Bros as being blank sheets of paper that he wrote upon. It's him that I'm interested in. Who Bros slept with is of absolutely no interest to me. *(Lie!)* I change the subject anyway and ask about the demise of Bros and why it all went so horribly, horribly wrong.

'We managed them up until about a year-and-a-half ago when they just weren't happy with the service that they were getting from us. We never look after any of our band's finances – that's the golden rule – and that was their road to ruin. They spent too much money, they screamed very badly when the finances started running out and their popularity started to wane somewhat, and we basically sued them for breach of contract.'

This was just after Craig left. Can you shed any light on why he went?

'It was the pressure of the work. It was so intense. The relationship was breaking down between the twins and him. He met a girl that he was particularly fond of and he'd had enough of the exhausting lifestyle that they led. He got seriously ill on tour which he just didn't seem to be able to get over . . . the man was totally and absolutely exhausted.'

Did you as their manager feel responsible for that?

'No. It was basically once the ball was rolling it was very hard to know when to put the brakes on or when to keep lubricating the passage. I think they were all egotistical maniacs and enjoyed every minute of the success until suddenly one of them couldn't cope any more. Whereas the other two still had an incredible hunger for it and I'm sure they still do. They're both incredibly strong and resilient characters.'

This goes against the grain of the image most people have of the Machiavellian manager and the poor exploited star, doesn't it?

'The idea of anyone having a Peter Cook role in management as portrayed in that film *Bedazzled* is quite ludicrous. The fact is that we work very hard for the percentage that we charge our artists. I understand the myth and it amuses me no end but it certainly doesn't worry me. I'm sure that's the misconception most people have, that you come along and you manipulate and you're this puppet master who creates the whole thing. But you can't make chicken soup out of chicken shit! Unless you've got the basic ingredients you're gonna have nothing more than a pile of shit.'

But looking at Bros – you dressed them up, you wrote their songs – weren't you ladling on the chicken soup until they were up to their necks in it?

'I'm very flattered that people should think that that's the case but the guys came to me with a degree of talent. With less talented people you don't have this success. I'm only as good as my last act. I tried to do it with three girls called Faith, Hope and Charity which I fell on my arse completely with. And the reason I fell on my arse was that the girls were nowhere near as talented as the guys in Bros were. You can lead a horse to water but you can't make it walk . . . er, drink!'

Whilst pondering the aptness of this slip-ette I ask after his other post-Bros act James Lee Wild.

'James Lee Wild was a complete and utter pillock,' he recalls fondly, immediately dispelling any remaining suspicions I was harbouring that he was fudging around Bros.

'The guy came along and he had a really wonderful voice, had a really good look, but he was more interested in going out with Page Three girls than in spending any kind of time in the studio. He thought we were going to wave a magic wand and it was all going to happen without him putting any effort into it, so as a consequence *it didn't work!* I didn't write the material so I can't take any of the blame for that. It was just one of those things – he didn't have, or rather we didn't recognize that he didn't have, sufficient talent to make it work.'

Why do you think there have been so many successful gay managers in pop? Are there many around today?

'I surprisingly don't associate myself with the music frater-
nity. I have a group of friends outside of that, and the ones that I
come up to professionally I'm not massively inquisitive as to their
sexual inclination. One hears of other obvious managers now that
are gay but I wouldn't say it's like a gay mafia, which I think at one
time did exist. The Sixties and Seventies were the boom time for
those kind of people. But I don't think anyone deliberately went out
to seek a gay manager any more than a gay manager went out to seek
bands. The fact that I'm a homosexual is really irrelevant to the kind
of role that I perform for my artists. It's like I think anyone having to
be known as a successful gay artist is really unfortunate. They
should be known as an artist or performer that happens to be
homosexual. You see ... '

(Oh God, he's going to say 'I hate the word gay'.)

' ... I loathe the word gay for a start. My performance as a
manager is really not affected by who I've fucked with the night
before.'

I deftly move on to ask if he feels vulnerable as an out gay
man to attacks from the press.

'I've nothing to hide. The reason that no one's done major
stories on me is because there's no dirt to dig. I've lived with the
same man for x amount of years, I don't go cottaging, I don't go to
Hampstead Heath. I was not a particularly promiscuous person. I
mean I was a fattie, love! *No one wants a fattie on the gay scene!* I'm
sure if I was better looking and had all the attributes that were
needed I would have done all those kind of things but I tended to shy
away from it. And I was ensconced in a very healthy homosexual
relationship for six years.'

A sadly childless marriage though – did you ever feel that you
were playing a fatherly role in management?

'Yeah, being forty-one years of age I most certainly could be
construed as being a fatherly figure especially to two children that
are sixteen and seventeen years old, as Matt and Luke were when
they came along. I never had any inclination sexually towards youth.
As far as chickens were concerned I preferred them from Colonel
Sanders. And I wasn't out there looking for love. I'd already found it
and was very happy about it so I wouldn't be out there cruising.'

76: *Seduced and Abandoned*

It's time to go. The interview gives way to chit chat. Tom talks about his other projects. He mentions the new band he's just signed, To Die For, and his new dance label, Atomic Records. But he's far more animated when talking about his antique shop ('a modernist gallery') or the book he's writing about the Thirties architect Keith Marriot. I look around his living room. Every *objet* seems to say 'this is one high class queen'. I ask if Tom ever feels a bit guilty about dirtying his hands with something as seemingly common and vulgar as pop music.

'No, I don't regard pop as being vulgar and I don't regard it as being particularly arty having an interest in the things that I do. They're quite commonplace and they're out there for anybody to enjoy. If they'll just lift up the rock they are there. Any finances and rewards that I've been given in the pop industry have enabled me to indulge myself in these artistic pursuits but my entire background is one of fine art and design. I had an appreciation of that at probably around the same time as I had any kind of appreciation of Hi-NRG or dance music … or the penis really. It all came at the same time.'

Gay Times, July 1991

Chapter fifteen

The Happy Wanderer: Jimmy Somerville

WHEN I think of Jimmy Somerville I think of wanderlust. He seems possessed by an inability to stay in one place for long. After six years he's passed through success with Bronski Beat, The Communards and a solo career to a fourth set of collaborators ('These two guys in California. One of them Brad is *so* spaced out and peaceful God knows how he's going to cope with me'). He has also moved from Glasgow through London to San Francisco. Perhaps permanently.

In conversation he betrays the same tendency. The interview was supposed to last an hour. We were nearly into the second hour before a distressed record company person came and broke it up. Jimmy would rattle out an answer to a question and then, without so much as a pause for breath, drift effortlessly onto another topic he felt more pressing. I guess that's what I like about him. He's one of pop's sanest and most sensible voices. Almost as if he only endures singing because it lets him do some more talking. Another fabby cover version at the top of the charts means another chance to spout off in *Smash Hits*.

We talked of many things, of politics and poofs and pop. Whenever I mentioned his new greatest hits album, true to form he'd talk about *Red Hot and Blue*, the AIDS charity album of Cole Porter covers to which he's contributed a version of 'From This Moment On'. For once he says he was glad to be involved in a charity project 'where the politics were right up front'. He's also added that refrain from 'I Feel Love' to it. Force of habit perchance Jimmy?

'No. That was deliberate 'cause there's something special about the song no matter what Donna Summer said. If you ever think about gay discos and gay disco songs you always think of "I Feel Love". And in a sense it represented a time when things looked like they could just go on progressively. So it's like a little historical point in the song.'

He'd flown back from San Francisco, that little mythical gay Mecca and Bethlehem all rolled into one, to do the publicity for the album and its trailer single, a reggae-ish rendering of the Bee Gee's 'To Love Somebody'. So, James, have you gone there for good?

'It's not actually San Francisco. It's across the bay 'cause I didn't want to live in another city after Glasgow and London. It's kind of permanent but because I have to come back and do work and stuff it makes it more difficult. The record company are OK about that. They realize if I'm not allowed to live my life then I'm not going to come up with anything worthwhile.

'Originally I wanted to be part of the gay ghetto. That was kinda intriguing as it was something I hadn't ever experienced. But the surrounding countryside is so magnificent. Also there's a unique liberalism that exists in California. It's quite radical there and I've met people who are really inspiring in their approach to the American political situation.'

Hmmm. But the land of the bland must generally be rather a disheartening place for a socialist.

'It is, but I don't find it any more sad than here to be honest. And if anything there's a few things which are a little more uplifting. Like the Robert Mapplethorpe thing in Cincinnati where the art gallery was taken to court and charged with obscenity. The jury upheld the First Amendment of freedom of speech and expression and used that to throw the case out. We don't have anything like that to protect us.

'Now there's a few things like that in London with groups like OutRage!, which I think is the best thing that's ever happened in gay politics in this country . . . apart from ACT-UP of course! But in America they're much more up for challenging any kind of discrimination and demanding their rights. I don't think America's brilliant but there are certain aspects of it which I really do like.'

Did you have any ideas about San Francisco, good or bad, that have been upturned?

'When I got to San Francisco and had been out a few times I suddenly thought "Is this what liberation is all about?" Being able to have little shops that sell useless things. Having this ghetto-ized district where you can hold hands for two blocks but you walk anywhere else and you get called every faggot under the sun. San Francisco has the highest rate of queerbashing in the whole of the United States! So it's no Utopia but it's something more than we have.

'There's a lot of young people there who feel alienated from that ghetto thing and they have their own cliquey scene. So it hasn't worked for everyone. It works for upwardly mobile gay men. But actually, now, there's a lot of lesbians who are starting to move into that district and that'll be good 'cause up until now it's been really male dominated. It's actually spreading out as well.'

Was one of the things that attracted you the relative anonymity you have there?

'Yes. Because I'm hardly known in San Francisco. I did something at the Castro Street Fair and afterwards this woman came up to me and said "Oh you were so great. I've never heard you before. Can I give you my card 'cause I organize parties and I'd like to book you?" That made me feel really ... humble. That someone didn't know who I was liked my voice or would be genuinely enthusiastic.'

You've always seemed very much the reluctant star. As if resigned to your fate because of the platform that fame provides you with.

'I'm a real exhibitionist though. If I go out dancing I can't just shuffle from side to side, I have to try and do ten different steps in two beats of a song. But yes I'm a reluctant pop star as I totally disapprove of what the record industry tries to promote through pop stars. That whole idea of escapism ... I mean what kind of escapism is it? It's like Noddyland.

'Once, when I was in Bang, this girl – she was obviously from out of town and it was a Saturday night – she came up to me and she was really sweet but then she said "I've never met anyone from the telly". And this is how they promote it. Almost as if you don't have any real existence but come out of the TV at the weekend to let rip.'

I suppose the flip side to that fawning approach to fame is the total resentment of your success some have. We all know that there exists this breed called 'The bitchy queen ... '

'It's funny you should mention that 'cause just last night I was at the Daisy Chain. I get all kinds of hassle but this time I didn't handle it very well 'cause my temper blows. I short fuse easily. I hate having to explain myself 'cause I think why should I have to explain myself to youse what I am and what I'm doing? I basically told these queens "Just back off and piss off!" I get hassled and abused and sniggered at by heterosexuals in the street 'cause to them it seems almost like a freak show, you know? I don't expect to go to a gay club and be treated in the same way. I woke up this morning and thought "Oh God!" It was my first night back and I just thought "I don't need this". There is a kind of bitterness in the city which is really sad. I think that energy these people have ... they shouldn't be turning it inwards they should be turning it outwards to benefit their own lives and to benefit everybody else. In the city there must be a million gay men and lesbians and if we can't get it together to organize some sort of resistance or some voice ... if I actually start weighing it up, I've had more aggressive encounters in gay clubs than I've actually had in the street from straight boys. There's something wrong there!'

Being the non-elected spokespervert of a generation is clearly a thankless task. We do seem by and large rather bad at acknowledging our heroes. Unless they've popped their clogs. Yet just as we wouldn't dare speak ill of the dead often, it seems we're unable to speak well of the living. I asked Jimmy what he thought he'd achieved. Firstly, did he think political pop actually changes anything?

'I don't think music ever really does convert people but it can influence them and start them thinking about things. I actually believe Bronski Beat and The Communards influenced a lot of attitudes about lesbians and gay men. *Especially Bronski Beat!* I still think what we did is one of the most important things in terms of like music and politics in the last decade. I think we presented something like ... *so* radical. And we're constantly denied that recognition in the press. All of the newspapers and all of the magazines did these huge things about what happened in the Eighties and not one of them mentioned Bronski Beat. And we were such an important thing . . . we decided that we were gonna be this band and our songs were gonna be about the fact that we were gay.

'I mean we knew there were gonna be consequences from that 'cause most of society has that attitude "I don't mind if you're gay but don't ram it down my throat". But our reaction was that everyday heterosexuality is rammed down our throat. I felt we had a duty to represent the alternative and I think we did. People do come up to me and say things like "'Smalltown boy' helped me get through this terrible period . . . 'Smalltown boy' helped me come out . . . thanks for all you've done . . . and stuff" and I think that's what it's all about. It might only be one person a month but they're so important to me, those people. That's what it's all about.

'We presented this idea to people: "You are not alone". "We are everywhere". That was the whole thing. It's a real kind of namby GLF thing but it's true. Queers are everywhere!

'And that's what I still try and do 'cause so many people are still isolated. I just think it's criminal that so many kids have to go through that. It's even worse now because the whole AIDS crisis has created a dreadful new moral climate. It must be awful to be fifteen and to want to decide to tell people you're gay and they have this reaction where they ostracize you and call you every AIDS carrier under the sun.

'You know as lesbians and gay men we are so unique. We live our lives until we are sixteen or seventeen as one thing and then suddenly we actually have this opportunity to change our lives and we do actually become someone else. We're almost like born again. If you go with it in a positive way it's one of the most enlightening experiences you ever have. And that's why I think it should be allowed to be such a smooth transition, but you have to get through such emotional and physical abuse. Lesbians and gay men are some of the bravest people in the world because they are so resilient. No matter what happens to them they always bounce back. It's really something to be proud of.'

'Something to be proud of' seems like a pretty good description of Jimmy. He's been banging our drum for so long now it's only fair that someone bangs his. Thanks for all you've done ... and stuff.

Gay Times, December 1990

Chapter sixteen

Homo Psycho Sexy Burlesque: My Life with the Thrill Kill Kult

I'M sitting in the world's smallest dressing room with those leading lights of the international sin set, Chicago's My Life With The Thrill Kill Kult, and we're talking about their new album *Sexplosion!* – whatever that means.

'It's an explosion of sex, silly!'

Of course. Thrill Kill Kult are the three horsegirls and the four horsemen of the erotic apocalypse, The Parental Music Resource Centre (PMRC)'s worst nightmare and my kind of wet dream. It's live that the band make most sense. They look like the last and the best gang in town: singer Groovie Mann throws himself around looking to all the world like Quentin Crisp has just woken to find himself trapped in Jim Morrison's body; Trash Cavity and Levi, the two big and brooding guitarists, all leather and attitude, could have just stumbled in off of a Tom of Finland drawing; Buzz swings around his keyboard attacking the thing like it's trying to get away; and then there's the three upfront backing singers and self confessed 'Go Go Butts', The Bomb Gang Girlz – Jacky, Kitty and Secret Dame – a riot of costume changes, coming on to the audience, pawing the boys and mauling each other. These are not gigs. This is a show.

'The live thing is very visual, like a documentary revue,' Groovie explains before the rest of them all join in. 'It's a kind of homo psycho sexy burlesque. There's a lot of interaction – people playing off each other and living out the songs.

'This is our introduction to Europe and we've brought over a scaled-down version of our American stage set, The Continental Club. It's like a leather disco bar and a strip club, with a glitter ball and a bartender. The whole bit.'

Thrill Kill Kult started life in 1987 as a film project that Groovie and Buzz were working on ('We share a common interest in bad films. Stuff like old Spanish occult movies with bad dubbing. *Sisters of Satan* – that was one of my favourites.') They gave up halfway through, on realizing that a band would be a far better vehicle for their concept of 'Total Sensory Overload'. Way back then their music was labelled 'Industrial hardcore dance', but all that remains of that legacy now are the beats that crash as hard as Hell. Chicago is home not just to the Kult but to the gay-run Wax Trax label – from which sprang all things Industrial. But whereas other acts like Ministry and Nine Inch Nails have got butcher over time, the Kult have just got nellier and nellier. Now they're like a Hi-NRG rock act. Their third album *Sexplosion!* is a *tour de force* exploration of a neon lit, twilight world of S&M, leather, sex, drugs and magic. It's where trash meets thrash, glam meets grunge, tease meets sleaze and rock gets into disco and gives him a damned good shagging.

'This is our sexy album. It's total Disco. We've left it really open for the listener to fantasize into. And it's real genderless. It doesn't make judgements.'

So if someone has the good fortune to come into contact with My Life With The Thrill Kill Kult what do you want them to come away thinking?

'That was fun. These guys are crazy. Do what you want. Be yourself and someone else too. Live out your wildest dreams. Don't just sit around – figure out a masterplan and break out.

'We don't take ourselves seriously and so serious people don't like us. But we don't want to convince anybody. And that's probably the secret to us – if you don't get it then you don't get it. If you have to try and figure it out, then forget it.'

Thrill Kill Kult feign a disinterested disdain for just about everything in keeping with a Sex Pistollian credo of '*and we don't care*'. And they claim that they don't even worry about those that seek to stop their fun, such as America's pro-Censorship lobby and the PMRC.

'That really doesn't affect anybody. Kids are gonna listen to what they want to listen to anyway. Putting a sticker on an album doesn't make any difference. It promotes it. It's like "Oh, my parents won't like it ... I better buy it then!"'

The Kult's first release was the delicious PMRC-baiting single 'Daisy Chain For Satan' and they've even promised to sticker their own record sleeves with the legend 'We promote the use of drugs, murder and homosexuality. That's fine by us.' And their next big project is – wait for it – *a rock opera*.

'It's a heavy metal Satanic rock-suicide-through-drugs funky *West Side Story* soap opera kind of thing. We're gonna call it *A Rendezvous With Destiny*. We just wanted to do something so that when people look back on the Nineties they'll go "Ohmigawd. What a mess!"'

But if you can't hold your breath till then *Sexplosion!* should be more than enough to keep you satisfied. On the sleeve, squeezed in between the pictures of Fifties muscle boys and glamour girls, is the invitation 'Come and get it'. Go on, get it and come.

Gay Times, December 1992

Chapter seventeen

Hope I Get Old Before I Die : Pop and AIDS

POP music should have been better placed than any other cultural form to offer a positive response to AIDS. At its best, it has been concerned with sex, youth and rebellion, and the influence of gay men upon it has always been paramount. But by the time it became clear we were in the middle of a crisis, pop's sexiness and faggotiness had been de-primed.

In part, this was the result of AIDS and pop themselves. In the early Eighties the likes of Boy George, Frankie Goes to Hollywood and Bronski Beat had dragged the genre, kicking but mainly screaming, out of the closet on an unprecedented scale. They were, though, merely symbolic of changes occurring in the real world outside; a new sense of assuredness and a heightened visibility of lesbians and gay men that, to our enemies on the Right, signalled that we had finally gone too far. The result was an all out war waged against us that peaked with Section 28's Eleventh Commandment, 'Thou shalt not promote homosexuality', and which had consistently used AIDS as 'proof' of the threat we posed.

Although the fight against the Section exploded in the face of its backers by giving lesbians and gay men an even greater sense of their own strength, pop responded with uncharacteristic obedience to the new moral puritans. The time when pop screamed 'polymorphous perversity' with New Romantics and Gender Benders, or sang joyously of sex with 'So many men, so little time' and 'Relax' now seem such far off days.

This was due to an unrelated change in popular music which happened during the same period. In the Eighties we witnessed that Fifties construct 'The teenager' waning in both demographic and economic significance. The social grouping with the largest disposable income were now the thirtysomethings. Cue the phasing out of the single and the irresistible rise and rise of the CD. Pop was forced to grow up in order to appeal to this new market. They didn't want sex, youth and rebellion. They wanted safety, nostalgia and conformity. It would prove difficult to accommodate AIDS into their concerns as, in line with Rightist thinking, 'it had nothing to do with them'.

In tandem with the growth of this 'Mortgage Rock', real pop music (chart music) threatened to discard the separate youth identity that it had been a major force in forging since the Fifties. All hail the new penis-less pop, with stars extolling views that merely mirrored those of their parents. The Bobby Sox mentality came back to haunt us, prudery was in and even a kiss on the first date seemed out of the question. By 1985 pop was reflecting the irrationalist AIDS panic with songs like Jermaine Stewart's 'We Don't Have To ... ' ('take our clothes off to have a good time'). The song managed to gain an amusing dimension, despite its scaremongering, because Jermaine came across like such a gloriously unreconstructed nelly that he seemed incapable of anything more saucy than 'drinking some cherry wine'. He would have found an ideal partner in Janet Jackson who urged her lover 'Let's Wait A While' ('before we go too far').

This sense of sexual retreat can be best seen two years later when George Michael tried to launch his solo career with a 'Relax'-style hype over 'I Want Your Sex'. The desired brouhaha came but he swiftly extinguished it. The lyrics had declared George's profound observation that 'Sex is natural, sex is good, not everybody does it but everybody should', but he tried to assuage the moral minority by claiming the song was about monogamy, and came out with such horrific quotes as 'The sense of fear has got to be made more specific and directed at promiscuity'.

The more worrying response has been the anti-gay sentiments which some voiced. Most infamous was Donna Summer's 'AIDS has been sent by God to punish homosexuals' (which she now claims she never said), proving once and for all that being born again gives you a brain the size of a baby's. The rap act, Public Enemy, have consistently spouted a Muslim line of moralism and hatred of difference which has them declaring 'gays are sticking things in places that they don't belong. They don't know what they're fucking with.' Countering this sort of religious rubbish Diamanda Galas recorded a trilogy of albums centering on *The Divine Punishment* which used Old Testament imagery and texts, not to support notions of a biblical plague, but to give a Job-like image of the suffering saint to a gay man with AIDS.

The most blatant homophobia has come from the all-male preserve of Heavy Metal, such as Guns 'n' Roses ('One In A Million'); and the merit-free Skid Row had publicity photos taken with one of the group proudly wearing a t-shirt with the slogan 'AIDS kills faggots dead!' Ho-hum.

But as ever, the real crime has been silence. The Party II, a big fundraising concert in 1988, had to be scrapped because no major act could be found to headline it. The previous year's Party had been well supported (leading the organizers to wryly conclude 'It seems that AIDS is no longer fashionable'), but when that was televized its most moving moment, Carlton Edwards singing 'The Last Rites' (about a young man dying of AIDS), was censored out by TV chiefs as 'it was not entertaining'. Earlier this year Radio One, in their finite wisdom, cut the intro to the FPI Project's 'Back To My Roots' which urged the listener 'Hey you don't be silly, put a condom on your willy!' Thus conceding nothing to the change in public attitudes during the 12 years since they did much the same thing to The Specials' 'Too Much Too Young' and Gang of Four's 'At Home He's A Tourist'.

In a similar vein *Top of the Pops* presenters would announce at the end of Elton John's 'Sacrifice' ' ... and all the proceeds from that record are going to ... charity'. Almost as if they thought merely saying the A-word would expose them to the virus.

Despite the central role of charity in pop post-Live Aid (in keeping with the Mortgage Rocker's Thatcherism they are all 'Active Citizens'), as far as AIDS has been concerned the relationship has been somewhat fraught. There have been noble efforts by Dionne Warwick ('That's What Friends Are For', a huge hit in the States in 1985) and Elton John, who in his dedication almost stands alone, but the most common response has been the sort of apathy that scuppered The Party II. *Red Hot and Blue,* a double album of Cole Porter covers by such luminaries as U2, Annie Lennox and Sinead O'Connor was almost scrapped, and delayed until this month, as no sponsor could be found ('because of the stigma of AIDS', according to its co-ordinator). Yet another megastar AIDS charity album *Nobody's Child* came out two months ago with no such hitches. That the latter was in aid of 'Ceaucescu's children' (Romanian babies infected by unscreened blood) seems to indicate that people are still preferring to think in terms of innocent victims and of guilty ones, undeserving of help.

Such records as 'Sacrifice' and the many small benefit concerts staged for AIDS charities, though laudable, are often problematic as they forget the reasons that necessitate their existence. Health care, scientific research and education are the responsibility of government. The good eggery of the Live Aid crew might forget this but we need to offer a more radical response in which all these fundraising efforts announce as loudly as possible that respective governments are reneging on their duty.

That pop has reneged on its duty to talk about AIDS cannot merely be because we have lost so few to it. Liberace, Sylvester, Jobriath, Esquirita, the B-52's Ricky Wilson, Level 42's Alan Murphy, Man 2 Man's Miki Zone, producer Patrick Cowley and Klaus Nomi (who seemed to be articulating his fears on his hauntingly beautiful last album *A Simple Man*) are surely sad enough losses.

Perhaps pop's main problem is that it's never had to deal with death before. Dying was always seen as something that old people did. (Although it could be eulogized, as with the deaths of James Dean, Jimi Hendrix or Jim Morrison, in keeping with The Who's line 'Hope I die before I get old' or 'Live fast, die young, leave a beautiful corpse'.) It is this equating of youth with recklessness, feigning a lack of concern for one's own welfare, that may prove one of the hardest struggles of all.

Apart from such youthful bravado, pop always found it difficult to consider death without lapsing into either kitschy melodrama ('Leader Of The Pack') or a sickly sentimentality ('Ebony Eyes' by the Everly Brothers). Both evoked not tears, but giggles.

This has changed. With AIDS, mourning – the making of that most private experience public – became a political act. Not only by acknowledging and documenting the losses but, more importantly, because the emotional response provides a necessary disavowal of the myth that the people who are dying just don't matter.

Noel's 'Silent Morning', easily the subtlest and saddest pun to enter pop's lexicon, and The Communards' 'For A Friend' both did this well, Somerville echoing W. H. Auden's 'Musée des Beaux Arts' with his bewilderment at how the world fails to be as moved as he is, and carries on as normal.

Noel's, however, remains the more poignant, as 'Silent Morning' also laments the passing of a whole way of life. The change about to affect gay men so dramatically was also taken up by Sylvester's last single 'Trouble In Paradise' and The Blow Monkey's 1986 hit 'Digging Your Scene'. In the latter, Dr Robert tries to reconcile his love of the gay scene with the propagandizing he hears, that the wages of such 'sin' are death. On both 'It Couldn't Happen Here' and 'Hit Music' the Pet Shop Boys comment on how two years later, sex had sadly walked off the dance floor.

Few have attempted to do that which is most necessary: to use pop as a vehicle for propagandizing AIDS. Jimmy Somerville tried with 'Read My Lips' but achieved as much good by clearly aligning himself with the cause. Not just by making a necessary nuisance of himself on ACT-UP demos but by talking to the media about the activist group and using his own fame to give them the much needed oxygen of publicity.

Pop has to present AIDS from a sex-positive viewpoint – against the elders and no betters who seek to use it for promoting prudery. What has to be done is to rail against their message and to show that the fight against AIDS is a fight against those who hate sex-as-pleasure, and against authoritarianism.

There has been but one attempt to do this – 'All You Need Is Love 1987' by the JAMMS (later known as The Timelords, now The KLF). A beautifully inspired and *angry* piece of sampling that juxtaposed snatches of Sam Fox's 'Touch me' with ones taken from the government's dire 'Icebergs and tombstones' AIDS TV ads – who'd have thought Marcuse's theory of repressive desublimation could sound this good? It made the obvious crystal clear; that the fight against AIDS is a fight against the establishment. Was it a hit? Of course not. As the chorus so rightly put it; 'Shag, shag, shag! *What the fuck is going on?*'

Gay Times, September 1990

Chapter eighteen

The House
That Frankie Built:
Frankie Knuckles

GOD you have to deal with some vile people when you do
this job. I first tried to set up this interview last year when Frankie
Knuckles had just charted with 'The Whistle Song'. His then press
officer seemed to think that single would be a good footing to launch
Knuckles as the Acker Bilk of a generation and offered me the
interview on the condition that 'you won't ask him about anything
gay, will you?'

I'm not too sure what there is to talk to Frankie about except
'anything gay'. This is the man they call 'the gay godfather of
House'. The current dance boom began in gay clubs, clubs where
Frankie DJ-ed. So central were they to the movement's genesis that
it even took two of its names, Garage and House, from two of those
clubs; New York's Paradise Garage and Chicago's Warehouse. If
you hate that music then blame Frankie. And if you love it, then it's
him you have to thank.

He's usually associated with the latter town. In America
dance music went underground after the late Seventies disco boom
and was reborn in Chicago, with Knuckles and the Warehouse
acting as its midwife. But he's a native New Yorker; it's where he's
living once more and where he first started DJ-ing. Frankie's first big
break came in the early Seventies when he had a regular spot at the
now infamous Continental Baths.

'To young English gay men it must sound kind of strange,' he says of that temple of casual sex. 'It was more than just a bath house, it was an entertainment complex with a disco and a cabaret. A bit of everything really. People would check in on Friday and they wouldn't leave until Monday morning when they'd go to work.'

In those days the music that faggots danced to was Philly Soul – breezy, carefully structured songs (the song is a continuing obsession of Frankie's – more of which later) shot through with lyrical themes of high camp and high drama.

It's a sound that has wrought a deep influence on successive generations of gay music makers. David Bowie and Elton John both made their Philly records, Jacques Morali, the man behind Village People, made his first records with Philly imitators The Ritchie Family, and The Communards had their biggest hit with a cover of Harold Melvin and the Blue Notes' 'Don't Leave Me This Way'. Remember The O'Jays? Frankie does.

'That was pretty much the basis for everything then. I still favour it personally, though I don't work with it so much any more. I have everything that ever came out on the Philadelphia International label. All the material they did – especially in those early days – was produced so well, to the point where 20 years later it still sounds so good. And Gamble and Huff very much influenced me as a producer.'

Just as Disco was reaching its commercial peak in 1977, the Continental Baths closed down. Frankie moved to Chicago to take up a position as chief DJ and part owner of the Warehouse. Within five years he'd turned it into arguably the best club in the country, pulling in a crowd of mainly young, black gay men. It was a place he famously described as 'church for people who have fallen from grace.'

'I had a lot of offers in New York, but nothing that would offer me a percentage. That's the biggest problem about this business – a lot of people think it's very glamorous being a DJ, but most of them are so underrated and they're definitely underpaid. Especially in the United States where the DJ is basically holding up the whole evening and attracting so many people.

'The Warehouse originally started in 1975. They were like gypsy parties really, they floated all over the city. By the time I

moved to Chicago they'd become stable and pretty much a legiti-
mized business. In those early days it was a non-profit organization
– it was a private club and all the revenue that was generated went
straight back into the business to make it a better club.'

So what made the place so special? What was it like on a good
night?

'It's hard to explain, you had to be there really. On an
average Saturday night we'd get anywhere between 1500 and 2500
people. In the beginning it was a very energetic evening. The audience was very dedicated – people would be lining up outside at 11.30
p.m. before it opened and there'd still be a line outside at seven in the
morning. It was the energy level that made it; there were never any
fights or any hassles or anything negative going on. Everybody was
having a good time.'

This was pre-Ecstasy, and many of the clubbers were drop-
ping trips. So much so that the music later earned the name Acid
House. Acid was adopted for several reasons specific to the young
blacks; it was cheap and cheerful, and was easy to conceal on your
person. The latter was especially important for a people as heavily
policed as they were.

'Acid was quite a big part of it. I didn't do it but quite a
number of people in the audience did. That type of drug kept them
going for all those hours.'

Knuckles wasn't just playing records. He was making live
music, not just through mixing but by using his own drum tracks,
samples and sound effects.

'At that particular time I found a sound effects record of a
steam train that was recorded in stereo. We had a really amazing
sound system and the first time I played it, it was the height of the
night. I had the entire room blacked out and switched off the lights.
I'd turn up the bass and cue the train sound. You'd hear people
scream as if the train was coming through the walls. It really freaked
a lot of people out.'

Which, seeing as most of them were tripping their nuts off, is
hardly surprising. Nonetheless the train sound became Frankie's
signature tune. The music he played was equally idiosyncratic, his
wide eclecticism formed the basis of the House sound. The first
records combined the trance-inducing effects of repetition and dub

production with the metrenomic rhythms of electronic Eurodisco. The notion of 'the song' came from Philly, the soaring voices from gospel ('I hated the way people would try to steal my singers. They could find their own in any church'). In the early Eighties just about the only contemporary music he favoured was coming out of, not America, but Europe.

'At that particular time the Euro stuff that was coming through seemed like the biggest noise that was being made. There were a few things between '80 and '84 that had a big influence; "Burnin' up" and Imagination's first record.'

Hearing Frankie cite Imagination as a major influence is a bit like Neil Bartlett saying how much he was inspired by Barbara Cartland, but who am I to argue? Queens have always favoured their dance music a little faster, and many were surprised that the driving beats of House took off with a straight audience too. But not Frankie – 'It's just the beat of pop'. What else did this music have to offer that specifically appealed to gay men?

'From my own personal observation, the gay audience is looking for something that has a little bit more rhythm ... I don't even know if I should use the word rhythm because they like some things that are a lot more melodic; music that's orchestrated well and with hooks that are very appealing to the ear and songs that are sentimental. That's the problem with straight people, most straight men have a hard time dealing with the reality of being sensitive and enjoying something that sounds so sweet and as sensitive as a nice love song. They refuse to let themselves go with that.'

One of the most repeated lies about dance music is that the lyrics are unimportant. With House this was patently untrue. When Knuckles soon made the inevitable transition from DJ-ing to making his own records his lyrics always had a specific resonance for gay men. Most of the first House records were radically different reworkings of somewhat obscure Disco songs from the early Seventies; Knuckles' first hit was a version of 'Only The Strong Survive' ('You gotta be a man, you gotta take a stand 'cause ... '). Pride, defiance and liberation were common themes (Jackmaster Funk's 'Freeman'), as was sex (Jamie Principle's 'Baby Wants A Ride'), drugs (Tyree's 'Acid Over') or celebrations of dancing and the dance floor itself. It may be too oblique for some, but Frankie argues that when he cut his first record, a version of Teddy Pendergrass's 'You Can't Hide From Yourself', the boys knew exactly what he was going on about.

'The reason that particular song appealed to that particular audience so well is because most of those gay kids were out, they were no longer living at home with their parents. And even if some of them were they'd make it known pretty much that they were gay. They weren't trying to hide anything, so that the message "you can't hide from yourself, everywhere you go, there you are" was something most of them could relate to. Apart from the fact that the music underneath it was so great. To have that type of song that put forth that type of message that makes them react like that, why not?'

And like any subculture worth its salt, the House scene was developed enough to have its own argot – a once-secret language that the subsequent success of the music saw cross over into more mainstream use. 'That was the way a lot of the kids in Chicago spoke,' confirms Frankie. 'It was mostly gay kids. Words like "jack" and "pumping the box", that's just the way they spoke out there.'

House started around 1982 and took off in 1986. Ten years on the music's everywhere. Why do these things always take so long to cross over?

'Things have to come full circle first. In the beginning most of the major record labels wouldn't put any time or money into it. Here in England everything is so fad oriented, every three or four months trends and bands are changing and everyone's looking for something new, as opposed to hanging onto something longer to try and cultivate it. I can understand that, as the music really needed time to legitimize itself. In the early days most of what we called House was basically stripped-down rhythm tracks with nonsensical vocals against them. Nothing really major was being done to them to create a song. Over the years what's happened is a lot of people that were making House music in like 1985 have fallen by the wayside. There's only a few people left that were making music in those days; myself, Steve Hurley, Larry Heard, Jamie Principal ... just a handful.'

But what of the music that's being made today. Has his baby turned into a Frankenstein's monster?

'I'm not going to pretend I know anything apart from the particular form of music that I make. I know that a lot of the straight DJs that are making records these days still gear the records to a gay audience. It's much easier to get accepted on that particular level. If it happens in a gay club for a gay audience, especially in the United States and *especially* in New York, then it's easy to break through. And most of the straight DJs recognize that and they use that. I don't see anything wrong with it. If they can take a song that might not originally appeal to a gay audience and turn it into something that will, then that's all for the better.'

Frankie left The Warehouse in 1983. 'I had all sorts of problems there and started to get more involved in production. I started to spend a bit more time hanging around recording studios and learning as much as I could. Then I got into remixing and working with Jamie Principle.' He moved back to New York in 1987 to take up a residency at The Paradise Garage. There he was able to properly establish himself as both a songwriter and a producer – making records like 1989's awesome 'Tears' (with his chum Robert Owens on vocals, who went on to record this year's anthem of the spooned 'I'll Be Your Friend'). Now Frankie's one of the most in-demand producers in the business, with the likes of Prince and Michael Jackson queuing up to work with him (a project with the temperamental Prince was abandoned before completion and Knuckles is currently remixing tracks for Jackson's greatest hits album). But he still DJs, and he's stayed loyal to gay clubs.

'In New York City right now the most important gay club is the Roxy. I play there every other Saturday and I play the Sound Factory every Friday. Ninety-eight per cent of my audience is gay and I'm gay also. I don't put myself on any kind of pedestal and I think that's the reason why I probably have the respect of most of them – even the straight people – because I'm not trying to hide anything.

'I play more songs than anything but that's always the way I've dealt with being a DJ all these years. Because in the early days, when I first started, songs weren't being styled to the dance floor the way they are now. People were writing songs and making songs and they just happened to be up-tempo and so they made you want to move. And that's the same approach that I take towards the music I make. I try not to think about the dance floor when I'm doing it. You could say I'm recapturing the sound and feeling of Disco, infusing it with what's happening today. I've been doing this 20 years and my music's pretty much the same. Of course the music's changed, but the style is the same, the style is the same.'

Strange boy that I am, I start wittering on about how much I love Techno. Frankie goes strangely quiet. Then he continues in a voice every bit as warm as one the Pope might use if I'd started discussing my favourite flavour of condom.

'Those are *not* songs. Not at all. Most of the gay crowds that I play for – and I have a pretty big audience – they're not into it. They like being able to hear songs with great voices, either male or female, that are saying something that they can embrace. A lot of noisy trash doesn't appeal to them. You know I've learned over the years that people react to certain music in certain ways. When you're playing an evening of very hard-edged, very hardcore music – especially Techno – you get a lot of negative energy coming out. Just like when you go into Hip Hop clubs and they're playing a lot of Rap. You're in a room full of people that get very intimidated. Immediately it's like their guard is up and you know you have to be very careful about how you walk around and what you say and what you do and how you look at people. And they're all like that because that's how everyone's attitude is and it's the music that's made them that way.

'At the Roxy you're amongst 7000 gay men. There's a lot of very positive lyrics that are coming through, dreams and fantasies, or whatever you want to call them, about love and about feeling that you're having a good time and that's all the music is telling you to do. So people react that way. The crowd gets softer and all they wanna do is hang on to one another and dance with each other and embrace each other all evening. And I'd rather have that type of audience any time. And I know plenty of straight DJs that would love to be able to play the same kind of room and play the same sort of music that I do.'

Although I could well imagine Ian Levine touting much the same line, Frankie's right. Forget the schism between House and its bad younger brother Techno. There's another one that should concern us more. In the Eighties a schism took place in American black music. A schism around sexuality. There's Rap – which was sexist, macho and obsessed with hate and violence. And there was House – which was sexy, sensual and obsessed with love and sex. Rap was straight. House was gay. Dance is massive now, more popular than perhaps any youth culture has ever been before. And the kids that love that music are in love with a queer music – the House that Frankie built.

Gay Times, August 1992

Chapter nineteen

Housewives' Choice: Female Fans and Unmanly Men

IT is 1926. And Valentino, the age of mass media's first great heart throb is dead. At his funeral there's a surging mob of women over one hundred thousand strong. But whilst the women were going mad for him, the men just couldn't see it. There was something about Valentino that wasn't quite right. He was a little too delicate, over concerned with his appearance – you understand?

Fearful heterosexual men had whispered in consternation: a few more chaps like Valentino could signal the collapse of Western civilization. These whispers first went public with an editorial in the *Chicago Tribune*. Beneath the provocative headline 'Pink powder puffs', the writer expressed his outrage at finding 'A powder vending machine! In the men's room!' and went on to squeal in an orgy of exclamation marks 'Homo Americanus! Why didn't someone quietly drown Rudolph Guglieme, alias Valentino, years ago? Do women like that type of "man" who puts pink powder on his face in a public washroom and arranges his hair in a public elevator?' Readers didn't have to be too intellectually spectacular to figure out just what kind of a 'man' he thought Valentino was. Putting on make-up! In public! And worst of all, oh horror of horrors, women clearly *did* like that kind of 'man'.

Valentino started off the great tradition of male stars who didn't seem overly concerned with appearing butch, and who built up a huge and fanatical female following while the rest of the world was united in the suspicion that he was, well . . . not as other men. It's one of life's great mysteries: what did nice, middle-aged women see in men who, to the rest of us, just didn't seem like the marrying kind?

Take Liberace. In 1956 he successfully sued *The Daily Mirror* for printing an article that he claimed 'implied I was an unmanly man'. For someone who seemed to have dedicated his whole career to implying that he was an unmanly man, that seems rather an odd thing to do. Nevertheless, when the *Mirror* dismissed him as 'the biggest sentimental vomit of all time . . . a deadly, winking, scent impregnated, luminous, quivering, giggling, fruit flavoured, mincing ice covered heap of mother love' they also had to concede he had an uncanny hold over 'teenagers longing for sex and middle aged matrons fed up with sex'.

Sex isn't the first word that comes to mind when one thinks of Liberace – with Valentino, heavy-lidded, perfumed and pouting, cute romantic little Latin fool that he was, yes – but *Liberace*? The latter was, if anything, sexless, playing up an image that exuded safety and homeliness. Here was a guy who dyed the hair at his temples grey to make him look more mature, a professional mummy's boy whose television show had just three props: a piano, a nice candelabra and his dear old mom, who'd stand there with the patience of a saint as he assaulted her with a constant barrage of dedications, naughty winks and flashes of that most cheesy of grins. But to the millions of women who watched and made his show the only real rival to *I Love Lucy* in the Fifties, was he more than just a nice boy who was kind to his mom? Did they reach the same conclusions about him as the gangs of teds who picketed venues on his first British tour brandishing placards proclaiming 'Queer go home'? If all those women thought the same about him as *The Daily Mirror* then why was he receiving over a dozen marriage proposals a week?

Sure, they knew he was unmanly but that didn't mean he was 'you know' – and besides, they liked him that way. They even thought it best that he didn't marry (according to one fan magazine's readers' poll), because that meant 'he can love his mom better'.

Liberace soon changed, proving perhaps that deep inside of every mummy's boy there's a screaming queen trying to claw her way out. By the Sixties, he had lapsed into complete self parody ('Pardon me while I slip into something more spectacular') and began coming on like a man in real need of a taste transfusion. It was a sort of strategy. 'I began to disarm my audience and say what people were thinking before they had a chance to say it. I heckled myself'. Thus he slipped out of one great showbusiness tradition and into another: the queen as a figure of fun, indulging in wild, over the top campery that is forgivable because it's all but act and affectation.

His fame waned until the Eighties – when he found himself selling out bigger venues than ever before, leading him to comment wryly that in the age of Boy George he'd become safe once more. This second wave of success survived his celebrated 'palimony' case and lasted right up until his death from AIDS in 1987.

Both Johnny Mathis and Johnnie Ray found that fans can stay steadfast, loyal and true even after their homosexuality is made public knowledge. Mathis told *US* magazine in the early Eighties that he had two male lovers, and yet his fans still turn out in their droves to hear him warble his way through 'The Twelfth Of Never'. And Johnnie Ray's British fans stuck with him right up until his death last year – in spite of not one, not two, but a mighty *three* arrests for cottaging. Could it be that such artists' homosexuality, suspected or real, is a major factor in their appeal and that this phenomenon – The Liberace Syndrome – is no more than fag-haggery on a mass scale?

Poor old Johnnie Ray was certainly one 'unmanly man'. His whole act, indeed, his whole fame, rested on his breaking a great taboo: he showed that big boys *do* cry. Actually *all* that Johnnie did was cry. He'd walk on stage, the girls would start screaming, he'd put his hand over his hearing aid as if it had started howling feedback, then he'd let rip with that huge tidal wave of a voice – but before he'd reached even the end of the first verse something in Johnnie would click and he'd remember what a rotten old life it was and begin to blub away, banging his pretty little head against the piano in unconsolable grief.

Johnnie was important for lots of reasons. He was just a teensy bit too early for rock 'n' roll, but was one of the people who dictated its shape and eased its passage. He was a heart throb who showed that it was OK for a man to be vulnerable and sensitive and hurt. He also showed that a lot of women like a man like that.

You can still hear the echoes of his sobs in the charts to this day. But he also influenced those who operate more or less outside of pop. The housewives' choices who trade on their personalities, on the singer not the song. Barry Manilow is the prime contemporary example. He's got the largest and the most fanatical following. He stresses that he's not pop, he's *more* than pop. He's showbusiness, a professional. He's charismatic. A little bit naughty, but basically nice. Boyish and self mocking, he's sincere and humble. And his fans? They like Barry's bum.

Manilow started out in 1972 playing piano for Bette Midler while she sang to a crowd of men wearing nothing but moustaches and towels at New York's Continental Baths. His act borrows heavily from hers. It's a lot less brassy and a little less camp but it's basically cabaret: big ballads with death-defying key changes and, most important, lots and lots of on-stage chat. 'I try stopping myself,' he said unconvincingly to one interviewer, 'but when I'm out there it's like I'm sittin' in my living room talkin' to my friends.' Like Liberace, Manilow excels at creating the illusion of intimacy – at making Mrs Average feel special, as if he's performing just for her.

It would be too easy to reduce all this down to 'nice personalities'. Because the men seem to be 'nice boys' (nudge, nudge) and 'mummy's boys' (wink wink) it becomes difficult for many to see them as possibly representing anything other than a surrogate son to these women. Thus any sexual component to the relationship is conveniently negated. A similar reluctance to consider any kind of autonomous female sexuality – *especially* in middle-aged women – has led to the myth of maternalism, a belief that the only thing such women could possibly want to do with these men is mother them. But with Barry's fans, if these are maternal feelings then they're of a deeply Oedipal hue. You don't scream at and chase after and mob someone you want to mother. You certainly don't swap and collect 'bum shots' of them with your friends. You knit them sweaters and take spit-sodden kleenexes to the chocolate smears on their face. What we are talking about with Barry is lust, pure and simple.

A singing crotch like Tom Jones holds little appeal for most women – with the only attraction being the thrill or the giggle of the girl's night out. Like the current vogue for those troupes of American beefcake strippers such as The Chippendales, what they provide is a 'girls together' environment. A space where heterosexual women are allowed (or, rather, allow themselves) to behave in ways that they usually can't. The act is not the focus of attention – they are merely providing the women with an excuse for being there, for congregating with other women. What is true for the macho performers also holds true for today's more nelly entertainers.

We can even trace some kind of progression from Valentino (cinema and theatre matinee performances were tailored towards and attended almost exclusively by women whilst their husbands were away at work) through Liberace (beamed into the home in the early evening or a concert attraction to which women would drag their reluctant husbands as chaperons) to today, when it's no longer taboo for women to attend, say, a Cliff Richard concert with their female friends rather than their husbands. This progression has been a search for space, an escape from the home – somewhere that for most women is still a place of work rather than rest.

There's also been a marked progression in the way women behave in the concert hall. Fans of Liberace exercised decorum and restraint. Johnnie Ray's concerts marked a watershed – women let themselves go. Today a Barry Manilow concert is a scene of near debauchery. The sexual component in the fans' adoration is made resoundingly clear – though how much of it is for real and how much of it is simply play is vague. As is the more interesting question of how much of it is really directed at him. Here's Manilow on why he persists with his 'sexy' stage antics even though he looks so uncomfortable when he's doing them: 'I do it because they want it . . . wiggling my ass – that's the bit I really don't like. I've never enjoyed that part of it . . . the only way I can think to get round the problem is by camping it up and fooling around. That Liverpool gig was uncomfortable for me. They wouldn't allow me to do the job. They wanted me to be cute and wiggle my ass and tell dirty stories. I was disappointed because I take the work I do seriously and now and again I fall into the trap of pandering to them.'

Compare that sorry tale of woe with a fan's experience of a concert: 'It's a real sexual thing . . . but it isn't only that, because I've been to lots and lots of concerts but I've never felt that kind of atmosphere and that kind of closeness. Complete strangers catch hold of your hand and you are united as one. When they start singing "We'll Meet Again" and all join hands you can almost feel the love. Something runs between us like an electric shock. It's just wonderful.' Perhaps it's this collision between the sense of female solidarity and the eroticism that Barry acts as a catalyst for, that creates the fabled 'Manilow magic'.

What becomes clear is that there are widely disparate reasons for why women adore Valentino or Liberace or Johnnie Ray or Barry Manilow or whoever. It would be foolish to try to seek out one unified reason. They are, however, a variety of responses to just one type of man, an 'unmanly' one. The attraction is rarely a presumed homosexuality – for we know that people have a quite remarkable capacity for self deception (and many of these fans are more than likely rotten old homophobes) – it's more perhaps an attraction towards these men's 'homosexual-ness'. Many of the artists may be straight, but their popularity rests on them being 'gay-acting, gay-looking'. It should be borne in mind that not everyone automatically equates 'unmanly men' with homosexuality and that one man's camp is another's good taste. Some see a gay man up there, others a gentle straight man. Some see a silly queen, others the perfect son. Some see an ideal lover, others a humpy stud. They can represent danger just as easily as they can safety.

All this belies a certain lack of compatibility between straight men and straight women. Between how 'men' are and what women want. A shortfall betwixt ideal and reality. A Liberace or Manilow is derided for homophobic reasons. Their fans for misogynistic ones. In so doing their critics are seeking to avoid facing the fact that, like it or not, some women like their men unmanly, perhaps even somewhat androgynous. There's a need to dismiss these women's opinions because what they are saying is something deeply threatening: *real* men are crap.

Gay Times, June 1991

Chapter twenty

I'm Not Like
Everybody Else:
The Kinks

Kinky (kinki) *adj.* having kinks; (coll.) eccentric, queer, weirdly attractive, sophisticated, perverted, mad.

The Penguin English Dictionary, 1965.

EVEN though we're sitting in a windowless room at Konk Studios, Ray Davies is keeping his sunglasses on today. He says he spent last night in a ditch. It's a good line. The ninth line of *Waiting for Godot* to be precise, but never mind. Maybe he did. He's also got a toothbrush in his jacket pocket. It's far more him.

We're here to talk about his book. As you'd expect from someone with a 'basic distrust of orthodoxy', *X-Ray* is not a conventional autobiography; an unnamed young journalist is despatched to write the biography of a septuagenarian, Raymond Douglas Davies. Past meets future, innocence meets experience, and all that kind of thing. RD tells the boy all about his life – how this kid from North London started a band with his brother Dave, and how, by recording some of the strangest and most beautiful records ever made, The Kinks became The Beatles' and Stones' only real rivals.

If the Sixties are now seen as one big party, then Ray Davies was the party pooper in the kitchen writing songs about the sink. He questioned the rampant neophilia of the time ('Village Green Preservation Society' – a frightening premonition of John Major's 'warm beer and cricket' speech), mocked the Sixties swingers ('Sunny Afternoon', 'Dedicated Follower Of Fashion') and celebrated those left standing still ('Dead End Street', 'Autumn Almanac', 'Shangri-la').

Ray Davies was also – from 'Well Respected Man' onwards – the first pop star to sing in an English accent. He wrote about England too. And you can't have England without queers, can you? When Britpop had barely got past wanting to hold girlie's hands, Davies sang about sexual identity crises ('See My Friends', 'Fancy'), label queens ('Dedicated Follower Of Fashion'), schoolboy crushes ('David Watts') and drag queens ('Lola'). The Kinks were all about identity, be it sexual, national or class; Ray's own as well as other people's. He kept asking 'Who am I?' But the closest we ever got to an answer was the song 'I'm Not Like Everybody Else'.

'In my childhood I was told that I probably would have a physical disability. They said "when you're old you'll be a cripple", knowing that made me feel a bit of a victim and an outsider. I found myself looking for other people who got banished. I really did walk down the street one day when I was 19 years old and say "I will not be like everyone else. I will not live the way they want me to". And I was speaking out loud like a mad person. I was quite driven. I wore a tie to art school because everyone else wore pullovers. I was confused obviously.'

About what?

'Everything. Sexuality, the world, umm, the cost of cheese rolls in the canteen. I can still taste those cheese rolls. Crusty on the outside. I was confused why we got a special deal there and yet at the ABC coffee shop around the corner they were 10p. I was confused about everything but that's part of growing up.'

Ray Davies does this a lot. He says something he didn't really want to say, and then says anything – the madder the better – to try and take your mind off it. I just say 'Moving on . . . ' and Ray, camp as ever, smiles and chirps back 'Shall we?' Probe. Flannel. Probe. Flannel. Probe. Moving back . . .

As time passes it becomes almost impossible to imagine the shock of the new. When The Kinks first appeared in 1964 they looked like such a bunch of girls. They started out in pink tab-collar shirts and dark blue corduroy trousers. They had hair down to their shoulders, leather caps, plastic capes and Cuban heels. They pouted, they preened, they minced. Lots of people thought The Kinks were queer. And the Kinks didn't care what people thought.

'Someone said a very odd thing to me. It's a very true thing as well. When we did "Dedicated Follower Of Fashion" on *Top of the Pops* – it must have been the way I sang it or whatever – but people started smiling differently at me, and saying that the campest person in the band is Mick Avory because he was trying to look so straight. I don't think it's play acting. We just find it very hard to be any other way. I can't be one hundred per cent man. I think everybody has two sides. With The Kinks there is a genuine sexless bonding, a kind of unity. I'd go up to Mick Avory now and say "hello dear", and he'd say "hello luv". That's the way we are. It comes, I guess, from being yourself. You can only be yourself. I once asked a girlfriend "why do you like me?", and she said "because there's nothing macho about you whatsoever".'

It wasn't a kind of rebellion then?

'Possibly. At school everybody else was trying to look like Rock Hudson and Tab Hunter. The girls thought they were the real men. Now we know the real story. It's something I can't define. We didn't give a shit about what people thought. It's odd though, a lot of people liked the campness. Men weren't threatened by us, girls liked us. It wasn't a wind up. Sometimes it was the only way we could deal with the world. There was nothing premeditated. Remember we didn't go to college to learn how to be pop stars. We had our own little unit, and that's who we were. We just never had a problem with it. Sometimes we wound people up. We definitely wound Mick Avory up at the audition, and when Mick joined the band he just carried it on.'

The Kinks' heyday was neatly bordered by the Profumo scandal and the Sexual Offences Act. It was a time of immense change. When Ray used the word 'gay' in 'David Watts', the word itself was in transition. The Sixties saw the rise of the straight/gay dichotomy. True to form Ray resisted this, suggesting things weren't always quite so clear cut. When he sang about homosexuality it was always as a source of confusion and doubt.

'I can't define what I am at all. And I don't want to and I don't want to have to ever in my life. That's part of my . . . fear I guess. I don't want to define what I am.'

Because it would be conforming or because you can't?

'I'm not out. I'm just out there. It's a different thing. It doesn't bother me too much. The only thing that concerns me is that I want people to feel free to be whatever they are sexually and not do it because of peer pressure. People shouldn't be pressured to be straight. People shouldn't be pressured to be gay. I guess it dates me a little to think a world will exist where people exist together. It's still a very tormented world. That's why The Kinks didn't care. "See My Friends", for example, I don't know how people put the gay thing into that.'

Why do you think they did?

'Because it's patently obvious that the friends I'm singing about are not girls. And they're across the river. *It's a gulf! Again!* People looked at it as a separatist thing. There's a side of me, there's a lot of man in me, there's a lot of woman in me, and I don't care. It doesn't bother me.'

What was going on in your head at that time?

'I was thinking I have the choice to go there if I want, to go across the river if I want. But I can't analyse other people's analysis. That's for them to decide. It wasn't playing on. I just suddenly found wonderful things I could write about. We were pursued by a lot of teenage girls, but rather than write "Baby come back to my place in your high heels and give me a blow job", I wrote "See my Friends". Ha! And possibly that's been the problem in The Kinks' career. We haven't written what people would have expected us to.'

Ray created characters in his songs. But he also wrote a lot about himself. Trying to work out which is which can be a tricky business.

'A lot of audiences think because I'm singing in the first person, it's me. I've had big problems with that. People don't realize that I'm like a novelist, I write characters. It worries me when people think that I am those characters. It's similar to those old tough guys in Hollywood. Everybody wanted to pick a fight with them.'

Ray Davies raises his eyebrows. I know this because I've now managed to reposition myself so that I can see behind his sunglasses.

What Ray means, and it's all there in the book, is that the band got invited to some marvellous parties. At one, given by the real David Watts, an old school, muscular homosexual and Northern promoter, Ray tried to marry his brother off with the host.

'I must clarify one thing. I totally admire David Watts. It's a song of admiration. I do wish I could be like him. About two years ago I went up in the car to try and find him. I searched and searched and searched. Finally I found this guy and he's dead. I cried and cried. He added so much to my life. I really did admire him. It wasn't mocking. I think people misinterpret things a lot of the time. It's going back to this sly wit, you know, cynicism? I never betrayed my subjects.'

Why were you so keen to marry off Dave to him?

'I felt that would be the right thing for him to do. I genuinely felt that this was a perfect match. I felt I could trust David Watts with my brother.'

What did Dave think?

'I think now he wishes he had.'

We never get to hear the story behind 'Lola' in the book. RD promises to tell his biographer the truth but he never does. So was 'Lola' as real as, say, 'David Watts'?

'It was a mixture of a lot of things. It was a secret affair and it was also a true incident in a wonderful club in Paris called The Carousel. Robert Wace, one of our managers, was dancing with this beautiful black woman, who was wearing this tight dress. Incredible. And I stole her. It was back to my place and there was the stubble. I'm just not mad about stubble. It makes your face very red. But it's many things, and again it's what I felt I had the right to write about. There was a sense that you couldn't write about it.'

Ray's never said this before. As with his songs he usually only talks about having desires, never following them through. When I ask him how often he acted on his feelings, Ray wibbles on about dinner party etiquette for a bit. Does that mean you're not going to answer the question?

'Umm. Umm ... err, phew. Phhh. You didn't think of it as sleeping with men. It's a dangerous thing to answer. I can not sleep with men because it's a gay situation. I think I'm more of a voyeur. I like watching people.'

Watching them do what?

'I observe people. I take it all in. I've got a really good recall system. It's just being part of the experience. And this could be said about my whole attitude to the Sixties. Yes I was there but I was watching it happen. I won't knowingly make it happen. The same applies to sexual activities. I was there but I was not part of the action in the sense that I was the lead. I was married then and I was trying to have a family life which was very difficult. I continually used to watch my wife sleep and wonder why she was there. I was trying so desperately to have a semblance of normality. But there's always been part of me that goes off into the night and becomes not Mr Hyde but Mr Mysterious.'

For my last trick I ask Mr Mysterious if I can run through the dictionary definition of 'kinky' with him. Just answer yes or no Ray, are you now or have you ever been one of the following?

Having kinks?

'Having kinks? Yes.'

Eccentric.

'Yes.'

Queer?

'In the sense of the definition of queer, yes.' Pause. 'What's the opposite?'

Erm. Normal?

Ray thinks. 'I can not answer that in the straight/gay definition. Okay? I would not say queer, I would say . . . odd.'

Weirdly attractive?

'Weirdly attracted to.'

To what?

'Anything weirdly attractive.'

Sophisticated?

'Yes and no.'

Perverted?

'Perverse.'

Mad?

There's another pause.

'Yes.'

Ray looked so anguished when I asked about 'queer'. Other pop stars would have said 'I won't answer that question'. Ray

Davies said 'I can't'. *X-Ray* is the autobiography of a man who says 'I don't know what I am ... but I know I'm not like everybody else.'

I get up to go. Ray Davies stands up and sighs and then gives me this great big bear hug. It feels really strange being hugged by God. I go weak at the knees, say goodbye and wobble out of the room. I've wanted to go for a pee for the last half hour. As I wander round Konk Studios trying to find the loo, I keep asking myself who I've just interviewed? Was it an ordinary bloke pretending to be a rock star, or a rock star pretending to be an ordinary bloke? On my way back out I pass by Ray who's now moved to another room. He hasn't seen me. He's taken his sunglasses off, but that toothbrush is still in his jacket pocket ...

Gay Times, October 1994

Chapter twenty-one

Just Good Friends?:
Take That

One thing that interests me is the problem of friendship.
For centuries after antiquity, friendship was a very
important kind of social relation...I think that in the
sixteenth and seventeenth centuries we see these kinds of
friendships disappearing, at least in the male society. And
friendship begins to become something other than that.
And one of my hypotheses, which I am sure would be
borne out if we did this, is that homosexuality became a
problem – that is, sex between men became a problem – in
the eighteenth century ... Once friendship disappeared as a
culturally accepted relation, the issue arose, 'What is going
on between men?' And that's when the problem appears ...
Well I'm sure that I'm right, that the disappearance of
friendship as a social relation and the declaration of
homosexuality as a social/political/medical problem are the
same process.

Michel Foucault

We're here to bring the sex back into pop!
Gary Barlow, *Smash Hits,* 24 June 1991.

(IN their first video, 'Do What You Like', Take That wear
lycra shorts, little caps and leather jackets with nothing underneath.
As the video progresses they wear less and less. At the close they are
lying down naked. The camera pans across their arses. They've just

had a food fight, smearing jelly over each others' bodies. It's so funny. It's so Athletic Model Guild. It made me think of that Barbara Kruger photograph which shows a group of men fighting, with the caption: 'You construct intricate rituals which allow you to touch the skin of other men'.)

> Now as they queue up noisily for food and cups of coffee they crowd round the counter and do something quite weird. They distractedly touch each other. And no, it's not because they're gay. It's almost as if they need to keep reassuring themselves that they're still there for each other. Jason's arm stretches across both Gary and Mark, Howard rests his hands on alternate shoulders, Jason's other hand plays with Gary's hair. Gary in turn holds on to Robbie's ears, then Howard's. Mark rests his arm on Howard who gives Robbie a cuddle. They stroke and nudge and cuddle each other constantly. It's really quite touching.
> *Smash Hits*, 25 November 1992

(Take That can't keep their hands off each other. That's one of the reasons I like them. They're all so touchy. It's so touching. 'And no, it's not because they're gay.' So that's alright then.)

> Without realizing they have one of their now infamous touching sessions. It's purely heterosexual, in case you're wondering. Jason strokes Mark's hair and neck while Mark rubs Jason's back. They do this quite absent mindedly while looking out the window. Gary joins in crushing them in an almighty hug and flicking their earlobes.
> *Take That in Private*

('It's purely heterosexual, in case you're wondering.' Come to think of it I wasn't. I've heard the rumours though. All 9, 765, 845 of them.)

> Jason: So the rumour is we're all gay now, are we?
> Gary: Am I gay? I am. Why? Oh good, just so long as I know.
> Howard: Does anyone think I'm gay?
> Jason: No, you're the only one people think is straight.
> Howard is insulted.

Howard: Why aren't I gay? What's wrong with me?
Jason: It's because you're such a fine figure of macho manhood.
Howard: Well, I want to be queer like you lot.
Take That in Private

(Note how the lads' unflustered good humour is presented as a kind of denial. They couldn't possibly be. Or could they? Every queen I've spoken to 'knows' the truth about Take That. But each one gives me a different cast list. 'Oh, it's just Robbie.' 'Gary's the only gay one.' 'Howard's the only straight one.' 'They all are.' 'None of them are.' Some of it's just wishful thinking. The ones we'd most like to be gay 'are gay'. The ones we'd most like to sleep with, usually. Their young female fans don't doubt their heterosexuality. But they like the fact that Take That, whatever their sexuality, are 'gay acting, gay looking'. Much of their appeal lies in their homosexual-ness. They are sweet and soft. Such nice boys. *Smash Hits* even calls them 'the kings of girliebloke pop'.)

I wish men could be more like women.
Jason Orange, *Smash Hits,* 22 January 1992

(During the Nineties gay men began to use the self-description 'boys'. The word suggests much. If being gay was once about being denied the spurious privileges attached to being a man, we've recently turned it into a rejection of those self same 'privileges'. Now we refuse to be men. We are *boys*. We are free of adult responsibilities. We are forever young. We are perpetually teenage. Why, we even like Take That. And Take That are a 'boyband'. They are not 'men'. But what is going on between *boys*.)

A real weirdy moment comes during 'Why Can't I Wake Up With You?' Robbie and Little Mark's faces are blown up on the huge video screen. They're singing to each other. Gazing into each others' eyes and smiling. And then they kiss! On the ruddy lips!!! And it gets the biggest cheer of the night!!!! These girls' minds are just plain filthy. They're even worse than me.
Richard Smith, *Melody Maker,* 17 December 1994.

Boys snogging is the Holy Grail of the Modern Girl. It's been an open secret between us for a long time, when the lights are low, the Malibu is flowing and the guys are safely tucked up in bed, we are just as interested in watching attractive men get acquainted in ways the most intimate of Masonic handshakes just won't reach, as men are in two babes get Babylonian.
Julie Burchill, *The Sunday Times*, 4 December 1994.

What better way could there be to mark World AIDS Day than a concert by Take That? Watching the world's first and foremost cock pop group is the safest – and the best – sex around. Tonight Take That made every other band on the planet look slightly pointless. They were pop. They were porn. They were panto. They were perfect.
Richard Smith, *Melody Maker*, 17 December 1994.

(I love the video for 'Why Can't I Wake Up With You?' Take That are in a hotel. They're staying in separate rooms. Each member is shown alone and distraught. But who are they singing to? Who is 'you'? And I adore the one for 'Pray', it's just so fucking sexy. Both Julie Burchill and Suzanne Moore invoked the name 'Bruce Weber' when writing about Take That videos. So much male flesh, so beautifully shot. And *Smash Hits* these days is just like a gay soft porn mag. I get it every fortnight. But you don't have to be homo to be homoerotic. Or do you?)

You get a few funny comments, but I haven't – touch wood – had anyone who wanted to smash a pint through my face. You get lads singing bits of songs but I think it's funny. And lads shouting 'faggot' every now and then. I blow them a kiss.
Mark Owen, *The Face*, December 1993.

(I guess it's just straight boys and gay boys who like to think Take That are queens. But unlike the straight boys we think it's a fabulous thing to say about someone. And Take That, bless 'em, take it as a compliment.)

Gary: I've heard lots of rumours that we're gay. I like that, it's a bit of controversy. I've heard rumours that I'm going out with someone at MTV.
Robbie: Some gay friends of mine, all their gay friends have slept with me. And I was crap.
The Face, December 1993.

(Fact: Fiction is better than fact.)

Nigel reads *The Daily Express.* In it Gary is quoted as saying: 'Our manager is gay. It's very open'. Nigel isn't happy. He talks to Gary, who claims he didn't say it. 'It must be one of the others,' Nigel frumps. He talks to me about it, says that he protects their privacy and they should protect his.
The Face, December 1993.

AIDS KILLS LOVER OF GAY TAKE THAT BOSS – Manager and male model lived together ... The news will come as a shock to Britain's thousands of Take That fans. The five heterosexual lads, with a clean cut 'boy next door' image, are worshipped by teenage girls. Their pictures adorn bedrooms throughout Britain. But at the beginning of their career they played gay clubs and freely admit they still have a homosexual following.
News of the World, 22 August 1993.

('But?')

Take That's pretty-boy looks and athletic dance routines have won them a lot of gay fans. From the early days the band performed in gay clubs and those shows, together with the fact that no member of the band has a steady girlfriend, led to the inevitable, but wrong, rumours that the band might be gay. 'The rumours started because I've always insisted that the boys play in gay clubs,' admits Nigel. 'They are five good-looking lads so the gay clubs offered a lot more than the straight clubs. My attitude was "Why not?"'

Performing in gay clubs was certainly an eye opener for Gary who admits that he – like the other guys in the band – was chatted up all the time. 'We've always done gay clubs and people always used to cheer and wolf-whistle when we'd go on stage. Before the band I didn't know anything about gay people, their views or how they lived. But now I feel I've lived a whole lot more.

'Guys would chat us up all the time and they were quite forward. They'd want to know if I was gay and when I said "I'm not" they used to say "that's cool" and keep on talking.'

The gay rumours posed no problem for any of the band members. Says Mark: 'I like gay rumours because it creates a bit of mystery about the band. We also get lots of letters from gay men saying they fancy us but we're not bothered by that.'

'We basically play to people who like our music,' adds Howard, 'and we just happen to have a big gay following. I don't see what's wrong with that.'
The Take That Fact File

(One of the great clichés you find in interviews in the gay press is the line 'I love my gay fans'. What people usually mean by that is 'my career has gone so far down the dumper I only have gay fans', or 'my career is at such a low ebb no one else can be bothered to interview me so my press officer fixed up this interview with some crummy fag mag.')

Did you deliberately set out to become gay pin ups?
Gary: No, we never aimed for anything in particular. We just think that whoever likes us can come aboard.
Jason: I'm really proud of the gay following. We get a lot of letters from gay fans, and I love reading them.
Robbie: I just find it very flattering that both sexes seem to fancy us. Gay audiences like having a good time, which we like as well.
The Face, November 1992.

(Is this just a queer sales pitch? Tom Watkins once said: 'the only people who buy pop records are young girls and gay men. Why? They both like cocks. That's all.' Maybe it's all incredibly cynical, just a way of getting those pink pounds rolling in? 'Well, we *might* be?' Maybe Take That are just playing Zelig? 'Any way you want me, that's how I will be.' I really don't think so. I really don't.)

> This most stridently heterosexual of men (Robbie Williams) is very protective of his gay friends and is physically affectionate towards all men and women regardless of their sexuality.
> I go out with Mark, our make-up guy a lot – he's gay. So what if we go to gay clubs? I'll hold his hand going down the street if I want to. I'm just naturally affectionate. I always kiss the other lads in Take That hello and goodbye – no tongues though.
> *Take That in Private*

And finally the conversation turns inevitably, to the subject of homosexuality . . .

(Inevitably?)

> Jason: I think the newspapers think it would be the biggest scoop of the year if one of us were really gay.
> Howard: Yeah, it's a shame we're not really.
> Robbie: No, but it would be a good news story.
> Howard: Or if we had steady girlfriends.
> Robbie: Hey, maybe when our popularity dies down we can say one of us is gay just to get the interest back up.
> Gary: I'm not saying I'm gay.
> Howard: I'll say I am.
> Jason: I'll kiss you Howard. We'll have a picture of us kissing and people will think we're having an affair. I love it that loads of people think we're gay! I spent the first few years of our career not denying just to get people going. It really used to amuse me.
> *Take That in Private*

(Take That came 'to bring the sex back into pop'. In fact, they brought homosexuality back into pop. They are not Jason Donovan. Donovan took *The Face* to court in March 1992. Take That broke through in the following months. Jason may have won the court case but he lost the pop war. Everyone hates him now. And the world loves Take That. I love Take That because they don't care and because they do care. Through Take That the subject of homosexuality is discussed unhysterically, as a matter of fact, a possibility. Take That promote homosexuality. This is a good thing. I really love Take That. Really. I really love Take That.)

> Gary: If there was a gay member of this band he would have had a nervous breakdown and left by now!
> Howard: Are you going to Harvey Nichols tomorrow then or what, Gaz? 'Cause if you are can you get us some scented candles?
> *Take That in Private*

(Really?)

April 1995.

Chapter twenty-two

Kerrang!
The Sound of Confusion:
Heavy Metal

IT had taken more than two weeks before I had the courage to buy the magazine. I didn't dare go to a newsagent near my house so I'd decided to make a special trip into town. On finding a sufficiently empty shop I shuffled in and scanned the magazine racks. There it was, all glossy and lurid looking, on the cover a man with no shirt on. After one final furtive glance over my shoulder, I rushed to the counter. Unable to look the assistant in the eye I handed over the money then beat a hasty retreat as soon as the change had been tendered. I walked on a couple of streets then peered inside my brown paper bag. I felt pleased with myself, and appalled at the same time. But I'd done it – I'd bought a copy of *Kerrang!*, the self-styled 'world's most dangerous heavy metal magazine'. I just pray that no-one saw me, I'd be so embarrassed. Heavy Metal's just so embarrassing.

This traumatic experience directly paralleled one I went through at 16 or so. Having decided to throw my eyesight to the wind, a slightly shaking and slightly drunken me attempted to buy a copy of *Men! Naked!*, or some such magazine, from a Baker Street newsagent. You'd have had a hell of a job trying to convince me at the time, but I suppose I was lucky. At that tender age I was certain of one thing that, for once, my head, my heart and my dick were all in perfect agreement on. I fancied men.

For most boys, though, adolescence is a time of crisis and confusion. And that these boy-virgins, these inbetweenies, comprise the sole audience for Heavy Metal is of course no coincidence.

Usually, when people talk about music, when they try to locate the source of that special thrill we feel when we hear our favourite songs, they are prone to warble on endlessly about 'heart' and 'soul', even sometimes 'brains'. But good Heavy Metal, we're assured, 'has balls' or 'kicks ass', yet it allows another body part to take centre stage. Heavy Metal is obsessed with cock to an extent that would embarrass even the likes of you and me.

People use their choice in music to announce something about themselves to others, taste is a tool we use to construct an image of a desired self that we wish to project – sophisticated, zany, rebellious, sensitive, whatever. The fans of Heavy Metal use their allegiance to it to announce their 'manliness'. It's music for boys who are tired of being men in waiting.

For some two decades now its appeal has lain with one group of people – there's been a constant turnover of fans who have been almost exclusively young males between the ages of 13 and 16. Stuck in the painfully slow transition stage from boyhood to manhood, they're left desperately wanting to be something they're not. Heavy Metal appears to offer a magical solution to their crisis, a way out of their state of flux. For them, being a Heavy Metal fan means being more manly. To them its twisted notion of what being a man means is totally convincing. For the rest of us, it's just a ridiculously transparent pantomime.

These young boys have a fantasy image of what comprises life as a straight adult male, that's not so pure and far from simple, and it comes across not only in their own behaviour but in the whole elaborate mythology of 'the rock 'n' roll lifestyle' which the songs celebrate and the musicians profess to live out. It's a last gasp attempt to romanticize male heterosexuality – where men are all free and wild spirits with no commitments to tie them down, inhabiting an all-male environment that women impinge on only to be used as sex aids. There's not so much a reality gap in operation here as a gaping chasm between how men are and how the boys need to believe them to be. As Aunt Ida once said, the world of the heterosexual is a sick and boring life – straight men have wives and kids and mortgages and boring jobs and Black and Decker drills. But the fans demand to be lied to and Heavy Metal obliges.

It's not too fanciful to suggest that for many fans the need to embrace Heavy Metal stems not from the aforementioned crisis of status but from a crisis of sexuality that is closely linked to this. These are boys at an age where sexuality is at its most fluid and the fact that these boys might be doing rude things with one another, or even thinking about doing them, must be kept hidden. Heavy Metal provides just such a smokescreen

The genre's clear homoeroticism only further confuses things – it raises our suspicions in the way that any all-male preserve does. At the centre of all its rituals – the live concert – one can almost hear the testosterone fizzing. When all those boys get together in a woman-free zone they are free to let themselves go and – big, tough, straight boys that they undoubtedly are – show their adoration of those 'real' men up on the stage.

And there, far more so than in the still slightly self-conscious audience, is the wildest orgy of male bonding outside of a rugby team's changing room. A riot of phallic imagery: guitar necks, microphones and clearly visible phalluses where they should be, in the genital area of those frequently thrust hips. It's a place where men are men and the women are, unsurprisingly, elsewhere.

Women are excluded by the sheer farce of it all as much as by the rampant misogyny. They are both hated and feared – the great unknown, dismissed as mere sperm receptacles, big breasted 'boilers' who 'are only good for one thing'. It's a world without love, silly love songs like Extreme's 'More Than Words' are still the exception. But such talk rings hollow, for where exactly are the 'foxy chicks' who supposedly hang around the stage door? It's the language of your average playground boast – it's about needing to remind everyone that you GET LAID LOADS and that you're NOT A POOF, RIGHT?

The fashion of Heavy Metal's fervently anti-fashion fans is one of pop's few true uniforms and is by far its most rigid. Individuality is surrendered in a sea of tight, frayed jeans, hair as long as headmaster will allow, tour t-shirts and leather or denim jackets festooned with patches advertizing your favourite bands. The look echoes a gay fashion, behind both, a desire to look like a 'real man'.

But whereas a gay man steals the symbols with his tongue stuck firmly in his cheek, the poor Heavy Metal fan is absolutely serious.

Fans may dress down but the stars are allowed to dress up in more flamboyant, often surprisingly feminine styles. Indeed Heavy Metal's folklore is littered with tales of groups who were literally run out of towns in the Deep South by Rednecks who mistook them for 'faggots'.

Their look comes from a unisexual one of 20 years ago that they have stubbornly refused to change. Tradition is important to these people. Much of the appeal of Heavy Metal lies in the way it appears to blunder on oblivious to the vagaries of fashion. Being swept along by the next big thing is to them a girlie thing to do. Just as the fans' clothes stress utility over style, which is seen as the unnecessary in dress, mere feminine adornment.

Pop music remains interesting because it keeps absorbing influences from all over the place and thus keeps evolving. Not so Heavy Metal – rock 'n' roll dinosaurs who'll defend the purity of the same seven chords and of the voice, bass, guitar, drums line-up to the end.

This mistrust of progress carries through to Metal's politics. It's about the only place where it's perfectly OK to be a right wing gumby. From songs like Ozzie Osborne's 'bombs-not-jobs' anthem 'Thank God For The Bomb' (with its jolly chorus 'Nuke ya, nuke ya') to Rush, a Canadian band whose entire repertoire consists of nuggets of wisdom from the far-Right philosopher Ayn Rand set to hard rockin' fugues.

Given all this we shouldn't be surprised at Heavy Metal's almost institutionalized homophobia. When the American band Skid Row release photos of them with the singer wearing an 'Aids kills faggots dead' t-shirt it is 'funny'. When Guns 'n' Roses sang in 'One In A Million', 'Immigrants and faggots they make no sense to me/They come to my country and think they'll do as they please/Like start some mini Iran or spread some fuckin' disease', it is 'social comment'. Two years ago, Jon Bon Jovi, was charged under Ireland's recent Prohibition of Incitement to Hatred Act after an onstage outburst in Dublin about 'homos' and 'faggots'. It was, we were assured in a whimpering apology, only because he was upset as his football team had lost a match. So that's alright then.

Just as we shouldn't be surprised by Heavy Metal's homophobia neither should we be surprised by the existence of Heavy Metal homos. Some of its seminal figures are also some of the best kept closets in pop – though they're hardly the only gay men to be employed in an anti-gay profession. This year saw the emergence of the first out group, the not-that-famous American band, Helot's Revenge (Motto: 'In your face – up your butt!') and the German group, Accept, have for many years been writing explicitly and approvingly about various queer goings on. Their lead singer Udo Dirkschneider (like Judas Priest's Rob Halford one of the few stars to support a crop instead of the near obligatory long, flowing locks) went solo in the mid Eighties, but not before barking his way through songs like 'London Leatherboys', 'Take Him In My Heart' and 'Head Over Heels' (about cruising in a park). They'd employed an Englishman to write their lyrics and one can't help wondering if they knew exactly what they were singing about. Heavy Metal bands can be pretty clueless – when they were first starting out AC/DC's ambiguous moniker got them booked in to play at some of Melbourne's more 'bohemian' niteries.

But by far the most spectacular camp intervention into the genre has of course been that made by the excellently named Queen. When they started out in 1973 they swiftly succeeded in making the then burgeoning pomp rock scene a little bit more preposterous, and though 'Bohemian Rhapsody' was a horrible thing to inflict on an unsuspecting world, they proved that any musical form can be made a little more bearable by the simple addition of a little bit of glitter and a good deal of mincing. They're not the only people who have liked the idea of playing guitars very loudly and shouting a lot, but who have felt embarrassed by all the machismo. The most obvious example of this conscious self-distancing from Metal's nastier elements and brutalist past is Glam – the bastard son of Metal and bubblegum – which cut a new seam that's been furrowed in more recent times by the likes of the extremely silly Hanoi Rocks and the extremely wonderful Manic Street Preachers.

Glorious though such Jessie Metal is – in theory if not always in practice – such bands usually find themselves marginalized and excluded from Metal's main project (*No Glam Fags!* screamed one American band's album title). Though there's a current vogue for Metal bands that it's cool to like (the bleak Nihilism of Metallica, the great Nirvana and Public Enemy chum's Anthrax) who bravely deviate from the notion of what a Heavy Metal band is allowed to do, generally speaking, rules most definitely is rules.

Heavy Metal does not like outside influences for the same reason that it doesn't like change – it has no room for doubt. That's why it's the scene that celebrates itself. No other type of music spends so much time writing songs to reassure the fans how great it is, extolling its own virtues and going on and on about how wonderful they, the fans, are. Is there a single Heavy Metal video that doesn't feature a mock in-concert performance cut with film showing cheery scenes from 'life on the road'? Heavy metal is music made in a vacuum. Good pop indicates a better way of doing things. Heavy Metal wallows in the worst. Good pop is about men being unmanly, Heavy Metal exalts a garbled view of the status quo of gender relations. It is conformity masquerading as rebellion.

There's this constant cry at Heavy Metal gigs, where the singer shouts 'Aww-right?' and all the kids go 'Yeahh!' Perhaps the real answer that those barely broken voices would like to emit is 'Actually no, not really'.

For Heavy Metal is the sound of confusion. Little boys playing at being real men in a homophobic, misogynist, phallocentric Never Never Land. From its clothes through to its entire world view, Heavy Metal is butch-drag-made-music. Luckily though, for many of the fans this is only a phase they're going through, the tragedy is that it's also a training ground ...

Gay Times, January 1992

Chapter twenty-three

Let's (Not) Talk about Sex: Sex, Pop and Censorship

THERE'S been a lot of sex in the charts this year, but same as it ever was: 'I Wanna Sex You Up', 'I'm Too Sexy', 'Let's Talk About Sex', 'Sexuality', 'People Are Still Having Sex', 'Sex Drive'. For pop records to deal in sex is no novelty – but for so many of them to come out of the closet and use the S-word certainly *is*. Of course the irresistible rise of dance music has put the emphasis back on the physical in pop, but it has always been sex music. If we had to put a date on when the whole thing started we couldn't do much better than say it was when Elvis first swung his magnificent hips (and was promptly banned) or when Little Richard first emitted that shriek of ecstatic queeny abandon 'Awopbopaloobop alopbamboom' and a whole new generation of kids knew exactly what he meant.

In this proscriptive, sex-negative society pop has always been a place where the discussion and celebration of sex has been central, and where the sexually dissident have been given a platform. Anyone that's cocked an ear to the noises pop's been making over the last thirtysomething years has had a ringside seat to a lively contest over sexual and gender identities. And one where the good guys and girls keep winning.

Pop has always been subjected to a barrage of abuse for not addressing itself to the 'real world', for being reluctant to comment on politics with a big P. Such critics, though, are our enemies – for them the issue of sexuality that pop has consistently dealt with is not a political issue but a personal one, and therefore peripheral.

Which is not to say that pop's attitude to sex has been an 'in your face' one. Many of pop's messages have worked best as a kind of code – automatically understood by its intended audience and intending to baffle all those that it doesn't embrace. And most times, pop is so smart that it feigns being stoopid just to pull the crimplene over granny's eyes so she doesn't realize what naughty things it's telling the kids. And when those who aren't in the know are oblivious to what's going on, they are in no position to stop it.

Our society is not a particularly censorship-friendly one. It has far more efficient and subtle ways of controlling our access to information and ideas. But censorship is by no means unknown – even with regard to the 'trifling and inconsequential' sphere of pop music. As with the other arts – and despite the myth that political freedom of speech is sacrosanct – anyone who starts to say something in the least bit contentious about so called 'moral issues' will find the forces of reaction hurtling down on them quicker than you can say 'Piss Christ'.

In the United States, record companies have long been obliged to mark products with 'Parental Advisory – Explicit Lyrics' stickers. This move has been the biggest victory so far for the right wing lobbying group the Parent's Music Resource Centre (PMRC) who have also succeeded in having the rap group, 2 Live Crew, prosecuted for obscenity, and in banning MTV in Texas. Although such cases are immensely worrying they are quite different from what's happening over here. Over in the land of the First Amendment, the PMRC have a hidden agenda of trying to cultivate a culture that is less hostile to censorship by beginning with attacks on the repugnant and misogynist statements expressed in the lyrics of bands like 2 Live Crew or Niggers With Attitude: i.e. the very people that liberals would be the most uncomfortable defending.

In Britain there has been no such conspiracy, only an uncoordinated clumsiness. In June this year the Obscene Publications Squad impounded 13,000 copies of Niggers With Attitude's album *EFIL4ZAGGIN* – it's interesting that such heavy-handed tactics were not used over in America where the LP swiftly rose to number two. The Squad referred the album to the Crown Prosecution

Service, citing songs like 'Findum, Fucum And Flee' and 'I'd Rather Fuck You'. But there might well have been another reason why the police took such an unprecedented step. The band's best known song is called 'Fuck Tha Police'.

As the rash of sex records shows, bands are usually allowed to talk about sex all they want so long as they do so in a language other than that which people normally use when talking about 'it'. Which goes some way to explaining why many of this current crop ultimately say so little.

After almost a decade of AIDS, though the chaos and crisis are still with us, we have recently entered marginally less proscriptive times. Though not actively encouraged to have sex, we are discussing it with a freedom never seen before. Which is partly why there is a glut of records around with a liberal, liberated patina that sound nothing like the noisy, sweaty bump, thump and grind of the dirty deed itself ...

The female rap duo, Salt 'n' Pepa reached number two in September with their spritely invitation 'Let's Talk About Sex', but – title apart – they could only come up with unremarkable observations that sex isn't dirty (*phew*) and that everybody indulges, concluding with the spoken line 'Yo Pep, I don't think they're gonna play this on the radio'. Such speculation on their own possible controversy was just plain laughable.

But it wasn't so long ago that the mere mention of the very word 'sex' sent blue-faced Radio One controllers off in search of their blue pencils. In 1987 people were a lot more jumpy. A climate that George Michael tried to exploit by attempting to kick start his solo career into controversy with the release of 'I Want Your Sex'. But life is cruel and our pop kids know a naff record when they hear one, so few of them bought it even though Radio One kindly refused to allow it to be played before nine o'clock in the evening. Such is the advance made since then that Color Me Badd reached number one this summer with 'I Wanna Sex You Up', raising barely an eyebrow. Radio One decided that it should only be played after 8.30 *in the morning* (when the kids have left for school). The station's change in attitude is also due to the slow realization on their part that if you're trying to pass yourself off as a happening radio station, coming over all fuddy duddy at the very first sniff of a reasonably risqué record is not the wisest of moves. When Radio One banned Frankie Goes to Hollywood's 'Relax' seven years ago they just made themselves a laughing stock.

While British radio may have learnt the error of its ways, it's still very much par for the course for music television to be censorious whenever sex threatens to rear its pretty little head. Presumably, images pose a far greater threat than words and music. Just one year ago, Madonna's predictably fabulous video for 'Justify My Love' was banned by all stations, but only a week after this there began a most undignified scramble for the very same stations' yoof programmes to give it a late-night airing in its saucy entirety. What was deemed offensive about it was not that it featured a few flashes of flesh but that it included erotic and tender (though not explicit) lesbian imagery. The great woman commented at the time with characteristic perspicacity: 'Why is it that people are willing to go to a movie and watch someone getting blown to bits for no reason and yet nobody wants to see two girls kissing or two men cuddling?'

A similar outcry is inevitably induced whenever the viewer is offered a swift glimpse of a soft dick. Bruce Weber's very ... Bruce Weber-ish video for the Pet Shop Boys' 'Being Boring' was refused an airing on *Top of the Pops* because the opening shots showed a naked man bouncing on a trampoline with his flaccid appendage bobbing up and down in the way that flaccid appendages do when naked men bounce on trampolines. But then the cock has always been the film world's most closely guarded secret. Overexposure of said member would take away its mythic powers and potency for, as Richard Dyer has famously noted: 'The penis is not a patch on the phallus'.

If you need further proof then witness the recent *Banned* season of films on Channel Four. The only scheduled film to be withdrawn was Jo Mennel's short *Dick* (pardon the pun) – featuring as it did one thousand of the little things. And the only complaint from the public that was upheld arose because of the broadcast of a clip from Derek Jarman's *Sebastiane* that flashed, you guessed it, an ever so vaguely tumescent willy.

Two months back when David Bowie released the long unawaited *Tin Machine II* album, the sleeve got him into hot water in America and had to be redesigned. The record company over there bowed to pressure from retailers and proceeded to airbrush out the four pricks that hung between the legs of the four Kouros statues the cover art depicted. If only getting rid of the four pricks that made the album was that easy ...

When Billy Bragg brought out his new single 'Sexuality' the record itself passed, but when it came to the video, both *Top of the Pops* and *The Chart Show* utilized some careful and clever editing to ensure that shots of Bragg looking into another man's eyes in a way that could just about be construed as wistful were not shown. The lines of the song that led into this tiny and not very touching vignette ('Just because you're gay/I won't turn you away') were not problematic for either radio or TV programmers. Which only goes to show that if you're glib enough then you can get away with almost anything.

Such glibness is far from being an isolated incident in the wonderful world of pop, but it is indicative of a still-emergent, yet deeply worrying trend within it. 'Being nice to poofs' is slowly becoming part of the ragbag of worthy causes close to the bleeding heart of rock's guilty conscience.

Bigotry, and racism in particular, have always made the big rock beast rather cross. Now its baby brother pop is starting to get slightly annoyed about homophobia. In 1990 both ABC ('One Better World') and Aztec Camera ('Good Morning Britain') nudged the Top 40 with songs from the 'let's all be nice to one another, I'd like to buy the world a Coke' school of political thought. And both introduced into this for the first time sickly sentiments such as: 'It doesn't matter if you're gay or if you're straight/and if it does you'll only fill the world with hate'. Oh, and indeed, dear, I guess one has to accept that at some point along the rocky road to liberation we're going to have to put up with being patronized by liberals. Thanks boys, but no thanks.

In the midst of such nonsense there are still people making useful comments. For a song about female masturbation, like the Divinyl's 'I Touch Myself', to go Top 10, is pleasing but problematic. Pleasing in the way any paean to female sexual autonomy is, when so many men would prefer to go on pretending that it does not exist. But it's problematic as the song – by becoming a kind of public property – reduces the sentiment to voyeurism. It ceases to be something a woman is doing for her own pleasure and becomes something done for the titillation of men.

La Tour's 'People Are Still Having Sex' is a simple and rather uninteresting dance record made fascinating by its spoken vocal. A cold, perplexed 'voice of authority' says in a tone that is all doom and gloom 'have you noticed that people are still having sex? / All the denouncements and absolutely no effect'. The judgement, one of moral indignation and revulsion, is not in the words but in the delivery. The lines are read, though, as humorous instead of as ominous. And although irony rarely works in pop music, we laugh at the narrator and the moral authoritarianism he symbolizes.

It's worth pointing out that La Tour actually chose to censor himself, changing the line in the original American version (where it was not a hit) from 'this AIDS thing isn't working' to the more ambiguous 'this safe thing isn't working'. Indeed such was the boy's fear of British prudery that a third version was even recorded *just in case* entitled, and I kid you not, 'People Are Still Having Lunch'.

La Tour's fears were unfounded. For in this country, at least as far as pop is concerned, the would be censors have slowly come to the realization that censoring almost always backfires. It is part of pop's *raison d'être* to annoy the proverbial fuck out of such people. So nowadays the 'too raunchy for TV' video and the 'warning! lyrics may offend' sticker are just another bow in the press officer's quiver. There's always been a schism in pop between those who shock because they are outrageous and those that shock because it helps to shift records. George Michael may have tried and failed but there's plenty of other acts out there who provide testimony to the fact that these days censorship *sells*.

Pop may have begun as a genuinely radical and dissonant voice but like anything it soon creates its own orthodoxy. Now pop is tolerated as 'sex music' for this is what we have come to expect of it. We like it to be a little bit naughty, to talk about sex but ultimately to say nothing. This is true now more than ever – the threat of AIDS has forced people to face up to the fact of sex. The ostrich position has been by and large abandoned, and yet sexual orthodoxy must still somehow be maintained. We have all of us done a great deal of growing up in the last few years and this has been mostly led by young people and gay men, who have throughout the crisis shown not recklessness but a refusal to opt out of the pleasures of sex. Their culture, pop, has been the music of this resistance movement, of the celebration of sex.

If you need proof of this, those songs with 'sex' in the title aren't the best place to start looking. Pop has never stopped talking about sex and saying all the things that all the old duds don't want to hear. But it's smart enough to say them in a voice that they can't hear. Like someone pretty smart said not so long ago 'If you gotta ask, you'll never know'.

Awopbopaloobop alopbamboom ...

Gay Times, November 1992

Chapter twenty-four

Little Town Flirt: Suede

'HIS present image is to come on like a swishy queen, a gorgeously effeminate boy. He looks camp as a row of tents with his limp hands and trolling vocabulary. "I'm gay," he says, "and I always have been ..."'

That's not me on Brett Anderson. It's Michael Watts interviewing Brett's hero, David Bowie, for *Melody Maker* back in 1972. Talking to Brett for the same paper 20 years later I could have used much the same words. But Brett wouldn't. The line that's going to haunt him for some time is 'I see myself as a bisexual man who's never had a homosexual experience'. What's often lost is that he'll qualify it with the declaration that he's straight. But if you think it's odd that the biggest girl's blouse in pop is actually heterosexual, don't blame him. Blame David Bowie.

'I come from a background where any excitement or any degree of extremity came through records. If you took me when I was 13 and said "show me something glamorous or sexually bizarre", I'd have pointed you to my Bowie records. If you listen to it every day for five years it's imprinted on your memory cells. You can't help it.'

That excitement and extremity-free zone was Haywards Heath – one of those tiny towns that scatter the hinterland between Brighton and London. 'It was a horrific little place and I was a very timid, terrified child. Throughout my whole time of growing up, there was a very vivid undercurrent of violence.' Like all good children he was swiftly marked out by his peers as different, and like all sensible children he soon began to wear this as a badge of pride.

'They always called me "queer". It started when I was about nine or ten and just carried on. I always quite liked it, actually, because when you're insulted by someone you consider to be a complete piece of shit, how can that be an insult? I always enjoyed the attention of being excommunicated from the lads' gang.'

One of pop's more tiresome clichés is viewing the enactment of stardom as some kind of revenge fantasy. Though Brett claimed that 'even then I had the idea of the band I was going to be in. I was just waiting for it to happen', it's unlikely that there was any all-consuming ambition. Rather it's that one day Brett woke up and discovered that his daydream had come true.

At 19 he moved to London with a long-time friend Mat Osman. With Mat on bass he formed Suede with guitarist Bernard Butler and Simon Gilbert on drums – both found via the classifieds section of *Melody Maker*. It's Simon who's the only gay member of the band. He's out but it's never mentioned – either because no one cares about drummers or because, for many, the likes of an ambisexual like Brett is even better than the real thing.

The band have been playing together for three years now. By the time their first single, 'The Drowners', was released last May, an overwhelming consensus had already been reached that this was 'the best new band in Britain'. Another single, 'Metal Mickey', followed in September which got them into the Top 20 and on to *Top of the Pops*, no problem. The first album, for which the phrase 'eagerly awaited' would be the understatement of the century, is out later this month. Now Suede are simply called 'the best band in Britain'.

The praise is well placed – but the group did fit perfectly into three current obsessions of the music press. Suede are a guitar band – albeit a very good one and one that doesn't hail from Seattle – and their sound is almost Glam, a big plus for all those currently trying to prove that 1993 is, in fact, 1973. Most of all, Suede seem to be what many have been desperately searching for since 1987 – the new Smiths.

Brett knows how important figures like Bowie and Morrissey were to him and has recreated himself in their image. To paraphrase what he said about an earlier stage of his life, he became the first rock singer in an age to consciously try and 'excommunicate himself from the lads' gang'. Then as now he's fully aware that, if nothing else, it's a very effective way of drawing attention to yourself. He dresses like a fop – Corduroy and Crimplene might have been more accurate monikers than Suede – and is glad to be fey, though he says he'd hate 'to be seen as simply some mincing effeminate prancing around in a blouse – there's a lot more to me than that'.

Just at the very point when Morrissey has tired of flirting with faggotry, along comes someone who is bold enough to sing on their first release about 'lying back and taking it, relinquishing control – which isn't considered manly, but about emotional submission too'. 'The Drowners' was a tale of sexual obsession that begins when 'we kissed in his room to a popular tune' and ends with Brett wailing in defeat 'You're taking me over'. Flip the thing over and there's 'My Insatiable One'.

The most important word in that was 'he' ('*He*'s my insatiable one'). Brett's not a great lyric writer ('I often write whole lyrics in the studio. The idea of sitting poring over a typewriter bores me') but like all our best songwriters (Ray Davies, Neil Tennant and, again, Morrissey) he deals with Englishness – something Brett once described as 'madness, perversity, repression and shyness'. Suede songs are about the twitching net curtains, the fumbles in the dark, the hysteria that's just below the surface, but only *just*. And it's all delivered in a fake cockernee wail that's Brett being Bowie being Anthony Newley.

The songs, he'll stress, are not autobiographical – 'they're often imaginary situations based on real sentiments, or real situations taken to their logical extreme.' Brett says he uses the word 'he' in 'virtually all our songs', and when I say that he must have realized this would be contentious, he begs to differ.

'No, what I wanted to do was express sexuality, but not in a straightforward way, because I think the very idea is quite … transient. Too much music is about a very straightforward sense of sexuality whereas, in reality, sexuality is completely deviant. Twisted sexuality is the only kind that interests me. The people that matter in music are more knowing, more deliberate. They consciously don't declare their sexuality, and I really don't think you have to declare your sexuality absolutely. Morrissey never has and he's all the more interesting for that. It's not surprising that, after you've been fed on a diet of heterosexual icons like Springsteen when someone comes along expressing something different – no matter how blatant or subtle – you jump at it.

'I happen not to be gay but I don't feel like a fully fledged member of the male sex. I certainly feel sometimes that I am a woman . . . I feel certain traits. Sometimes I feel like walking around my house lighting candles instead of going out playing football.'

But for all his claims of the importance of ambiguity, when I ask he'll say that *yes*, he's only posing as a sodomite. So isn't it somewhat insincere to shamelessly hijack gay and homoerotic imagery?

'I don't. I hijack *sexual* imagery. That's what I do because I feel *sexual*. If you're asking me am I insincere to pose as a sodomite because I haven't had a cock up my arse, then no, I'm not. You can still feel that way even though you haven't had that particular sensation. The sexuality you express is not limited to the things you've already experienced. If you're a virgin, does that make you asexual? I don't think it's dishonest but it might be furtive – a lot of English sexuality is.

'If people think I'm gay that's fine. I know lots of people definitely do and I get a kick out of that.'

What he learned during those lonely days in Haywards Heath is how pop thrills. 'Brett' is as much of a fiction as 'Ziggy Stardust'. 'I don't think it matters what you really are, it matters what you do. What you are is only necessary to you and your little satellite of friends. It's very narrow-minded just to make records for yourself and your friends.'

So what *is* Brett? A straight man who not only doesn't mind if you think he's gay, he really wants you to think it? A heterosexual who thinks poofs are just as exciting as you or I? What Brett is most definitely not is Jason Donovan. Jason's libel action against *The Face* was the end of a dark age in pop – Brett's appearance is like the first blossom of spring. In short, for all his faults, Suede *matter*.

Brett is still enjoying a honeymoon period with both press and public. I was the first to ask him awkward questions but there'll be harder ones to come. It's not 1972 any more – unlike then, the people he'll annoy most will be queens, not straights. Most of our favourite moments in pop may have depended on artifice but we're also quite big on authenticity. I've wondered before if there's that much difference between what he's doing and what the Black and White Minstrels did. The bottom line is, perhaps, does Brett really know what it feels like?

We've come a long way since the golden years of Bowie, but I'm still struck by how well Michael Watts's words about David in 1972 fit Brett in 1993. I cut Michael off in mid flow before – let's hear what else he had to say about Bowie claiming to be gay: ' . . . there's a sly jollity about him as he says it. A secret smile at the corners of his mouth. He knows that in these times it's permissible to act like a male tart, and that to shock and to outrage, which pop has always striven to do throughout its history, is a ball breaking business.'

Hey kid, just you be careful out there.

Gay Times, March 1993

Chapter twenty-five

The London Boy:
Colin Bell

COLIN Bell, the MD of London Records, was someone I'd wanted to interview for a long time. The most powerful and influential out gay man in the UK music business, his CV over the past 20 years reads like a mini-history of poofs and pop: from managing Tom Robinson in the Seventies, through signing Bronski Beat in the Eighties, to running London in the Nineties and turning it into this country's most successful singles' label. In 1994 one in ten singles sold in the UK was on London or one of its dance subsidiaries: Systematic, ffrr, ffrreedom, Internal and Junior Boys Own.

Due to some Network South Central fuck up, I was half an hour late for the interview. Colin Bell's an extremely busy man. But Colin didn't mind. I like Colin Bell.

'I'm 42 now. I went to university in the early Seventies where I discovered I was not bisexual, I was gay. I came to London – the city – and by the time I got here I was reasonably openly gay. I tried to get jobs in the music business. It was the Punk era and I was hanging around with a circle of people who were mainly gay and who were involved in various kinds of gay activist groups. I met Tom Robinson somewhere along the line. In fact I met him on Hampstead Heath, actually.'

Were you cruising or just walking the dog?

'Cruising. And we became great friends – and friends is what we were, not lovers. And he was in a group, Café Society, and my ambition was to manage acts. I helped Café Society out, but I didn't really manage them. It was a bit problematic because I had no money or anything like that. And then he left them and came to me and said he was going to form a new band and would I manage it? And I said "yes". He had written two songs which he played me on his acoustic guitar. One was called '2-4-6-8 Motorway' and one was called 'Glad To Be Gay'. So we had this concept – the first openly, politically gay rock band. We sat down and very mathematically said "that is what we want to do, let's find a group to go with it." So we put the group together and I started ringing up trying to get gigs.'

Why did you think it would work at that particular time?

'It just felt like the right time. We were kids and we felt there was enough interest and enough liberalism generally. There was more of an open-mindedness at that time than there was, say, five years previously, 'cause when I'd first come across the music business at the beginning of the Seventies where you had David Bowie, Elton John and the Glam Rock thing, there was a lot of gayness around but it was all pretty much ... camouflaged. You know, David Bowie "Oh, I'm bisexual" and all that bullshit.

'So we put the group together and started getting gigs in clubs and pubs and the big break was when we did a TV programme called *The London Weekend Show* which Janet Street Porter was producing. She did one on young gay Londoners and they booked us as the musical entertainment. We had one or two kind of vague offers on the table – everybody was a bit nervous about a gay rock star – and we did this show and then on the Monday every record company in town wanted to sign us. In the end we signed a deal with EMI because we thought that would be fun as they'd just dropped the Sex Pistols. And they wanted to get back and prove a point and felt that Tom was a good way of doing that. We started having hit records and it started all going rather well and some way into all this – I was very inexperienced and EMI felt that Tom was potentially the next Bob Dylan and in order to make him the next Bob Dylan in America they felt he should have a manager to suit. Tom and I have never fallen out from that day to this. We're still good friends. And I still have the utmost respect for him. But I then became like his assistant manager for a while.'

What sort of time was this, around *TRB TWO*?

'Yeah. And his career didn't ... flourish as it might have done.'

He says fame went to his head.

'He says that? I would say that's probably true. He wasn't easy. And then two years later we got involved in his management again for Sector 27. And that didn't go especially well. Then after two years I felt that there were so many problems surrounding them that unless he took on board his problems directly they were never gonna get solved. So I quit. He was on Phonogram and when I said I'm not going to manage him any more they said "oh, well, would you like to come and work for us?" Which is how I came to work in a record company.'

This was in 1980 when Phonogram had just bought London?

'Around the same time. They hadn't set London up at this time, they'd just bought Decca. And I worked at Phonogram for a couple of years as first of all press officer and then Head of Press. I was always involved in marketing and imaging the acts. I had a certain talent for taking up an act and saying "look if you're presented in this way it would probably work". And we had a very successful period.'

You worked with Soft Cell early on. Did you have any input into their 'sleazy' image?

'I arranged some of the photo sessions and did some imaging. But who's responsible for the idea? The group will always say it's them. But it was a natural idea to me and it was a natural idea to them. After doing this for about two years Roger Ames, the chair of Polydor-Decca now, who was Soft Cell's A&R man, moved over to London. They were setting it up properly as a record company. We'd always worked well together and he asked me to come with him and I did. Which was a very risky thing to do.'

London was in the doldrums wasn't it?

'Yeah, it had been a defunct label and they started to get it going when I went there. They'd signed Bananarama.'

I always thought that was you.

'No. I didn't sign them. I got involved with them later. They had them and Blancmange when we came on full time. We inherited a little record company that had two acts that didn't make much money. And we were shit scared. The breakthrough for London Records was signing Bronski Beat.'

And that was you?

'Yes, I knew a lot of people on the gay scene and this guy Alan Reid phoned me up one day when I'd just started at London and said "oh there's a Pink Arts Festival the GLC are financing and we're having a meeting to see how we're gonna spend the money. Would you like to come along – as someone in the music business who could give us some advice?" So I went along and there were all these skinhead guys down at the Oval House and I was sitting at the back listening to what was going on. And in the end they said: "well you're in the record business what do you think we should do?" And I had nothing to say because they were thinking of spending the money in creative ways, making records, making films, things like that. I said: "well you should get out and do what you like" – you know "sounds good" – and left. I didn't think any more of it. Then two or three months later Tracy Bennett came into the office and said: "I've seen this great band called Bronski Beat". I knew of them because they'd been in *Capital Gay*. You'd often see gay groups and I'd often be very sceptical about them.'

Why? Because they were usually crap?

'Usually, yeah. I think to really work it has to work both on a musical and a political level. And it can work on different kinds of political levels. But the two need to work alongside one another if you're gonna do anything that affects people. A lot of acts that we now talk of as being gay, for example Soft Cell, at that time they were implicitly perhaps gay, but they never said they were gay. Marc Almond would never do interviews with the gay press. But if you were gay you could see it. So anyway we went to see them at The Venue and thought they were phenomenal. Called them into the office the next day and they all walked in and – lo and behold – they were all the people I'd met at the Oval House a few months earlier.

'So we offered them a record deal and that's when it got really difficult because every record company in London caught onto this act. There was a huge race to sign Bronski Beat.'

Why? This was, what, 1983? The great Gender Bender boom.

'Yeah, but it was also the songs. "Smalltown Boy" stood out especially as being a classic song. Trevor Horne offered them a deal. Seymour Stein was very keen to sign them. Island Records were mad to sign them. What convinced them to sign to us was, I think first of all, I was the only openly gay record executive that they met. And we promised to sign them and market them as a gay act and not to interfere with them. And more or less we did that. But there was always a very difficult balance between being able to do and say just what you want and still sell records.'

Did you feel like you said about Tom Robinson – the time is now right?

'It was slightly different with Tom. BBC Radio and the media were much more conservative than they were by the time of Bronski Beat. For example "Glad To Be Gay" did not get playlisted on Radio One. In fact it was actually put out as a track on an EP because we knew they wouldn't play that cut. So they'd play "Don't Take No For An Answer" instead, and that was the only way that we could steer that record through to being a hit. And with Bronski Beat we had similar issues. "How far can you go and still have your record exposed?" I think you see that most acutely in the video for "Smalltown Boy" which says everything by implication and nothing ... you can read it two ways. You can read it that this guy got beaten up. Or you can read it that he got queerbashed.'

Is it true that the brief was that it had to be read as gay by English viewers but be more oblique for an American audience?

'No. I don't think it was especially made for an American market. But it was certainly true that it had to be readable in two ways. For example, the original storyboard had Jimmy being caught cottaging. So the cottage sequence became the street sequence. It was a difficult balance. Then the next record we came to was "Why?" and of course the first lyric is "turned to kiss his lips?" There was a lot of controversy about whether we'd get away with "*his* lips". And in the end we did, but it was touch and go. And you know, on the day I die if they say "did you do anything worthwhile in your life?" I'll say "well, I did two things. One was being involved with 'Smalltown Boy' at that time and the other would be being involved with 'Glad To Be Gay' at that particular time." Because both of those songs as far as the music business and gay awareness were concerned are important moments.'

Landmarks?

'OK. Landmarks (laughs). You still meet people today who say I remember hearing "Glad To Be Gay", or I remember being at home and that video came on and it changed my life, you know? And at that time we were pretty conscious of that. I have to say that working with Bronski Beat and Jimmy, it's not always been easy because they've always seen me as the big bad record company. 'Cause the role I've had a lot of the time is to take what they do and sell it to a wider audience, rather than just take what they do and present it as it was. And Jimmy, I think, finds that frustrating, but he recognizes that ultimately you have more impact if you can appeal to more people.

'So Bronski Beat were critical to the development of this record company. They put us on the map. They were our biggest act. They then went on to sell internationally. They were a huge act in every country around the world with the exception of America. They nearly got America. But Jimmy wouldn't open for Madonna. And there was a lot of conflict between the two other members of the band. And they split up . . . and we know the rest. Then Jimmy went on to The Communards and The Communards were as successful, but they didn't really have the political bite of Bronski Beat.'

How do you mean – in the songs?

'In some of the songs, yeah, but not in the hits. There's always a strange double standard about it all – which is "it's OK so long as you don't remind us."'

The Communards kept reminding people.

'Yeah, but a lot of the other things The Communards did let you think that it might not be that way. Take "Don't Leave Me This Way" – it had a girl singing with a deep voice on with Jimmy. Take the concept of The Communards, they had four girls as well. Yes, Richard Coles and Jimmy were both gay but there was an element of showbusiness about it that allowed you to forget that. Most of the successful gay artists have got both a level of showbusiness and credibility and are selling records to people who are older than the 13-year-old girls. The Communards did that, Erasure did that, Boy George did that. You can get to the gay market by other means, i.e.

be cool, in the way that all those other acts at some point were – Boy George, Pet Shop Boys, Erasure – just how open were those acts about being gay from the off? They weren't *that* open about it.

'But on the other hand The Communards did have something that Bronski Beat didn't have. There was an affectionate throwback to Disco music with them. Which maybe politicized Disco to some degree. You know – "it's OK to like this music". "Don't Leave Me This Way" was like the all-time gay anthem. And that was really what London was built on. There was a lot of other stuff obviously. We'd been doing dance music from day one.'

Were you involved in licensing the Sylvester and Patrick Cowley records and later the American House and Euro records on ffrr?

'That comes largely from Pete Tong. He was Head of Club Promotion and later A&R Man. His job was basically to find American dance records that we would put out. What I always have had, though, is a liking for dance music. I wouldn't claim to be an expert but maybe I have more understanding of the culture than other people in my position. In that I actively go to clubs which not many straight people my age do. Where do I go? Trade. Heaven. Not as much as I used to.

'So there was a House explosion in 1986 and the big acts? It was the re-launch of Bananarama. "Venus" and the boys on The Brits and all that stuff. I was very much involved with that and the whole repositioning of the act.'

Did you suggest they work with Stock, Aitken and Waterman?

'No. I wasn't A&R-ing them. Roger suggested Stock, Aitken and Waterman. What had happened was there was Frankie Goes To Hollywood, there was Bronski Beat and there was a consciousness that Hi-NRG was going to go overground. That was the time of all those "So many men, so little time" records. And what we saw in Bronski Beat and Frankie at a commercial level was the ability to take Hi-NRG influenced pop mainstream. Stock, Aitken and Waterman had been making Hi-NRG records with Dead Or Alive and Divine. And we'd come to the end of working with Swain and Jolley. So then they went off and made "Venus" which was Siobhan's idea.

And the record sounded like a smash and we'd been playing around trying to get a focus on the video . . . '

You see *Top of the Pops* nowadays and it's all muscled dancing boys, but 'Venus' was the first video to feature them. How did the idea come about?

'To be honest it happened by accident and I wouldn't take credit for it. It was Peter Care, the video director, and Siobhan's idea. It just felt right. Going forward it was obviously a plot that would work and when it came to The Brits and having 20 boys all dancing, that sort of stuff, then I was involved in all that. And from that point onwards I was deeply involved in Bananarama all the way down the line. Then later we had the Fine Young Cannibals, which did very well.

'Then we had a pretty rough period. We had one year that wasn't particularly good for us which was '88 or '89. And by this time Roger was gradually easing himself into the background. And Tracy and I were taking more and more control. The year of Shakespeare's Sister and "Stay" was a transitional year. And at that time East 17 came along. I bumped into Tom Watkins at Heaven and he said we must have dinner one day. I'd never worked with him before. He was one of those guys where he knew of me and I knew of him. He was no longer managing the Pet Shop Boys and was being sued by Bros and didn't really know what to do with his life. And he said "oh, I've got this new group, I might be interested in managing them", and he handed me a couple of photographs. And I came back here and said to Tracy "why don't you give them some money to put this band in the studio . . . "'

After you'd just seen some photographs?

'No, no, no. They were literally Polaroids and I didn't know if they were pretty or anything. It wasn't anything sexual, I assure you. It was more the look of them. They looked quite unique. And they still do – rough, East End street kids. So we gave them some studio time and I didn't think anything was gonna come of it. And I went off to Australia on holiday and came back six weeks later and Tracy grabbed me and said come in here, played me his tapes and there were two hits on there, "House Of Love" and "Deep". We thought, "well, we've got to sign them". And that was the start of this current period. When I've been running the company. We've aggressively tried to develop the roster here. We've particularly focused on dance. Successfully. We've always been a successful singles' label, we've never been this successful.'

How much is London Records Colin Bell's label?

'It's not my label. I became MD at the end of '92. But I don't own it.'

But the buck stops with you?

'Yes.'

How gay is the music business these days compared to when you started?

'I find it quite exciting now because when I first started nobody was openly gay. There were a lot of closeted gay people within it. Now there aren't many closeted people. Most people behind the scenes are open about their sexuality. Certainly John Reid and most of the Elton John camp are now out. Which helps. There's Simon Napier-Bell. I mean who cares now? For me the thing about this record company is that my gayness is an important part of the ingredients. In that it's very good to have someone that's got gay eyes, gay ears in the music business, and it complements people who don't have that. A lot of exciting music comes out of the gay scene. Whether it be dance music or alternative acts with a political vision. And being gay gives you a way into that. It gave us a way into it. My being one of the few executives in the record business who was openly gay, and one of the first, you know long before David Geffen did, was a positive asset. There's no question of that. We would not have signed Bronski Beat had I not been openly gay. We're not a gay record label as such but ... '

There's a distinctly faggy hue to it ...

'Perhaps (laughs). Most of the artists are entirely heterosexual, but that's the same in life isn't it?'

The time was right for Tom Robinson in 1978. The time was right for Bronski Beat in 1984. What do you think of the present climate?

'There are many more out gay artists than there were before. Apart from the old hands there are a lot of gay people around making records. I don't see many stars at this point in time. I'm sure there will be. But you see stuff like the Queercore movement – you wouldn't have had that ten years ago. And they came out and said "we're sick of all these fuddy duddies from the Eighties, we don't give a fuck", and that's good. I like that. People don't care so much now. And that's such a huge shift from the Seventies. It's now even becoming a non-issue in America. Melissa Etheridge, k. d. lang – now that really is a breakthrough. But I think it's often easier for lesbians in a sense. They're less threatening sexually. Men who fit a stereotyped gay image are quite threatening for heterosexuals en masse. Whereas a lesbian who wears frocks is not very threatening. There's been a huge shift in the late Eighties in America with people in public positions coming out. David Geffen coming out was one of the most significant things because he has huge influence and power. He's a man who can talk to Clinton – and does.'

You're obviously quite a political animal too.

'Well, Jimmy would say I'm bourgeois ... but I've always been political in the sense that I've always been politically aware. I don't think it's possible to be gay and true to yourself and not be political. But I've always understood the practicalities of living in a straight world and trying to win in the straight world. Because I think winning as a gay person in the straight world is a political act. And I choose to do it by being successful in my chosen line of business. And having some visibility and being open about it as much as is relevant. I go to Gay Pride and I will stand outside the Houses of Parliament during the Age of Consent debate, like anyone else will. And I'm still active in the gay scene. I lead a gay life, you know? And I always will do.'

March 1995

Chapter twenty-six

Murmuring: REM

I haven't said enough ...
oh no, I've said too much

REM, 'Losing my Religion'

A SPECTRE is haunting America. The spectre of AIDS. And they're dealing with this post-Cold War invasion of the body-snatchers in the only way they know how – by exhuming McCarthy. Whispering campaigns are set in motion that question the antibody status of any celebrity that dares to say anything in the least bit interesting.

Stars are rumoured to have AIDS if they're openly gay (Elton John), if they're fag friendly (Madonna) and even, in a nod to the classic hysteria of the Fifties, if they lose a little weight (Luther Vandross). The whisperers have even abandoned the middle ground of the old 'queer smear' to go straight for the new jugular. Rob Halford, the leather-bedecked singer with the heavy metal band, Judas Priest, paid the price of looking like an old man at The Block and recently had to call a special press conference to deny that he was HIV-positive. With the death of Freddie Mercury, lazy thinkers everywhere got some new ways to try and spot a star with AIDS.

When the American band REM released their new album *Automatic For The People* in September, the new McCarthyites ran through their checklist of suspicious behaviour. Singer Michael

Stipe failed the Mercury Test on three counts: the group announced that they would not be touring to promote the new record, press duties had been delegated to the other three band members, and seven of *Automatic*'s 12 songs were in some way about death.

It was left to his fellow band members to swiftly dismiss these rumours as 'bullshit'. They explained that REM was now such a huge multinational concern that their record company insisted they all take yearly health checks for insurance purposes and they had all tested negative just a few months back. But this mattered little – it might have been 'bullshit' but shit sticks.

The new McCarthyism, like the old one, uses AIDS as an anti-euphemism, as a way of inferring something else. Both witch hunts rarely rounded on their declared enemy – communists or people with AIDS – but were a fairly efficient way of hounding two other sorts of undesirables: liberals and gay men. Stipe stands guilty on the first count and has long been suspected of the second.

He has always been guarded about his personal life, and only the barest of the bones are known of the Michael Stipe story. Born in 1960 into a typically nomadic forces' family, he's often spoken of how he felt 'different' from other children: ('I was very, kind of, afraid of a lot of things ... I realized I was an outsider and felt separated from most people.') In his mid teens he says he went through a transvestite period, remaining completely oblivious to the world of music until he heard Patti Smith's *Horses* – a life-changing experience which made him go back and discover the Velvet Underground and the New York Dolls and to later get into the post-Punk scene. At the age of 18, he moved to Athens, Georgia, a big college town and a liberal oasis in the Deep South, to study art. It was there that he met the other members of REM.

Stipe used to tease journalists by telling them 'we're the American Smiths', a comment that said as much about their constituency as it did about their music – a brand of intelligent guitar rock as suited to bedsit listening as it was for stadiums. In the States REM were broken by college radio stations and by a diet of constant touring, playing initially, they've said, at 'pizza parlours and biker bars and gay discos'. *Murmur*, their first album, was released in 1983 and, over the course of a ten-year, eight-album career, they've grown steadily and seemingly inexorably both in stature and sales.

By the time of *Automatic For The People* they were shipping the proverbial multi-platinum.

Most usually described as 'eccentric' (though at least one journalist has called him 'surprisingly camp'), Stipe has kept an increasingly low public profile of late. The band have all stayed in Athens (unlike the town's other musical product of note, the B-52s) where Michael makes occasional forays into local politicking and runs a vegetarian restaurant. He's maintained his interest in art, specifically photography, and has directed several of REM's videos to much acclaim (there's homoeroticism aplenty in those made for 'Finest Worksong', 'Orange Crush' and 'Losing My Religion' – the Jarmanesque latter received the honour of being banned from Irish TV because of its high quota of male titty). Shunning the rock and roll lifestyle, the only other members of his profession he's close to are Natalie Merchant of 10,000 Maniacs and Morrissey. La Mozz was so shocked at finding another member of the human race that he actually liked that he wrote 'Found Found Found' (' ... someone who's worth it in this murkiness') in celebration of their friendship.

Depending on your point of view Michael Stipe's lyrics are either pure Dada, in the grand tradition started by Dylan at his stream-of-consciousness best, or complete and utter gobbledygook.

He's acknowledged a debt to William Burrough's cut-up technique: ('I kind of agree with him when he says language is a virus from outer space. I appreciate language and I appreciate the ways that we can use it or abuse it or twist it around to beautiful shapes at the ends of our fingers'), but as with his reluctance to fill in the details of his own biography it sometimes seems that he's trying not to give too much away, as if this guardedness was a strategy. 'I'm not about to split myself open,' he once explained, 'to gut myself and spill myself all over people. Number one, because there's not that much inside that people ought to see, and number two, I don't want to put myself in the position where my rib-cage is split open to people I don't know.'

However, following the re-election of President Reagan in 1984 he began to haul himself out of the alphabet soup school of lyric writing and came out as a liberal, addressing the usual ragbag of worthy causes (US intervention in Central America, the environment and so on) on stage, in interviews and in his songs. Though in the case of the latter he still encountered slight problems: 'I can write the simplest, most straightforward song in the world and nobody is going to have a clue what I'm talking about'.

Come 1990's *Out Of Time* album he'd already tired of the soapbox and had moved into the confessional. 'I wanted to call the album *Fiction*. I thought that was descriptive – all the songs are basically fictions . . . they're all love songs.' Genderless and unrequited love songs too, and all pretty much as impenetrable as ever. But Stipe promised that for the next album he was going to write some 'really straightforward words'.

That album was *Automatic For The People*, a quite astounding record that rightly topped just about every critics' and readers' end-of-year poll. Although seven of its tracks touched on death its overall mood was not morbid but curiously uplifting. Interestingly, at the very time that he'd stopped giving interviews he appeared to be giving more of himself away in his lyrics – almost as if he wasn't too keen on being pressed to explain a song like 'Fuck Me Kitten' ('You are wild and I am your possession/nothing's free so fuck me kitten').

There's little in his lyrics to fuel the flurry of speculation about Michael Stipe's sexuality – if you rush out and buy an REM album expecting some kind of Southern-fried Morrissey you'll be sorely disappointed – but one feels that he's more than happy for us to speculate in such a way. He's consistently cited Walter Percy's 'Metaphor as Mistake' as an inspiration, claiming 'anyone who really wants to figure out the meaning to our songs should read that essay then go back and listen. It talks about how people misinterpret something that's being said and come up with a little phrase or word that actually defines the essence of what the original was, better than the original did. My lyrics are a blank chalkboard for people to pick up and scribble over. They can make up any meaning they want to.'

Which also, perhaps, means that we can make up any Michael we want to. There are a whole variety of ways that singers who are not prepared to say 'I am gay' can tell us that they are. Lesbians and gay men soon learn the skill using their 'gaydar' to read these signs – we're constantly claiming people; sometimes we get it right, sometimes we get it wrong (dykes were packing out k. d. lang concerts long before she came out in the summer, and they'll undoubtedly continue to pack out Michelle Shocked's even though she's just got married). With Stipe, who is at best oblique, at worst impossibly obscure, the signs that he may be gay are there if you look, though perhaps they're only there *because* you're looking. In pop, in the past, taking what someone says too literally could be used to 'prove' that John Lennon's a walrus, putting what they say under too close a scrutiny has been used to 'discover' that Paul McCartney's dead.

Is Michael Stipe gay? I really don't know but I hope so. Has he got AIDS? Again I don't know but I hope not. On *Automatic For The People* there's a song called 'Man On The Moon', about the need to question everything and how willing people are to believe anything they're told. Michael Stipe tells us very little but he still has the courtesy to write a kind of nonsense that allows us to believe whatever we want, and indeed whatever we need to believe about him.

At least I think that's what he does.

Gay Times, February 1993

Chapter twenty-seven

The Odd Couple: McAlmont (Thieves)

DAVID McAlmont, the half of Thieves who's black and gay, has a voice that sounds like a gift from God. Only David and God aren't getting on too well at the moment.

'I was a Born Again Christian for years. I grew up in Guyana which is essentially a very boring place and the Church was pretty much the only game in town. I towed the line I guess. In the end I had to leave because it wasn't a good thing to be a gay man in Guyana.'

'In fact,' Saul Freeman – the half who's white, straight and somewhat swoonsome – interjects, 'when I first met you, you still described yourself as a Christian.'

'Did I? My how things have changed! Basically I was taught that homosexuality and Christianity didn't add up. Eventually I decided that my desires were a lot stronger than my faith. I met Saul about a month after I'd come out of my suicidal stage, and joining a band was part of the stand against all that ... deciding to use my voice because it was good rather than to praise the Lord. I found in Christianity you spend a lot of time denying yourself for the greater glory of God. I stopped that because I wanted to find out who I was.'

The name, as you've probably guessed, comes from Genet. They get compared to Jean's best mates The Cocteau Twins all the time ('It's beginning to bother us a bit'), but like all good thieves they plunder from all over the place. Thieves – white, black, straight and gay – are cultural miscegenation at its best, reviving the long lost art of gender bending. Influences they namecheck include The Associates, The Blue Nile, Jane Sibbery, Pet Shop Boys, k. d. lang, Aerosmith. Aerosmith??? Right, stop there.

I'll be surprised if you hear a more gorgeous thing all year than their second single 'Unworthy'. A record that's caused more than a few reviewers to wet their knickers with understandable delight. What's that line? 'It's no good I want you in my bed instead of my mind'. You sound a little lovelorn, David?

'That's one part of me. I'm not sure how interesting the joyous parts of my life are to anyone. I'd much rather be there for people when they're feeling down.'

Though they're now signed to Virgin, in many ways Thieves remain resolutely Indie in both sound and attitude. But isn't Indie the Millwall of music; let's keep it white, let's keep it straight?

'It is and it's a shame. I guess what Thieves could become is an expression of what I'd like to see. There aren't enough black gay men in pop full stop ... well, who are open about it. But I can't see the sense in being open and happy about my life and hiding it as a career move. There was a time when I wondered if I should play that game – playing it straight for a while and then come out dramatically. The strangest thing is that a lot of journalists want to do this nudge, nudge, wink, wink sort of thing. Or else they infer that Saul and I are lovers ... not that it bothers Saul at all. It doesn't help when I say "My Grey Boy" is about Saul and myself.'

It's a relief that David, the man, is so direct. Their songs can be a little abstract.

'Originally we took that very impressionistic Liz Fraser-esque view of words, but the songs we've been writing recently have been much more direct. That's probably due to the change in our relationship. We trust each other now so it's more easy to write songs about my life. Or about David's.'

I'm sorry?

'Oh yes,' Saul confirms. 'On "They Hide" we sat down and I would write a verse about David and then he'd write the next verse about me.'

You'll be sharing underwear next.

David, I had been expecting this big swishy thing. Why do you think journalists overemphasize your effeminacy?

'It surprises me that some people are so taken aback by me. The appearance of black men in pop is usually so studded and male ...'

Err, Little Richard, Smokey Robinson, Michael Jackson, Prince ...

'You know what I mean. That ladies' man soul singer or big tough rapper thing. I'm really disappointed that we live in a society where men have such a limited and boring idea of what a man should be. And of course people look at me and say "you're not that". But I think it's there to be contested. I'm a black gay man and this is the way I want to present myself as a black gay man. I tend to go on for hours about male behaviour. If you have a penis how much more male do you need to be?'

Gay Times, November 1993

Chapter twenty-eight

Out On Your Own: Kitchens of Distinction and Sugar

ME and Patrick Fitzgerald are sitting on Brighton beach. We're playing with the pebbles and talking about rock, but the conversation keeps coming back to this 'sense of belonging' thing.

'I always thought that whole existential angst of being an outsider was such an early twenties thing. Really studenty. And then it becomes desperately serious – when you feel that they actually don't want you to belong. It's like you start a club, you allow all the members in and then all the members sack you. Almost everything in my life seems like that sometimes. It's not just being gay, it's being human – you will always be alone.'

Patrick's not very good at being a gay man. He does all the things you're not supposed to do. He doesn't feel he fits into the scene. He doesn't like dance music, not only preferring to listen to rock music, but making it too. But why, Patrick, *why?*

'Rock's confrontational as opposed to hedonistic. Disco is all about having a good time, and feeling good about yourself. Fine. No problem. But I was always interested in the pain of people's lives. It's not that it's any more real or valid. It's just what I'm into.'

Patrick's very good at being a gay rock star. He does all the things you're not supposed to do. He's out. And moreover he was the only out gay man in pop to emerge during the late Eighties.

Starting out at the time of Clause 28, he says he had no other option.

'When we did out first interview with the *NME* we were asked if I wanted to be out. I was appalled but it was genuine concern – "don't fuck up your career boys". I didn't realize it was an issue. I thought it was being straightforward. I'm like this and this is what I want to sing about. I was completely unaware that anyone would have a problem with it. I hate lying. It's the one thing I can not stand. There's no point in doing what I do if I'm going to lie. That was Morrissey's strength on the first Smiths album. And it's his weakness now. He was never out. He was just confused and worried and it was so good to hear someone convey that confusion. It was outrageous at the time and lyrically it was a real inspiration. He was using a language that I understood. It was colloquial, it was from my home town and his experiences seemed so heavily interrelated with mine.'

Patrick's now thirty one. Born in Switzerland and brought up just outside Manchester, his mum told him he was gay when he was nineteen. He went through a 'serious self-pity stage', moved to London, listened to The Smiths a lot and studied to be a doctor. In 1986 he met guitarist Julian at a party and started a band with the worst name they could think of.

Kitchens of Distinction are now on their fourth album. *Cowboys and Aliens* is yet another big swirly guitar type thing. It's also their best since their debut *Love is Hell*. Patrick agrees with me that guitars are a great medium for expressing rage. The Kitchens make records that, to quote Allen Ginsberg, ermm, 'howl'.

'Our albums are always dictated by my emotional state at the time I'm writing them. Our last record, *The Death of Cool*, was quite dark and quite gloomy. I was having a very, very bad time. It's the only record I can think of that goes on almost exclusively about splitting up with your boyfriend. *Cowboys and Aliens* is mostly a journey into how the band's internal psyches are working. It's a very therapeutic record.'

Patrick's lyrics have been at their most affecting when they've been at their most personal – when he's sung about the hopes and fears of your average queer. But after some superb early songs like 'Prize', 'Four Men' and 'Hammer' Patrick became a little more oblique. 'The other two were surprised by the gay tag after *Love is Hell*. It was like "Hello boys, you've got naked men on your album cover!" Usually, lyrically, I have to make sure that I satisfy their concerns and write something that is pertinent to the three of us – like the single "Now It's Time To Say Goodbye" is genderless. It's lyric by committee sometimes. There's nothing on this album that's about being gay.'

I suggest that the constant Kitchens' concern with the battle between your heart and your penis, between security and promiscuity, is a very gay thing.

'Yeah, but that's relevant to straight boys as well. Pain? That's a common experience. Hets are very pained, it's just they don't talk about it much. They don't have that "love will kill you" though. That's not drummed into them. That trauma of waking up in the morning and finding a lump somewhere that all the gay boys go through.'

Patrick now has a solo project, Fruit, which gives him the chance to pop out of the kitchen and make 'my excursions into queerland. I just let go much more and I'm much less censorious. It's utter self-indulgent bollocks but it can be revelatory. I can really go off on a complete Patti Smith trip.'

A Fruit album should appear next year. Their first excellent single, which came out on the Rough Trade Singles Club in August, isn't really 'utter self-indulgent bollocks'. It's just Patrick being himself. The B-side 'Scatter Me' was written the day Derek Jarman died. The A-side, 'The Queen of Old Compton Street', is about – *you guessed!* – Old Compton Street. 'The song's critical but I also love and need it as well, and that's the paradox. I love the openness, the hand holding, the kissing on the street. The very public queerness of it all. All these pretty young boys being very scary by being themselves. But you've got to have money and it's fairly exclusive to the pretty Muscle Mary. And there is absolutely no agenda apart from fucking. I don't think there's anything particularly wrong with that but if that is the be all and end all then that's a bit blinkered. But I'll go there. What bothers me is that you can only do it if you look good and behave in a certain way and I don't.'

Fruit got it's first airing in the spring at a gig Patrick gave at Liz Naylor's shortlived Queercore night, Scum. Sadly it now looks like Queercore itself is all over too. Liz, a friend of Patrick's from her days as press officer at One Little Indian, has shut down her CatCall label as she's 'fed up with the music business'. Sister George's Elyot told me recently 'Queercore's still happening but a lot of people have taken what they needed from it and moved on ... now we're just concentrating on becoming the biggest rock and roll band in the world.' This side of the Atlantic some are still clinging to the wreckage, but Homocore continues apace in the States. As proven by the superb second album from Pansy Division, *Deflowered*, and the *OutPunk Dance Party* compilation.

'Queercore's brilliant,' Patrick reckons. 'I loved it and I really love Sister George. It's exhilarating and in your face and fun – the essence of pop. But then again I felt like some sort of uncle who's hanging around at their kid's show and embarrassing everybody just by being there.'

Uncle Patrick's now got quite a gang of nephews and nieces. Sitting a little away in front of us on the Beach is his friend David from Thieves. David's now split from his musical other half Saul ('it was all very messy, but I'm over it now') and the album, now billed as *McAlmont* by McAlmont, is finally out. Queercore and McAlmont apart, there's a brace of indie inverts from the ironists (Thrill Kill Kult, RPLA), to the bands on the margins (Blueboy, Boyracer, Shriek, Sexton Ming, Bandit Queen), and those on the margins of bigger bands (Debbie Smith, the drummer of Echobelly, Simon Gilbert of Suede, The Breeders and Hole bassist Josephine Wiggs and her girlfriend Kate Schellenbach, the drummer with Luscious Jackson).

But as far as the rock mainstream's concerned we still have to content ourselves with 'the claim game' we freaks have always played with pop. Nirvana's 'troubled' Kurt Cobain was embraced by some no sooner than the gunsmoke had cooled around his pretty little head. Brett from Suede – like a woman spurned – is more Thin White Duke than Ziggy Stardust these days, and is playing the role of rock star as junkie rather than rock star as queer. Suede's new album *Dog Man Star* contains far more gratuitous drug references ('Heroine', 'Daddy's Speeding') than pervy references.

Morrissey's changed too and is now more interested in thuggery than buggery. His stylings are increasingly masculinist –

both in terms of his recent records' harder guitar edges and blatant rockism, and his scrapping of his fey ways in favour of professing a predilection for boxing, skinheads, the Krays, tattoos and Herman Melville. Of course they're all as gay in their own way – though from a different tradition – as Oscar Wilde, gladioli and *A Taste of Honey*. But one can't help wondering if La Mozz realizes how ridiculously camp his association with all these things appears? Or does he think he now comes across as one dead butch homi?

REM's Michael Stipe has finally got around to admitting his sexuality is 'indecipherable' (i.e. he intends to keep it that way). Patrick's a big fan, especially of *Automatic for the People*. 'What an immensely great record that is. It's phenomenal that a band produces its best album on their ninth album. A whole record of nostalgia and soul searching. The sense of loss of innocence and youth that comes across on the record is [makes noise to suggest awe]. It kind of inspired the lyric to "Prince of Mars" – which started off as a list of nostalgic events for me but turned into the Little Prince coming here and me trying to show him what it was like not to be a little kid anymore.'

Somewhat surprisingly queer rock heroes are a problem for Patrick. 'Either they're very good at being gay and not very good at music. Or the other way round. Tom Robinson was very good at being gay but I didn't like the songs very much. Whereas Bob Mould's very good at music but not very good about being gay. He's really crap actually which is quite funny.'

Mould was outed by *The Village Voice* last year. The astounding thing was what a well kept secret it had been. And continues to be. The British music press have carefully avoided mentioning it, bar *Select* who broke the news by mocking up a cover of *Gay Times* with Bob on. The man's only comment thus far has been: 'Fifteen years into this [career] it seems like people are really interested to home in on one particular point which, if I thought it was germane or intrinsic in the work that's been created in the fifteen years, I would make a point about it. It just happens to be a very unimportant sidebar.'

Bob claims his sexuality doesn't necessarily affect his music – although it could explain why, like REM's Michael Stipe, his lyrics have thus far been so elliptical. But there is some sense of movement in his work: from the beautifully dumb rage of Hüsker Dü, through the absolute gloom of his two solo albums, to the way he's lightened up a little with Sugar – but that's falling in love for you, I guess. Immediately prior to being outed Bob can be spotted holding up a photo of his lover and manager Kevin O'Neill at the close of the video for 'If I can't change your mind'.

It almost looked like Mould was starting to out himself. Sugar's song 'Slim' described watching a friend die of AIDS, and the *Beaster* album dealt with how in our society the good and the innocent get crucified (*METAPHOR! METAPHOR!*). And he's currently writing the soundtrack to the movie of Dennis Cooper's *Frisk*. Free at last, eh Bob?

'I know Bob,' Patrick says. 'He's a real sweetie, but it's just not on his agenda. You've got no idea what he's going on about anyway, bless him. I really want to talk to him about it. He's really tortured and he's very serious about his torturedness as well. Whereas I'm quite flippant about mine. He's really hard work. He's just so closed. I spent an evening with him in London and took him and his friend to the Piano Bar which was just the wrong place. He was so sweet. He said, "oh yes we have places like this in New York". But you could just tell it had nothing to do with Bob. He just wanted to be in a coffee shop drinking coffee, not talking, and smoking lots of cigarettes. And that's okay. I know quite a few closeted rockers and I don't challenge them. They're quite wary of me. But I'd very much like to get off my cross as the only out rock boy. I'd be very happy to let someone else do all the talking.'

Gay Times, November 1994

Chapter twenty-nine

'Outrage and Boredom Just Go Hand in Hand': Manic Street Preachers

'PEOPLE that we know in the music press have told us they just can't believe the amount of letters that they get coming in saying "They're wearing fucking eyeliner they should be kicked in." *Really nasty stuff.*'

Richey James, the Manic Street Preachers' guitarist, is looking a little forlorn. Disarmingly charming and wearing a rather classy see-through blouse he's recently learned to expect this sort of crap. According to who you believe his group are either rock's great white hope or a distinctly ungreat white elephant. After a string of independent singles their noisy hybrid of glam and punk rock and roll has won them a recording contract with Columbia. Their first single for them 'Stay Beautiful', is released this month. Half the world seems to be hoping that it will thrust them towards megastardom whilst the other half wants to see the boys fall flat splat on their pretty little faces. Richey agrees with me that to provoke such extreme reactions is an encouraging sign.

'It's perfect. Just how it should be. I'm just as happy having people loathe me as I am to have them love me. Music's got so safe and ordinary it'd be good if a few more bands tried to get those sort of opinions forced on them.'

'All the groups people are force fed, like Happy Mondays or The Farm are so drab. They look like my father,' adds Nicky Wise, the group's gangling bass player. 'So they write good pop songs – well who cares? If you let pop be reduced to just entertainment for entertainment's sake then every government in the whole world's won. You've got to have something more exciting. It's like when Jimmy Somerville was arrested for giving someone a blow job in Hyde Park, I thought that was brilliant. It's much more thrilling.'

Whilst most groups these days make dance records and take every opportunity to remind Joe Public that this doesn't mean they're puffs, the Preachers fly in the face of fashion by playing 'manly' rock music whilst coming on like absolute Jessies. This has led some to call them musical Luddites, but Richey suggests more noble reasons for rejecting the indie dance ethos and its cult of the lad and embracing frock and roll instead.

'The problem with that scene is that the bands act out a kind of lifestyle without ever questioning how it comes about. The Happy Mondays getting pissed and beating up their mates then fucking their girlfriends is just not exciting 'cause where we come from it's just everyday life. And at the end of the day they're not even selling that many records. But someone like Guns 'n' Roses sell sixteen million albums.'

But they're really vile people too.

'I know, I know. Al those American rock and roll bands are just full of bullshit. We've got no respect for them. They might put on a bit of make-up but then they'll go around calling everyone a faggot. And people say we're clichéd!

'And it's tragic 'cause rock and roll is meant to be this great force for change. It still can be. You can reach a young audience that are untainted by all the bullshit that's gonna come their way later on. The first thing we set out to do was recreate the generation gap and I think we're succeeding. All our fans are really young. From thirteen to sixteen. And most people know what we're about, we are a really *obvious* band. But even if people just know that we're pissed off that's more than most bands.'

Indeed, there are a rash of bands who mistake reaction for radicalism. The Preachers recently played support to one of the worst offenders, the wildly homophobic Manchester band, First Offence.

'The first thing we did when we went on stage was kiss each other,' Nick recalls gleefully, 'then we blew kisses at them and said "What are you gonna do?" But they didn't do anything. They just stood there.'

The Preachers specialize in such shock tactics; it's as much in the way they dress as when their singer James makes an onstage invitation like: 'If there's any pretty boys out there in the audience who want to bugger me, I'll see you after the show.'

'When James said that there were a couple of bottles,' Nick confirms, 'but we like to threaten people sexually. Especially males.'

Although the band are currently all living – Larry Parnes style – at their manager's flat in London they hail from the tiny town of Blackwood in Gwent. It was there, Nicky explains, that the band was born out of boredom.

'If you're hopelessly depressed like I was, then dressing up is just the ultimate escape. When I was young I just wanted to be noticed. Nothing could excite me except attention so I'd dress up as much as I could. Outrage and boredom just go hand in hand.'

The Manic Street Preachers are so startlingly sensible, refreshingly so in the age of the bozo, that I cross every one of my toes in the hope that they'll be as big as they say they will.

'We just want to make one brilliant debut double LP that sells millions of copies,' says Nicky, 'and as long as we've made our statement and perhaps changed something then I just want to disappear and go back to live with my mam.'

Rock and roll. Phew!

Gay Times, August 1991

Chapter thirty

Pink Vinyl:
Gay Dance Labels
and Nu-NRG

I'VE got this theory that you're only two shags away from any other gay man in the country. You've shagged Boy A. Boy A has shagged Boy B. And Boy B has shagged Boy C. It's quite simple really. Gay dance labels are a bit like that – everyone's been in everyone else's bed at some point – metaphorically speaking. Trannies With Attitude were on React. Now they're on Out On Vinyl. Which was started by Tim Lennox. Who was involved with Flesh Records. Who have just signed Roger. Who used to dance with Gloworm. Who are on Hooj Choons. As are The Source. Whose first record was on React. And so on and so on and so on.

Let's start at the beginning shall we? In 1987 James Horrocks was one of the prime movers who helped this country's underground dance scene go overground. He co-founded the independent label Rhythm King which, after putting out Taffy's Hi-NRG anthem 'I Love My Radio', scored number ones the following year with Bomb the Bass's 'Beat Dis' and S'Express' 'Theme From S'Express'. He left Rhythm King soon after, but in 1991 produced a record – a boomphed up version of Candi Staton's 'You Got The Love' by The Source. He knew he had a hit on his hands and decided to put the thing out himself. 'You Got The Love' went top five, no problem. Not bad for a first release. And React was in business.

Then as now, James was running Heaven's Friday nighter, Garage, which despite the name was playing a steady diet of continental Techno. Fabulous music but with one little problem, as James explains: 'Most people don't know what the fuck they're listening to when they go out. They know they like it but they can't buy it as they've got no idea what the track's called. Particularly if it's an instrumental. We wanted to try and transfer the gay scene and the records that are big on that scene onto vinyl and put the best tracks together on a label that people would come to trust.' Together with his business partner, Thomas Foley, and DJs Daz Saund and Trevor Rockliffe, he compiled an album of 'Belgian Techno Anthems' called *Reactivate*.

Three years later and we're now on *Reactivate 9*, which, reflecting the evolution of gay men's tastes, is an album of trancey Techno compiled by James and Thomas with Garage and ff DJ Blu Peter. Or as we're supposed to call the music now – Nu-NRG. Although the term implies a debt to Hi-NRG and Nu-Beat, it was first applied to Blu Peter 'because the music I was playing and the way I was playing it had a "new energy", basically. People came and they heard a different sound. It's a mixture of various forms of Techno and Hard Euro, mostly from German labels like Superstition and No Respect. It's uplifting but intense, bouncy and happy but hard and fast the way gay men like it.'

React is now not just the première gay label, but has firmly established itself as the country's leading underground dance label. Its compilations now embrace Happy House *(Rush Hour)*, New York Garage *(Kinky Trax* and *Strictly Rhythm)*, Gabba House *(Technohead)*, Italian Piano House *(Extravaganze)*, Italian Energy *(The Power of Media)*, as well as albums put together by some of the scene's favourite DJs: Mrs Wood *(Mrs Wood Teaches Techno)*, Trannies With Attitude *(Let's Go Tesko)* and Rachel Auburn *(Freska!)*, with one from Princess Julia in the pipeline.

The DJ compilations are a good way of further establishing names before they release records in their own right. As has now happened with Mrs Wood ('The Awakening') and Blu Peter (Elevator's rather bouncy 'Shinny' and 'The Second Movement' EP). React's big project at the moment is MASH, 'an extended family of artists and performers' put together by Simon Napier-Bell, whose wilfully camp reworking of 'You Don't Have To Say You Love Me' went Top Twenty in May. James believes 'Techno is the Hi-NRG of the Nineties. Not just because it's the music gay men dance to, but because you can trace a direct line from the more Moroder-ish stuff and what we're putting out today. I think there's a terrible tendency for people in the music business to underestimate gay men's taste. React tries to be the opposite of that.'

The prime example of that tendency to underestimate has to be *A Saturday Night At Heaven* – a genuinely terrifying collection of Euro-tat compiled by Heaven's Ian D. The album was put out on the Hi-NRG label Klone in May and is proof, if you still need it, that heterosexuals don't have a monopoly on naffness. *Some Of These Were Hooj*, which came out at the same time, was every bit as beautiful as *A Saturday Night At Heaven* was ugly. A collection of some of the finest moments in the life of the label Hooj Choons – which is to Trade as React is to Garage. Hooj Choons sort of developed out of Trade Records which, after licensing the greatest record ever made, E-Trax's 'Let's Rock', promptly disappeared. Hooj have put out records by Felix, Hyper-go-go, Gloworm, JX (whose 'Son Of A Gun' is only rivalled by Atlantic Ocean's 'Waterfall' and Klatsch's 'God Save The Queer' as the gayest sounding record of the year) and Diss-Cuss – otherwise known as DJ Malcolm – not half bad remixer and one quarter of the quartet of Turnmills' DJs who've now moved effortlessly from spinning records to making them: Mrs Wood, Blu Peter and Paul Newman. DJ Malcolm's new single 'Love Will Save The Day' is out on Hooj, while Paul Newman, who started out on Trade Records as Decktition ('Love Rush') is now Tall Paul and on Effective with 'Rock Da House' – which was recorded at Hooj Studios. Confusing isn't it?

If this is all starting to sound like some new Gay Mafia, it's only fitting that up North the prime mover is Tim Lennox, 'the Godfather of Gaychester'. Tim was the man who first brought House to Manchester when he played at the Number One club and was one of the DJs at the early Flesh nights at the Hacienda. Now he's involved with Paradise Factory – with whom he started the Out On Vinyl label in March. Lennox, who had previously put out records as The Shy One, is both OOV's executive producer and the main force behind the in-house project T-Empo. Their first single, a chirpy cover of Thelma Houston's 'Saturday Night, Sunday Morning', went Top Twenty in May (interestingly after it was picked up by London Records – as gay a label as any, but that's another story). Tim says he chose 'Saturday Night, Sunday Morning' 'because I really wanted a record to close the night with at the Paradise Factory. I'd always loved the original and hearing Pete Tong play it a while ago sent me scurrying back to my record collection and digging my copy out. It's a perfect record really – it's a love song but it's also a love song to clubbing. In a club everything you create is your own – apart from the music. So why not create your own music?'

The nation's favourite big girls' blouses, Trannies With Attitude, from Leeds' Vague, have also been signed by OOV. Nick from the Trannies had previously assured me that their first single for the label would be called 'Goose? Snertigoose!' and had also instructed Tim to try and get clearance for a sample from 'The Birdy Song'. But he now assures me the record is called 'Freedom' and that it celebrates the same ethos as their club: 'It's got an "I Will Survive" vibe. The song's a positive anthem about the right to express yourself and to be who you want to be. There's another single as well, a melodic rap called "Nasty Girls" which is about all the different types of girls there are ... girls meaning boys, of course.'

This month has seen two new arrivals – London's Well Equipped run by Wayne Shiers and Rob Kean (with Thyone Girls' 'Keep On Pumpin') and Flesh Records which has, once again, sprung from a club and, like their fellow Mancunians OOV, is putting out much more mellow discs than the London boys' banging Techno. Paul Cons from Flesh assured me that this is a Northern thing: 'Flesh Records is a reflection of the musical tastes of the club. The music at Flesh is more New York, more black and more a part of that gay disco tradition. We deliberately decided to make the first releases a bit more out. I think it's important as a statement of intent to try and make something explicit like this work, rather than being clever and knowing. The second record is quite militantly gay.'

By which he means Tracy and Sharon's 'Filthy Hetero'. The record attracted a lot of attention when it first appeared last year as a white label (and as an equally popular t-shirt), and it samples Edith Massey's Aunt Ida speech from *Female Trouble* ('The world of heterosexuals is a sick and boring life. Queers are just better'). Tracy and Sharon's Tom Stephan sent a copy to John Waters who said he was thrilled to be sampled ('Now I feel like James Brown'). American-born Tom is yet another DJ and a film maker whose short documentary about the Sisters of Perpetual Indulgence, *21st Century Nuns*, was recently shown on Channel Four. Like the Trannies's singles, 'Filthy Hetero' is gay in its message, not just its sound. Though Tom stresses that the single is meant as a joke: 'I don't think the record's heterophobic. If it's aimed at anyone it's aimed at homophobic heterosexual people. But we're saying nothing compared to what's been said about us. It's just about being tired of being polite.'

Flesh's first release is a cover of Eleanor Mills' 'Mr Right', sung by Roger and produced by the Hacienda's distinctly unfilthy hetero DJ, Graeme Park. They've done a fine reclamation job on a knowing diva anthem: 'I'm looking for Mr Right, had enough of Mr Wrong.' Twenty-three-year-old Roger's from the Midlands but is now a London boy. He was one of the original go-go boys at Flesh when it started three years ago and has also shaken his booty at Kinky, The Daisy Chain and Ciao Baby, and for Hooj Choons acts Felix and Gloworm. But he doesn't go out dancing anymore. 'I gave up clubbing a year ago. You know how it is? You're this boy from the suburbs and you move to London and you go crazy. Then you wake up one morning and realize you don't know anything about the city apart from how to get to the Embankment or Soho.'

Roger had previously sung with Eat More Fruit and got involved with Flesh by accident. Or rather by misfortune. 'There were some compromising photos of me going around and I was trying to get hold of the photographer. So I called Flesh to try and get the guy's number and Paul mentioned the label. I was enticed by the name Graeme Park, auditioned for them and got it.'

There are two fabulous things about all these new labels. First there's the music. And second is their rejection of ambisexual fluffiness. These are records made by and for us, that have sprung from a culture where the coolest thing you can be is queer. Out of the clubs and out of the closet, as it were.

Anyway Roger, you were saying? 'I just think it's good fun to have a bloke singing a song like "Mr Right". It's not that shocking in this day and age. Every dance song that refers to love misses a big angle and it's good to open things up a bit. The track's entertaining first and foremost, with a hidden message. Well, it's not really that hidden, is it? That's the best thing about it. It's so bizarre when you see all these people with real problems about being gay. The main thing is that I have no problems. I don't mind people knowing what I am or what I do. My only attitude is "fuck it".'

Gay Times, August 1994

Chapter thirty-one

Preaching to the Perverted: Homocore and Queercore

Homocore

THERE'S a strange noise coming down the line from Toronto to Brighton.

When Bruce La Bruce explains that 'it's probably 'cause I'm calling from the tub', this boy's in nelly heaven. Anyone that's seen Bruce's movie *No Skin Off My Ass* and specifically the scene where Bruce gives skinhead wünderkind Klaus Von Brucker a damned good seeing to, will understand that talking to Bruce in the bath is every bit as much of an honour as Marianne Faithfull offering you a bite of her Mars Bar. La Bruce is now in the process of finishing his second film *Super 8½* but it's not movies I want to talk to him about today, it's music.

If this year's 'big thing' is Riot Grrrl, then Bruce is all those teenage feminists armed with guitars' bent big brother. Seven years ago when he was a nineteen-year-old mohawk hanging out at Toronto punk gigs, he started a fanzine called *JD's,* the house journal of a scene that as then didn't exist: Homocore.

'Over here punk was always very sexually adventurous – it was all about allowing people to express themselves. All the seminal bands at the time like Castrating Jesus and Ugly Americans were all completely groovy and they'd all have their own little song against homophobia long before it was trendy to do that. But as the Eighties progressed it just got more and more sexually conservative.

'We weren't really accepted in the punk places because we were gay, and because we looked punk we'd often get refused entry to gay places. We always thought that punk was meant to be anti-establishment and that people involved with it should be exploring sexual ambiguity.'

Punk didn't disappear during the Eighties in North America like it did over here, but went underground. Despite what Bruce says, the problem with most of the leading lights of that wave lay in their ambiguity. You were never sure if bands like the Circle Jerks, MDC, The Meatmen, Angry Samoans or Impotent Sea Snakes were homos or homophobes. As they never declared their sexuality most of their audience took their songs about homosex as a chance to laugh at the fags.

'Our reaction ended up as just "fuck 'em all" and we decided to create our own version of gay punk. The target audience for *JD's* was punk and teenage boys, both straight and gay. Both kinds were rejecting a lot of conventions so it was a good time to get 'em ... "while they're still young". But most of all it was about reaching all those isolated and confused kids from small towns and cities across North America who might just as soon have hanged themselves as come out.'

Bruce calls *JD's* 'a softcore zine for hardcore kids ... We wanted it to be about sex and unapologetically gay.' It owed a lot to the American underground paper *Straight to Hell*. Both were largely made up of (probably made up) readers' 'true homosexual experiences' (i.e. mucky stories). *JD's* helped to validate the readers' sexuality and also provided a platform for literally thousands of kids who'd until then thought they were the only little gay boy in Straightsville, Arizona, to come out and start talking to each other. His tactic of making out that the scene was much bigger than it was worked a treat and inspired countless others to start up their own 'fag-a-zines'. At the last count there were almost two hundred of the things.

Three years ago Bruce asked for bands to send in tapes from which he assembled two *Homocore Hit Parade* tapes. The songs veered between the sublime (Nikki Parasite's 'Male Call' and

Bomb's 'Be A Fag') to the appalling (England's own Apostles). Just as had happened with the zines, Bruce's championing of such bands led to a mini explosion – now there's even a label, OutPunk, dedicated to the release of all things Homocore.

'I created the label so I could produce music I could relate to.' Twenty-one year old Matt Wobensmith tells me. 'I just got sick of seeing ambiguous messages – not to mention bigoted ones. Basically I'm a pervert and I'm actively recruiting.' Matt was behind the compilation EPs 'There's A Dyke In The Pit' and 'There's a Faggot In The Pit', and his label is now home to many of the scene's leading lights: New York's arty polysexualists God Is My Co-Pilot, Fifth Column (led by Bruce La Bruce's former colleague at *JD's*, Gloria B. Jones) and Tribe 8 – a rough edged San Franciscan dyke five-piece, formed according to guitarist Lesley 'to validate cultural identity in the underground scene for dykes'.

Though singer Lynn adds helpfully: 'But we really started so we could get girlfriends. Being dykes and being out and playing music is political. It's not like we meant it to be, it just is.'

By far the best of these new bands is Pansy Division, who like OutPunk hail from San Francisco. The trio's new single, 'Bill And Ted's Homosexual Adventure', came out on that label, but their first EP and an excellent album, *Undressed*, were put out independently. When I spoke to singer Jon Ginoli they'd just played the March on Washington (' . . . so we should have got a few more people to hear about us.' Yeah about a million of them? 'Err, not all of them came to our show').

Jon had been in bands before, singing songs about persons of a non-specific gender: 'Then one night I went to see the dyke band Two Nice Girls play and thought "dammit – why aren't guys doing anything like this?"' – and then in true punk style, he went out and did it himself.

'I try to write songs that reflect the way gay men talk when they're together, so there's a lot of vernacular in our songs,' Jon tells me. Consequently most of their songs are about what gay men invariably talk about when they're together – dick. They're also very, very funny. Coming on like a bolder and much bawdier version of the Buzzcocks or the Ramones, Pansy Division are anti macho ('Fem In A Black Leather Jacket'), sex obsessed ('The Cocksucker

Club'), masters of the pastiche ('Smells Like Queer Spirit' – 'hello, hello, hello, homo') and absolutely fabulous.

Though Homocore started out as genuinely mixed between fags and dykes, the irresistible rise of Riot Grrrl has seen many women moving out to realign themselves with the latter. And just as with boys and punk, the scene's provided many young dykes with the camouflage to help them come out. Yet it's interesting that while Riot Grrrl's enemies are keen to demonize it as 'full of lesbians', many of its so called friends choose to overlook the lesbian content.

'The Riot Grrrl thing isn't particularly lesbian but it's perceived that way,' Bruce confirms. 'It has a reputation for being very middle class. They're like the girl scouts: "let's have a chapter in every major city". My friend and I went in drag to their big convention in New York as two very middle class uptown ladies who'd read about it in *Cosmopolitan* and wanted to check out.

'Leslie, who's in Tribe 8 was in ASF which was one of the only dyke Hardcore bands going at the time we were starting *JD's*. So it was like a spontaneous combustion, all these things are connected. The drag movement, Homocore, Riot Grrrl, they all intersect.'

Gay Times, June 1993

Queercore

Sister George hail from Walthamstow. The real face of East 17 are four queers: two girls, two boys, two white, one black and one Jewish. They stress that there was no positive discrimination involved in choosing the make up of their line up, though. More a combination of friends made at gigs and the trusty old *Melody Maker* ad.

This, the first homegrown Queercore act started playing together six months ago. They're as beautifully abrasive and angry as ever but have now transformed themselves into a lean, mean killing machine. Their debut album *Drag King* – a slightly more restrained affair than their blistering live shows – is released on Valentine's Day.

For singer Elyot, Queercore is 'a new generation that has got different politics and different tastes in music and in clothes and in life. People who weren't happy about what you're supposed to be like if you're gay.'

But perhaps Lisa, a woman with a brain the size of Scotland, and whose fat buzzsaw bass is the band's backbone, offers the best definition: 'Queercore is an attitude problem. Sister George started out of the Riot Grrrl scene. That opened the door for Queercore by creating a climate where loads of young girls could go to gigs which you couldn't do before.'

Sister George owe a greater debt to American Riot Grrrl bands like Tribe 8 than they do to the US Homocore scene which preceded it. When Riot Grrrl broke over here 18 months ago it led to a newly politicized indie scene, allowing not just angry young women, but Asian groups like Cornershop and Voodoo Queens, and queers like Sister George, to be heard. Huggy Bear, in their photos, slogans, fanzines and with songs like 'Pansy Twist', had already brought perverse sexuality into the arena. But whereas they made it OK to pretend to be queer, Sister George were the ones who made it cool to be queer.

In the summer Liz Naylor began CatCall records as a Riot Grrrl label, its first missive being a joint LP by Huggy Bear and Bikini Kill. Sharing the disenchantment of many over what Riot Grrrl later became, Liz has now turned CatCall into a Queercore label with Sister George as her first signing.

'I wanted CatCall to be as extreme a label as possible because I don't think we live in particularly ambiguous times. Fuck Suede *et al.* What I learned from Riot Grrrl was that people got scared and ran off to the safety of the indie establishment. I dislike that. You have to try and replace those alternatives. Rock music is a great forum for expressing discontent. It's really healthy that Queercore bands are forming and protesting against not only society generally but are also criticizing the gay establishment.'

In many ways Queercore sees itself as a direct reaction against Old Compton Street's put-your-money-on-the-counter culture, an alternative scene set up by those too poor to participate in it. New bands, Parasite and Children's Hour are, just like the scene that spawned them, more girls than boys, and incredibly young.

'The scene's run by gay men and if you haven't got the money then you can't be part of things,' says guitarist Linden who, like the rest of Sister George, is signing on. 'At the end of the day the people who run the pink economy are just there to rip us off.'

'Our song "Gold Plated Sparta For The Olympian Gods" is how we feel about the gay scene,' says Lisa. 'It says "just because you're gay it don't mean you're OK". We don't want to be nice and soft and safe and pink.'

Linden is equally unimpressed with other 'so-called lesbian and gay bands: Erasure and all those drab drag acts. It's just campy boringness. They say nothing to a lot of young lesbians and gay men who are often involved in struggles. And they don't say anything if you're black or if you're a woman.'

Featured on the album is a number called '100 x No', where Sister George take Tom Robinson's old punk chestnut 'Glad To Be Gay' and swiftly kick it to death.

Says Lisa: 'That song sums up our attitude. "Glad To Be Gay" is imprinted in your head from when you're little, like the film *The Killing Of Sister George* is. You get this idea that life's an apology. All tank tops and back alleys. When that song came out, coming out was the big issue. But we feel that is not enough. Each generation goes a few steps further. Just the fact that we are dykes and poofs playing together is political.'

The most successful song on *Drag King* is a piss-take of hetero mating patterns and courtship rituals, 'Let's Breed'. It's part of what Liz Naylor calls 'a wider-angle anger about sexual roles and a questioning of relationships. Queercore has just as much to say to straights as it does to queers.' Unsurprisingly, as the scene has finally come to the attention of straight journalists this aspect is often overlooked. A recent piece by *The Guardian*'s Caroline Sullivan tried to reduce Queercore to no more than a series of petty internal squabbles. Steven Wells in the *NME,* like Sullivan, conveniently overlooked everything that Sister George and their like had to say about heterosexuality, instead using them to mouth criticisms of gay men that he didn't have the guts to say himself.

Elyot's guitar sports a Tribe 8 sticker bearing the legend 'Assimilate my fist'. They're more than aware of the problems involved in dealing with the mainstream. Liz Naylor had been more worried that Queercore would be dismissed by its enemies as 'oh, they've all got a chip on their shoulder or that they're angry about being queer.' But as Lisa says, Sister George have already got lots they can feel proud about.

'I feel proud that we have created something that's not just a music thing. It's like we exist as a big snowballing gang. That's what we mean by the Queercore militia. It is a conscious gang, people are organizing to come to gigs. It's growing gig by gig and it's not just something you watch passively and then go away home. It's about people, both straight and gay, thinking about things like sexuality. I think the period we're in now makes all this inevitable. And that's good because it annoys so many people. All four of us have been waiting for something like this for ages.'

Capital Gay, 11 February 1994

Chapter thirty-two

The Queen of New York: RuPaul

'Man was born free and everywhere he is in chains.'
Rousseau 1762

'We're born naked and the rest is drag.'
RuPaul 1993

THE man is black. The wig is blond. RuPaul is six-foot-five-inches of fabulousness – 'but with hair, heels and attitude I'm through the goddamned roof!'

RuPaul's huge in the States now, thanks largely to the single 'Supermodel (You Better Work)' – a homage to Naomi, Christy and Linda. He looks as good as they do, but is less a Supermodel than a superstar-role-model.

'This is all very exciting for me, but it's also very exciting for me to think about what all those teenage kids in the middle of nowhere are seeing. Something must click you know? "If this guy's doin' this stuff then maybe I can get away with it". It's not that they all have to dress up in high heels and a blond wig – but you can follow any dream that you want to. You write your own ticket. And I'm the living example of that.'

All this is, of course, very American. But the pop process is the closest thing that the States gets to democracy. It's the way a piece of white trash from Tupelo, Mississippi called Elvis Presley can become King of America. And equally how a femmy black kid like RuPaul can become Queen of New York – 'I moved here with just a pair of high heels and a dream ... and look at the bitch now.'

RuPaul Charles was born and raised in San Diego and first slipped into a dress at the age of five. He remembers it was pink, but whether it was faggotry or frocks that came first is less clear: 'I always felt like that. I never felt I wasn't gay. I was one of those "very creative" kids and people never questioned that. I always got asked to entertain my mom's friends.'

At fifteen he ran away from California to Atlanta in the Deep South – funny, I thought you were meant to do it the other way round.

'San Diego's very Republican and very white and Atlanta's like the mecca of the South – a Black boom town. There's a lot of opportunities for African American people to move on up. There were visible people of colour doing exciting things and that was just the greatest thing to be around. You had the sense that it could be done. And that's why I'm so proud to be a role model for a lot of gay children, 'cause people did that for me.'

The big one for Ru was Miss Diana Ross. 'When I was a kid it was like "look momma there's a black girl on TV!" I like that thing of making it through adversity, and the songs she did later were so positive – "I'm the boss, it's my turn, I'm coming out!" ... of course she was a bitch but I love that too.'

In Atlanta RuPaul and some friends got into genderfuck 'Boppers' Drag' (smeared make-up, a nice dress and army boots), something he took to New York in 1984 when he joined the Wigstock generation. He got more and more glamorous and was perfectly placed to get more and more famous – as the Nineties dawned, drag started getting cool. Madonna appropriated Vogue-ing, Jennie Livingston made *Paris is Burning,* Jackie 60 became *the* club to be seen in and records like Uncanny Alliance's 'I got my education' took the scene's vernacular ('*Miss Thing!*') into the charts.

RuPaul comes across like he's swallowed American drag's three finest moments (Stonewall, Warhol, Disco) and spat them out into 1993. And it's cute that he's been working with that little triptych who kept US pop camp during the Eighties; Deee-lite, the B-52s and the Fabulous Pop Tarts.

The single 'Supermodel' you should already know and love. The coup is that the album is just as glorious – a camp popdiscogaragehouse sextravaganza. When Monica Lynch, MD of New York dance label Tommy Boy, says she signed RuPaul on the strength of the music, you better believe her.

Monica's compared him to *Sesame Street*'s Big Bird – 'he's so unthreatening, he's harmless.' It's a semantic error a lot of people make. RuPaul's genius is that he just *seems* unthreatening and harmless, which is a different thing entirely.

At present he is our cause's greatest ambassador. This is a TV who was made for TV. I really can't remember a pop star who's been this witty or this wise. When I ask if anyone's given Ru a hard time he thinks for a minute: 'You know what? There haven't been any. None. It's all been totally positive. I'm working with good energy and you can't go up against that. Not in your heart of hearts. Some people may try but they just look like a damned fool.'

This is the first gay man to reclaim the family on our own terms. On chat shows they always try and heterosexualize Ru's tale and ask what his parents think of all this. And Ru will stress how fortunate he was with his family, and how too many parents reject their gay kids.

'But they *were* very supportive. They knew this was my calling. Of course they would have preferred me to be a doctor or a lawyer. The next single "Back To My Roots" is all about this . . . well actually it's all about black hair care products, but the subtext is about coming back to where you came from. How you have to deal with your past before you can move on to your future.'

Ru never shies away from questions of sexuality, gender or race. The big word for this Big Bird is 'Love' – the phrase 'everybody say love' may once have belonged to Miss Ross, but now it's unmistakably Ru's. 'My act is all about loving yourself and learning how to love yourself, 'cause if you don't love yourself how you gonna love anybody else?'

The crap people amongst you will dismiss all this as hippy bollocks, but Ru's already one step ahead of you.

'It does get kind of New Age-y, mishy, moshy, mushy, bushy, but all I'm saying is people wanna live and the way to do this is to do the right thing.' These visions of love don't float in a vacuum. On America's best chat show, *Arsenio Hall*, Ru uses this love stuff to foreground a story about a march against the Klan ('I went down there in full drag baby'), and then to blast the Reagan–Bush years ('the pendulum swung so far to the right in the Eighties, now it's gonna come CRASHING back to the left'). By which time he's got the studio audience eating out of the palm of his perfectly manicured hand.

Ask him about drag and BLAM! 'I always say "we're born naked and the rest is drag". Any performer who puts on an outfit to project an image is in drag. Everything you put on is to fit a preconceived notion of how you wanna be seen. It's all drag. Mine is just more glamorous.'

Today he's wearing men's clothes. The voice is lower, but what's really noticeable is a slight dip in confidence, a little less *oomph*. It confirms what he says about how empowered the frocks make him feel. When dressed as a woman he says he feels 'like Superman – I'm castrated but I'm also more free. The first time I put on heels I became a god. I think everyone should give it a try.'

The world has fallen in love with RuPaul and I really don't care if it lasts for fifteen minutes or forever. But I pray it's the latter.

Everybody say *love*.

Gay Times, July 1993

Chapter thirty-three

Relaxed: Holly Johnson

ME and Holly Johnson go way back, you know? Both of us were complete girls stuck in a boy's grammar school. Different grammar schools in different decades, I'll grant you, but nevertheless our two stories are intertwined.

For some people it's the Kennedy assassination. For me it was the 'Relax' ban. I remember exactly where I was when I heard the news, on the morning of Wednesday 11 January 1984. I was fifteen and on the bus to school. Me and this boy Andrew were chain smoking Marlboro, copying each other's Maths homework and pressing our knees together. On the radio Mike Read, DJ and tennis-playing mate of Cliff Richard, was playing yesterday's chart run down. He ground to a halt at number six, and in a voice more indignant than angry said he wouldn't be playing 'Relax' because it was 'overtly obscene'. Oh, it was fab. Next week the record leapt to number one.

The ban spread like mould to all BBC radio and television stations. 'Relax' stayed at number one for five weeks. Not since the Sex Pistols' 'God Save the Queen' had a record so divided the nation. It wasn't gay against straight. It was young and sexy and naughty against old and prudish and 'nice'. And it felt great being fifteen and on the winning team.

Frankie Goes To Hollywood thrilled and helped lonely, little me in equal measure. Twenty years ago Holly Johnson was in much the same situation himself. 'I was desperately searching for some kind of gay identity when I was a teenager – and books and films and pop music were one of the ways I found that. It was like that feeling the very first time you go to a gay club – you realize that there are other people like you. It was all quite a revelation. I felt comfortable for the first time in a sense – not completely but it's important, you know?'

Indeed I do. You see somewhere between the pain of The Smiths, the politics of Bronski Beat and Frankie's sheer unadulterated pleasure I found myself. In 1984 neither me nor Frankie knew what was round the corner, that this would be the last gasp. But Frankie were the ones that made the future, my future, look exciting. And I was more than a little distraught when Frankie came, they said, and then they went away again.

The first half of Holly's autobiography, *A Bone in My Flute*, is a fabulous record of what it's like to grow up gay in this country; surrounded by cruel boys and crueller teachers, being dragged by his dad to football matches when he'd rather be ice skating in his brown bri-nylon catsuit, or wanking over the underwear section of his mum's Freeman's catalogue. *A Bone in My Flute* is the ballad of a teenage queen camping it up, carrying on and trying to get away. And it's about how you grab at anything you think will help you get through.

'I'm a big cissy,' Holly confesses. 'I was very young when I realized there was some difference to me. I remember distinctly waving at Territorial Army soldiers at the army barracks across the road, thinking "don't they look fab?" And me mother dragging me away, thinking "what's he doing waving at them men over there?" I must have only been four years old. And then there was the interest in me sister's *Bunty* comics. Wanting to join the sewing circle at school. Going ice skating was very effeminate in a sense, but that's more about theatre and performance, isn't it? Dressing up was a big part of it for me, whether it be a cub scout uniform, a bri-nylon catsuit or a choirboy's cassock.'

Holly found solace in pop. First came David. Then there was Marc. Then Roxy Music and Lou Reed. They helped him feel able to tell people. 'Oh, I'm bisexual, just like my hero David'. Holly wanted to say he was gay, but bisexual meant full-on-rock-and-roll-balls-out sexy glamour with knobs on. And gay meant Larry Grayson.

'Bowie was a more appealing stereotype to relate to. No one wanted to be like Larry Grayson or John Inman. We were petrified. That was our worst nightmare. I would have much rather turned into David Bowie, put it that way. The bisexual act was helpful, but it was bad in a way because those artists that did come out as bisexual in the Seventies were still colluding with the closet. It would have been easier if Elton or David Bowie had just said "I am gay".'

There's only one thing worse than ambisexual pop stars. Ambisexual pop stars' *fans*. There's a scene in the book where Holly's all dolled up to go and see Bowie play live at last. He's so excited, he thinks he's going to meet other people like him. Instead him and his friend, Honey Heath, get beaten up. 'I don't know if it was exactly queerbashed. We were bashed. The fact that we had make-up on perhaps was something to do with it. Perhaps it was because we were thirteen and we were just not as big as the other lads. Apparently there were a couple of other people in the audience that I met later. There were kindred spirits there but we just didn't find them.'

As the mainstream moved over and glamour became every-day, Holly found himself having to work that much harder to be different. 'The whole point was the outrage of it. Not to be like them. I was a complete exhibitionist and ego maniac. That's the only way I can resolve it in my mind. Because I hardly think I would have been sophisticated enough at fourteen to have formulated a kind of "I'm queer and I'm here" philosophy. Perhaps it was the lack of attention that I felt at home.'

Raised round the corner from Penny Lane, Holly had the good fortune to be brought up in one of this country's more homo-friendly cities, Liverpool. ('There's a wonderful bohemian aspect to Liverpool which is a throwback to the Sixties, but it also has an extremely sub-*Brookside* universe. There's a certain type of person that has a very macho, thick-as-pig-shit attitude to gay men as well.') Punk seemed to provide a haven for more open-minded, if not like, minded souls, and in the late Seventies he moved into the music scene. But, as with his experience of Bowie boys, the scene's homo-philia only really existed on the surface. 'There was tolerance of the way I looked because they all wanted to look like that. All the straight boys started to cut their hair funny all of a sudden. But there was still homophobia going down. I liked the attitude, but it was all very lads together. Pete Shelley of the Buzzcocks was the only musician that I met that showed any sympathy for gay men.'

Finding Bowie boys, Liverpool and punk had all failed him, Holly ran away to London. He hitchhiked his way across the UK, plucked his eyebrows on the way, shaved his legs and then he was a she. Or something.

'Me and my friend Cathy moved to London when I was eighteen. It only lasted two weeks. But it was such an adventure. A bit later I used to travel down a lot with this boy Jake. We went to the Black Cap and the Coleherne, and those places held such an immense glamour for us. But then when I first came to London I thought it was glamorous to get the tube. It was like "Wow isn't this fab?" We weren't exactly hicks, we were more sophisticated than a lot of people are at our age, but it was exciting seeing these rather masculine-looking men in leather. And me and Jake started wearing leather caps and leather this and leather that.

'The S&M was a uniform. It was another kind of dressing up. Punk had become mainstream and I never really was a punk anyway. I didn't actually like many of the records. Tom of Finland was quite a big influence. And Mapplethorpe – that really powerful imagery. There's a sinister aspect to Mapplethorpe. But with Tom of Finland there's a kind of beauty and inner happiness with his figures, and that comfort with who you are was an extremely attractive trait. Perhaps it was the first glimmer of sexual happiness that I ever saw in the homosexual world.'

When Holly joined his first band, Liverpool's arty shock rockers Big In Japan (with Jayne Casey and the KLF's Bill Drummond), they were more perv rock than punk rock ('I was obsessed with William Burroughs at that time. I thought I was a Wild Boy. Andy Warhol and Lou Reed and Holly Woodlawn and Candy Darling. They were the stars in my imagination.') When they split up due to ego differences, Holly formed a band with three straight lads he'd bumped into in Virgin Records. And with a name nicked from Guy Peellaert's *Rock Dreams,* Frankie Goes To Hollywood were

born. At an early gig an old friend of Holly's, the newly mous-
tachioed Paul Rutherford was so impressed he climbed up on stage
to join them and never left.

Liverpool was the land of a thousand bands. Holly thought
the only way to get noticed was to outperv them all. 'We did it to
attract record company interest in London. I knew that it had to be
more than Bow Wow Wow had just been, and the only way you
could do it was by thrusting not only flamboyant or ferocious
homosexuality but the whole lifestyle that went with it in people's
faces. That was the kind of thing it needed to get A&R men to sit up
and notice.'

Frankie formed during the Gender Bender boom, which was
by and large cautiously sexless. Frankie were the ones who put the
sex back into homosexuality, though Holly insists 'that wasn't really
our intention. Nothing so worthy. I'm not going to pretend that the
position I was in then was anything but selfish. I was never interested
in being politically correct like Jimmy Somerville was. My view of
"gay libbers" as we called them was that they were just ugly queens
who couldn't get laid. Between the ages of fourteen and twenty-four
all I was interested in was having a fabulous time, taking drugs and
having sex and going to Amsterdam.'

Frankie were also the first to say the unsayable, and to
declare what the Gender Benders had only hinted at. Holly and Paul,
the queen and the clone, were the first bona fide out gay pop stars.
This worried those who were still in the closet. Boy George, who at
that time was still claiming to prefer a cup of tea to cock, wrote an
open letter to *Record Mirror* attacking their 'Hilda Ogden type view
of homosexuality'. Claiming they were 'not educating people only
telling them being gay is like a four-letter word sprayed on a toilet
wall – cheap, disgusting and very childish'.

'I couldn't believe how we were attacked by Boy George as
soon as we stuck our heads out of the trench,' Holly remembers.
'Although I didn't express it at the time I was extremely upset. I
thought "what's wrong with her?" you know? She's had a couple of
hit records and we're just queens on the dole.' A year ago Boy
George told me it was the likes of the Frankies that made him stop
faffing around and come out. But at the time he clearly felt threatened. 'Of course,' Holly says, 'I understand that now, but at the time

I didn't realize what it was. Now I know George is well adjusted to all of that and will be the first person to admit that he was slightly hypocritical over that situation.'

People might expect all the pop queens to stick together – but there's very little solidarity. One of the surprises of the book is how Paul Rutherford always sided with 'the lads' against Holly. 'That was a real illusion though, "the lads" and "the queers". That was a media invention. And it was encouraged for a while by ZTT as part of the unfolding soap opera of Frankie Goes To Hollywood. Paul found it difficult to play second fiddle in the group and that affected our relationship, unfortunately – perhaps he hoped that if I left the group then he would replace me.'

I always thought the lads were overcompensating – having to assert their heterosexuality as initially people presumed they were gay as well. 'They were quite macho. But they were nice lads who were thrust upon this high-pressure situation where people thought they were gods all of a sudden. And they were just like lads on a council apprenticeship. That's why they all went off the rails for a bit. I mean I'd been off the rails since I was fourteen.'

Things weren't helped by the group's somewhat fraught relationship with their record company. ZTT had been formed by producer Trevor Horn in association with music journalist Paul Morley. Many assumed Frankie were mere puppets, which pleased Horn and Morley no end. 'They were just out to make a name for themselves, exactly the same as I was. I don't think it was merely exploitative. ZTT didn't have to tell me or Paul to play up our homosexuality. There was no need for that. But Paul Morley wasn't interested in promoting the band. You see we'd presented this image to him of this outrageous gay rock band that wanted to be a dance band, but he had his own agenda completely. His agenda was to publicize ZTT and Paul Morley.'

Despite Morley's claim to be the band's *auteur provocateur*, even he couldn't have hoped for a gift like the Frankie ban. Holly remembers he actually 'felt very disappointed' when he heard the news. 'I thought our lovely beautiful pearl of success had been tainted with a kind of negativity. That was for a moment. And then I thought "Oh fab! It's much more romantic now." What I couldn't understand was that it had been played about a hundred times on the radio. And I thought they can't get us because I only use the word "come" in the lyric, and it's only the imagined context of what the word means that is perhaps filth. I really did think it would slip through the net.'

It looked like Frankie were anticipating a backlash and had started to tidy up their act. I seem to remember on their first *Top of the Pops* appearance, just before the ban, they'd already ditched the leather and perv gear for Yamomoto suits. But Holly corrects me. 'No, that's not true. Our first *Top of the Pops* appearance wasn't Yamomoto suits. It was borrowed leather trousers and borrowed leather jackets and hired Moss Bros suits. It wasn't Yohji Yamomoto until mid '84. But I was genuinely sick of wearing leather knickers, I can tell you. Have you ever gone on stage in a pair of leather knickers? It ain't easy. It might be for the fabulous muscle boys we see in gay clubs today. But you had to have quite a bit of balls to do it in them days. So I was dying not to wear leather knickers. We'd done that.'

Sweaty pants aside, being a queer cause célèbre 'was kind of wonderful. It was a very exciting and optimistic time anyway, 1984. Not just for me but for a lot of people. It just seemed anything was possible. It was that feeling of being on a surf board in the sunshine. There was a whole positivity vibe that was coming out of the gay clubs. Records like (Sharon Redd's) 'In The Name Of Love' and 'Beat The Street', all this kind of ebullience and celebration of life.'

1984 was also a time of hard times, of the sort of strife and conflict typified by the miners' strike. But Holly remembers the gay scene as pursuing its own agenda. 'It was reaching a peak of post-Seventies San Francisco celebration. Gay men weren't suffering, they had good jobs and were making money and they were partying. It was the Thatcherite dream in a sense.'

But were people partying so hard because they knew that it might soon be over? Holly, for one, was unaware of the black cloud that was looming on the horizon. 'I wasn't the sort of person to read *Capital Gay*. I know there was an attempt in the gay media to highlight things like this new gay cancer or whatever they called it in those days. But I was more interested in where the next MDA was coming from or what to wear next Saturday night to really pay attention. I didn't see anything threatening on the horizon ... oh, perhaps I did. I remember one night my gay mother and father took me to Heaven and I had this bizarre LSD experience where I saw Heaven as this Babylonian nightmare slave market and I was being brought down there and they were trying to sell me in this kind of sinister world. I never took a chemical drug again after that.'

You use the line in your book: 'I didn't want the tolerance of bigots.' Did you feel like a folk hero, and were you aware that some of it was quite superficial? That, like your run-in with the Bowie boys, liking a gay star doesn't always equate with liking gay men. 'Yeah, but for a while I was completely swept along by it all and thought I was living this wonderful gifted starlit life. I thought it was a good thing that people liked the divine cheek and sheer arrogance of that record. That was great. Although it could have turned into a football chant as well. The fact that it had become mainstream and was number one shocked me, actually. 'Cause it was all of a sudden "Oh dear it's tupperware now". Although it wasn't tupperware, it was black rubberware.'

You also say you felt straight journalists were making too big an issue of your homosexuality?

'Well that's how I felt then. I didn't really want to be a preacher for gay rights. And I felt I didn't want to set myself up as a spokesperson. I remember talking to other gay people about it and none of them had any answers. Some would say "play it down, play it down". Some would criticize and say we weren't waving banners enough. It was a difficult course to travel. And it was territory that hadn't really been sailed before. We weren't particularly well equipped at twenty-four-years-old to handle it. Although we're still here. Do you know what I mean?'

After 'Relax', Frankie left the sex wars for the Cold War. 'Two Tribes' spent nine weeks at number one in the summer of 1984. 'Relax' dutifully climbed back up the charts to snuggle up next to it at number two. They also sold a quarter of a million t-shirts and got two other number ones with 'The Power Of Love' single and the *Welcome to the Pleasuredome* album. The world was their lobster. Then it all started to go horribly wrong. A second album, *Liverpool*, was made without Trevor Horn, and Holly acquiesced to the lads' demand to make a rock album. The band began to look about as appetizing as yesterday's sperm and promptly fell apart. In the meantime Holly had fallen in love with a German man called Wolfgang Kuhle. Wolfgang was presented as Holly's Yoko Ono – a foreign agent who hastened the band's demise.

'There's definitely hostility to the existence of a gay partner in a person's life, and he's had to take a hell of a lot for being the partner of a gay man who's lived part of his life in the media. And also for being the manager of a gay singer. I wouldn't be here speaking to you now if it wasn't for him. I would have died several years ago if I'd continued the course of my life that I was leading. Wolfgang's support and the guidance that he's given to me has been really important. And it's always underplayed by other people. Or they make excuses, they say "Oh, that person has taken you away from us." Because you see before I had this relationship with Wolfgang I was at everyone's disposal. I was there to work for the band and they couldn't really handle that. And the fact that Wolfgang's German – the racism that brings out in British people really is quite incredible.'

After a ground-breaking court case against ZTT, Holly was freed to pursue a solo career. Going 'ha, ha, ha' in the face of his detractors he scored a number one album in 1989 with *Blast*, but when the follow up, *Dreams That Money Can't Buy*, died a death, Holly decided to step off pop's merry-go-round. Then in November 1991, the same week that Freddie Mercury died, Holly was told he was HIV-positive.

'From the beginning, the diagnosis I was given was actually an AIDS diagnosis. And seeing pictures of Freddie Mercury on the cover of the papers looking emaciated, that was really vile. Just knowing that the tabloid journalists were going to wait until they got a really bad picture of me and print the story anyway. And I didn't want it to come out in a negative way like that. Because there's been enough of that kind of badgering, let's face it. But I was also scared, I'd read stories where gay men's flats had been burned to the ground. Horror stories. I didn't know how people were going to react.'

So in April 1993, in a lengthy interview with *The Times*, Holly came out a second time. 'Kenny Everett was forced out several days before I made my announcement and that kind of defused the media attention slightly, which was perhaps a good thing. I'd done the interview a good week before, and I'd been talking about doing it for a year. I had it set up but I was absolutely petrified. I thought women would grab their children and run to the other side of the road.

'My fears were on the whole unfounded. It was a huge relief. But it was like a pressure cooker exploding and I went off my head again for a while. Three months after the announcement I was really aggressive. Imagine all this pent-up anger and shit in a pressure cooker for sixteen months, not being able to talk about it to your friends. And then it just comes out. I wasn't a particularly pleasant person to be around at that time.'

You've said that your being out in Frankie was selfish, was this more public-spirited?

'Well it was Derek (Jarman) really. I've always been a huge fan of his and he just made me feel ashamed that I hadn't already made the announcement and that I was farting about in my own psychological suffering when I could have been communicating ideas. And apart from that there was Wolfgang saying to me every day "You've got to tell them, you've got to tell them . . . " Because he knew that it would come out in a negative way eventually if I didn't and that I'd feel much better. And he believed that there was nothing to be ashamed of in my condition, and that was part of my struggle, coming to terms with what I'd discovered about myself.'

Do you think there's some parallel between what you did in 1984 and what you did in 1993? Has this country moved on at all, or did we just take one step forwards and one step back?

'This country is retarded, I'm afraid. I only feel like that because of the vote on the age of consent. It's absolutely outrageous how we can openly just trail along behind the rest of the world and feel proud of that.'

Do you think this country's fucked-upness about sex was a factor in Frankie's rise?

'Yeah. It couldn't have happened in Germany, could it? Cause it would have been "Oh so what?" It did happen but it didn't happen in the same shock-horror *News of the World* kind of way. They just got off on the music and the vibe and on what we wore.'

You said as a child you craved attention, but once you'd got it you walked out of the limelight. Was it really that ghastly?

'It was just the superficiality of it all that got to me. The way people reacted to the fame and to the money it generated made me quite cynical. So there was that and there was the business problems. I started to withdraw.

'And it was also the advent of AIDS and HIV infection. All of a sudden it was no longer fashionable to be a gay man. It's been a strange position for me because the first record company I was involved with actively wanted to exploit my homosexuality and the second wanted to downplay my homosexuality. They didn't want Elton John, they wanted Robert Palmer! Two extremes really. I also wanted to make *Blast* a pop record and some people saw it as me selling out. Wanting to make a record that wasn't banned, that wasn't controversial.'

The Times' sister paper *The Sun* hijacked the HIV story, and trailed it with the line 'for the man who boasted of the joys of promiscuous gay sex it was the ultimate punishment'. Did you expect all that 'wages of sin' crap?

'It was a bit like that, wasn't it? I remember being asked about that in about 1985 in Japan. Someone asked me "Aren't you afraid of getting AIDS?" And I did a freak on this poor Japanese woman. My psychology and the way it was set up at the time couldn't quite cope with that question. There was a lot of denial going on in my life.

'But yes, I knew that was going to happen. That was one of the things that was said to me in my very first counselling appointment at the clinic. There I was sitting there with this big fear and the health advisor said: "Oh they're gonna say the propagator of gay promiscuity has now got his just desserts." Which I don't think really was the right way to go about counselling me when I'd just received that news. But there is a branch of counselling that believes we must voice our greatest fears immediately and get them out into the open.'

You stop the book at the point you receive your diagnosis – saying it's too soon to consider your feelings ...

'Well, look at my position. I started to write the book as a way to cope with the diagnosis and hopefully to release a lot of the shit that I had lying around. The negative ideas and the bitterness and the way that I felt treated by the world. So if I'd have wanted to deal with the last eighteen months of me sitting on me arse waiting to die ... 'cause that's what I felt. "I've got six months to live I'd better write me memoirs quick." I didn't want to re-examine that. Maybe I'll do it in the future.

'I'm not saying I completely feel pure now. Or clean, or that all my problems are resolved. They're not, you know? I'm as imperfect as the next person. But there is the sense that some things are better out than in. Definitely.'

Gay Times, April 1994

Chapter thirty-four

The Rhythm Divine: Jon Savage and Disco

WE are all into dance music nowadays. Arms that once shunned it now embrace it. It's enjoying an even greater popularity than it did during the Disco boom of the late Seventies. But now it has something it never had back then – 'credibility'. Today the rock snobs and the pop snoots want to cut a rug with the rest of us.

The general public's fondness for dance music has constantly waxed and waned. But for gay men it has always been a constant. There's a clear dialectic relationship between the two groups, with dance moving forward as we move from the margins to the mainstream and back again. We set the trend with Motown, Northern Soul, Philly, Disco, Eurobeat, Hi-NRG and House and *they* assimilate and popularize them.

Now that the ball is in their court, for many it becomes necessary to Stalinize dance's past. The integral role that gay men have had in the music's development is denied. It would be criminal to let them get away with this, not least because it is one of the few things that we can point to and declare 'ours'. For twenty years it has been the soundtrack to our lives and we have used it to help shape a separate and specific gay identity. Since the late Seventies the disco has been the main focus for gay life, the closest thing many of us get to a genuine feeling of community.

Next month Channel Four are showing a programme that's going to upset rather a lot of people. *The Rhythm Divine*, made by Paul Oremland, Kevin Sampson, Jon Savage and Sarah Stinchombe, is a history of dance music that tells the truth. It is also a total hoot, and packed with what Jon Savage calls 'Squeal value'. Eartha Kitt, Sylvester, Village People, Bananarama, Deee-lite ... squeal, squeal, squeal, squeal, *squeal* ...

Jon explained to me how the documentary came about.

'Two years ago I made an item for *Out on Tuesday* called *Disco's Revenge,* the point of which was very explicitly within a gay series to talk about the gay roots of Disco and specifically House music and to make a polemic out of it. It ended with Frankie Knuckles saying "Gay people have always set the standard in popular culture. End of story" ... "Eat shit!" effectively.

'We only had a twenty-five minute slot and we uncovered much more footage than we could use, and had such a great time doing it that we decided to expand it into a more general history of Disco music. In a way I think it's a gay programme in the best sense, in that it shows in the wider sense how gay people inform mainstream styles and how mainstream styles then take over and change something that has started in gay culture. So the gay stuff gets mentioned because it's there. You can't ignore it.'

I wondered if it would be true that the programme can be made now, or rather be taken notice of, only because they are currently on dance's side. So now we are *allowed* to reassess the Seventies and have a good old rummage through its wardrobe and its record collection. Jon gives a somewhat maudlin pout and looks to the floor for inspiration.

'I don't really have a problem with popular culture mining the Seventies because basically popular culture mines everything. It's such an endemic process that the thing to do is enjoy it and roll with it. The fact is that a lot of the people we interviewed in America just did have a fabulous time in the Seventies. It was a time when, as far as they were concerned, it was a good time to be gay and gay people were strong, and to some extent you see that going into popular culture with the Village People being the most obvious example. Now you could argue a lot about whether or not it's a good thing to have 'YMCA' at number one ... '

Oh alright then. There was a problem with a lot of ' gay disco music' in that it was only gay to gay people. The Village People for instance leapt back in the closet at the first sniff of a hit. I'm wondering if we get anything out of the music beyond pleasure?

'Well all that stuff was '78, '79 . . . a very different world, and what has happened in the last eleven years hadn't happened. I think it's difficult, but we shouldn't judge the products of the past too much by what has gone on since.

'Obviously you can point at the Village People and say "Well they did that dreadful film with Valerie Perrine", but you can say for whatever it's worth that they did occur at a point when gay people were, or seemed to be, more powerful and perhaps more tolerated within society. I think even the difference between 'YMCA' and *Can't Stop The Music* is quite big. *Can't Stop The Music* was a flop. By the time the film was made disco was dead.

' I don't think we can underestimate the simple impact of gay visibility. Particularly then. You didn't get that before . . . except with those pretty-boy pop stars. The Village People weren't overtly gay but it was obvious pretty much, because even the heterosexuals who saw them must have said "What the fuck are they wearing those clothes for?" It's a very, very stylized and unreal image but . . .'

And a somewhat problematic image. There are always some problems when straight people take something that was once ours, like Disco, to their hearts.

'In popular culture there's always this trade-off between gay visibility and commercial assimilation of a previously deviant sub-culture. It's a complicated trade-off because it's not just simple exploitation and on the other hand it's not just simple pride being expressed. But I think a lot of people understand that and deal with it how they will. Frankie Knuckles and Jimmy Somerville are very overtly gay and will not change that or modify their opinions within the music industry.'

How aware do you think the music industry is of a gay audience?

'There are certainly a few intelligent people in the music industry who are, like Colin Bell at London Records. They'll promote a record in stages, so if you release a Bananarama record, a core audience like a gay audience will rush out and put the record in at number thirty-seven. And then they can boost it and make it cross over. I find it very interesting that there is acknowledgement of gay people buying Disco, but there is no acknowledgement of gay people buying rock. So within Disco terms if you're making a gay programme, people in record companies will give you stuff 'cause they recognize that a gay audience buys the records. When you're dealing with rock like the programme in the last *Out on Tuesday* series about punk nobody wants to know because rock is much more "heterosexual". Gay people *"don't buy rock."'*

There's a germ of truth in there, though. Dance music has been very important to us. It's meant something to us that rock music hasn't.

'Yes, basically dance music is community, togetherness and a lot of rock music, listening to it is very atomized. The archetypal kind of rock thing is The Smiths and people listening in their bedrooms. Coming together to see concerts but not really linking up to the extent that the dance community does. The gay community became visible and was able to some extent to find itself through dancing because of the nature of the music. Its whole rhetoric, the way it works, is about community.'

The programme ends with bands like The Farm and Happy Mondays. The indie dance scene. What do you think of those attempts to fuse dance and rock?

'With a lot of that stuff I like the music but I have a problem as it's very macho. I greatly relish that period '83, '84 where you had androgyny. Soft Cell, Boy George . . . a very different image to that traditional lads down the pub masculinity.'

Surely that's necessitated by their knowledge that they are engaging in something as historically 'unmanly' as making dance music?

'Yes there's obviously some disavowal going on somewhere . . . '

For me, though, that's the exciting thing about Disco, about pop music really. That it *is* unmanly.

'It's the business of pop to be unmanly. Because English society is so stratified and palsied, pop is an arena where sexuality and gender can be discussed. Which you just don't get in other places.

'It's why English pop in particular is so completely riddled with camp. I mean why did I thrill when I saw The Kinks in 1964 and the bass player had such long hair that I thought he was a girl?

I thought that was great just as I thought it was great when Marc Almond minced all over *Top of the Pops* with 'Tainted Love'. That's kind of thrilling.'

And so, if I may say so, is *The Rhythm Divine.*

Gay Times, January 1991

Chapter thirty-five

Seriously:
Pet Shop Boys

LAST night I had this really strange dream. French and Saunders were doing the Pet Shop Boys as one of their piss takes of pop stars on *Star Test*. Jennifer Saunders was an aloof and queeny Neil Tennant, and Dawn French was an enthusiastic but dim Chris Lowe. When it gets to the final round where they have to choose the words on the screen that they think best describe themselves, they're having a little trouble.

They take turns to hover a hand over the screen. Jennifer Tennant is thinking really hard. Dawn Lowe looks like it's all too much for his tiny brain to cope with. After a few minutes Jennifer Tennant admits defeat.

'Well, what on earth are we?'
(Pause of Samuel Beckett-type proportions)
'We're the Pet Shop Boys, Neil, ... '

The new Pet Shop Boys' album is called *Very*. As with *Please* and *Actually* the joke will be lost on most people, but the likes of you and me will think it's *very* funny and *very* Pet Shop Boys – whatever that means.

The duo collect labels the way lesser groups collect gold discs. I can't think of anyone else that people have tried to hammer into as many different pigeonholes at once. Usually the line goes something like – 'Ooh those Pet Shop Boys, they're ever so post-modern and clever and camp and ironic, aren't they?'

But are they?

I see us in the tradition of Joe Orton and Noël Coward, in
that we are serious, comic, light-hearted, sentimental and
brittle, all at the same time.
Neil Tennant

... and then in my dream Jennifer Tennant presses the
buttons marked 'serious' and 'comic' and 'light-hearted' and 'senti-
mental' and 'brittle'. All at the same time! The show cuts away to a
video of the Pet Shop Boys playing a storming Hi-NRG version of
'There Are Bad Times Just Around The Corner'. But in this clip Joe
Orton and Noël Coward are the Pet Shop Boys. When we return to
the studio the computer asks Jennifer Tennant: 'Didn't Coward and
Orton have something else in common?'
'Drama?'
'You're getting warm,' the computer replies helpfully ...

Actually, *Very* is a bit of a disappointment. Queens like me who'd
fallen in love with *Behaviour* and wept along with its electro ballads
on an almost daily basis may find it all a bit too up-beat and up-
tempo. It's as jolly as *Behaviour* was sad. Strangely, the only track
that makes you want to go wibble is 'To Speak Is A Sin' – 'strangely',
because it seems to be little more than an update of 'Ballad Of The
Sad Young Men'. The song's set in a bar where some strangers in the
night are exchanging glances; 'you look first then stare and once in a
while a smile if you dare ... ' Nonetheless it's curiously affecting,
though the real sadness is that there's anyone who still thinks gay
bars are like this.

I'm assuming that the bar is gay, though the word isn't
mentioned in the lyrics. But with the Pet Shop Boys there's always a
lot of things left unsaid. We fill in the gaps and invariably jump to
the right conclusions, just as straights often jump to the wrong ones.
Their songs mean different things to us, and that's why they've
always meant more to us. For although the Pet Shop Boys are
extremely popular they've been much misunderstood.

I always maintain that we're completely misunderstood
anyway. People often say "it's wonderful it's so camp",
and I just smile politely because I'm a bit disappointed
really because it wasn't meant to be camp. Actually real

camp is when something is totally sincere. There's no cynicism or trying to be clever.
Neil Tennant

... Dawn Lowe smiles and presses the words 'misunderstood' and 'disappointed' and 'sincere'.

The computer asks why they haven't pressed 'camp'.

'We're having enough trouble trying to define ourselves,' Jennifer Tennant barks back. 'If it was beyond Susan Sontag I'm sure it's beyond me.'

'Going to Sarajevo and putting on a production of *Waiting For Godot* – that's camp!' Dawn Lowe interjects.

'All the more so as she's no idea how camp that actually is. It's much easier to name things that are camp than it is to define it. Actually, even in "Notes On Camp" Sontag resorted to making a list. *King Kong*, Firbank novels, feather boas.'

Cut to scratchy old black and white film of Christopher Isherwood reading from *The World In The Evening*: 'You see high camp always has an underlying seriousness. You can't camp about something you don't take seriously. You're not making fun of it. You're making fun out of it. You're expressing what's basically serious to you in terms of fun and artifice and elegance.'

Back in the studio Jennifer Tennant presses 'fun' and 'artifice' and 'elegance'. 'I always liked his Berlin novels,' he says, 'and I adored *Cabaret*. Hence Liza Minnelli ... '

You have a certain quality that really is unique,
expressing with such irony although your voice is so weak,
but it doesn't really matter 'cause the music is so loud.

Pet Shop Boys, 'Yesterday When I Was Mad'

'Yesterday When I Was Mad', one of the songs on the new album, has Neil singing of how they are often damned by faint praise. In the above chorus he mocks the most common misapprehension about the duo – that they are ironic. Sorry – 'ironic'.

Part of the problem is that Neil Tennant *is* clever (Chris Lowe's a bright young thing too but affects a Warholesque 'Gee, I don't know' air and generally comes on like the simple Northern lad he so clearly isn't), and brains are a pretty rare commodity in pop.

This acts as a distancing mechanism which means that liking the Pet Shop Boys was never quite the same as liking Kylie or Take That or any of the other 'rubbish' in the charts. They became 'the pop group it's alright to like'.

A band started by a man like him – the former assistant editor of *Smash Hits* and all – could be seen as just a contrived exercise in manipulating the pop process. If they recorded a Village People number it was just a great camp statement. And if Chris said he really liked the lyrics to 'I Should Be So Lucky' he was only being ironic. It's alright, it's not meant to be taken seriously.

Except it was.

... they don't press 'ironic' ...

These days the idea of a pop group embracing post-modernism is no longer a novelty. Even U2 have given up authenticity and sincerity for artifice and irony. But I guess that's what happens when you hang around Brian Eno for too long. There's a certain amount of overlap between camp and post-modernism and irony – seeing everything in quotation marks, the love of playfulness – so much so that Andy Medhurst has suggested post-modernism is merely camp with A levels. But they're not the same thing.

The Pet Shop Boys were perfectly placed to be seen as a thoroughly post-modern pop group. Appearing as they did in the late Eighties – a time when I saw the worst minds of my generation destroyed by post-modernism. But it was more than just a matter of timing. If post-modernism was the great leveller in culture, they've attempted this in pop, continually refusing to show reverence to the rock canon: be it in turning the Elvis Presley 'classic' 'Always On My Mind' into a throbbing House anthem (with cowbells on!), or by giving U2's 'Where The Streets Have No Name' an equivalence with Boystown Gang's 'Can't Take My Eyes Off You'.

The thing was, many thought the joke in the latter was on Boystown Gang rather than U2.

... We cut away to a clip from U2's *Zooropa TV* film. Bono is dressed in his golden Elvis suit and crooning a few lines of 'Can't Help Falling In Love' before launching into 'Where The Streets Have No Name'. All this is disrupted by fast cutaways to Susan Sontag saying 'the ultimate camp statement is "it's good because it's awful'", a drunken student dancing to 'I Should Be So Lucky' and rasping out 'it's so crap it's *brilliant*', Neil Tennant saying 'I always maintain we're completely misunderstood anyway', and finally a scene from Coward's *Private Lives:* Elyot says to Amanda, 'Nasty, insistent little tune'. Amanda replies curtly: 'Extraordinary how potent cheap music is'.

Back in the studio Jennifer Tennant has a satisfied look on his face. He doesn't press 'post-modern'.

'For many people, camp is the same as tacky or kitsch but I don't think they are really. Being camp isn't just being a snob. "Kitsch implies a recognition of high aesthetic values" – Roland Barthes.'

Dawn Lowe looks unimpressed.

' "Eat my shorts!" – Bart Simpson.' . . .

The Pet Shop Boys hadn't come to bury pop, but to praise it. Like Noel Coward, Neil Tennant knows the potency of cheap music; 'pop music,' he's argued, 'is rubbish in a good way.' Long before Björn Again had become a permanent fixture at Freshers' Balls, Neil was claiming that Abba were the best songwriters of the Seventies (he's said 'Knowing Me Knowing You' came from 'their Ingmar Bergman period'). However much Neil Tennant loved artifice, most of what he said and sang wasn't a sneer but utterly sincere.

It's bizarre how readily people saw some ironic intent when you consider what a rare commodity irony had previously been in pop. Everything used to be taken at face value ('*Hooray!* Randy Newman hates short people too!'). The Pet Shop Boys were even victims of this literal approach themselves. When they released their first single 'Opportunities (Let's Make Lots Of Money)' they were written off in some quarters as Thatcherites. Two years later some still rushed to judge 'Shopping' as celebration rather than critique. And many still labour under the misapprehension that the 'girls' in 'West End Girls' were really, well, girls.

But even before everyone discovered how clever and post-modern the Pet Shop Boys were being, when they weren't yet the darlings of the music press and the sort of dim people who only like 'intelligent' music, straights were already claiming that they alone knew what the pair *really* meant. Their name was leapt upon as being a gay slang phrase for gerbilophiles. It wasn't (if the phrase existed at all it was an exceedingly obscure piece of American gay slang for S&M rent), but the story was irresistible and gossip soon became gospel. In interviews Neil would have the 'evidence' put to him, he'd look stunned and say he didn't know this when they chose the name, and – hey bingo! – here was the 'proof' that the Pet Shop Boys had *something to hide*.

A whispering campaign began in the straight press claiming that the Pet Shop Boys weren't telling us the whole truth – and not just about their name. Things came to a head with an interview in the *NME* at the end of 1986. The boys were given the cover ('Queen's Award for Industry' – geddit?), and the paper did something the straight press had been doing for years before we discovered it. It tried to out them: 'In anticipation of denials-a-go-go let's marshal the evidence ... studied ambiguity ... hamsters up your bum ... homoerotic possibilities ... ' It even wondered 'are they lovers?' – something that's never crossed the minds of any queens I know, but is automatically assumed by your average hetero hack.

But there were no 'denials-a-go-go'. Just Neil completely unflustered replying quite matter-of-factly: 'We've never said anything about our sex lives to the newspapers or to magazines and we don't intend to – and that's not a clever ploy to appear mysterious – although if it has that effect I don't mind'.

Despite his unashamed love of pop, Neil refuses to allow himself to be just another pop star. 'If you decide you want to be a star, you have to be prepared to share your private life with the public ... however if you decide you don't want to be seen as a star there are loads of things you don't do. You don't do lots of interviews, you don't do lots of cosmetic photo shoots for *My Guy* or whatever, you don't do glamorous videos, and you definitely don't talk about your private life.'

'Being in a pop group isn't about being presented as two real people. It's about being the Pet Shop Boys ... what we do in private doesn't matter. Only the songs,' Neil's said, though I'm not sure he believes it. He talks too much about how the public property of the songs are personal statements: 'Obviously people are going to look at our songs and read this or that into them. Some of them are quite direct, they're written from experience so it's quite embarrassing really. But the end result of people just speculating about things is far more accurate than them thinking one thing or another. I just don't know why people want to bracket you in one way or another. It's not what I want.'

To their credit though the Pet Shop Boys still readily talk about the things that matter to them, be it gay clubs, gay disco, AIDS or Clause 28 (they were the only pop group to play *Before The Act*). And if they won't put the fact of their sex/love/private lives on record, they don't seem to mind putting it on their records.

... Jennifer Tennant arches an eyebrow and says wryly, 'I'm surprised you didn't put "animal lovers" on there,' before smiling to himself and pressing both 'self-mocking' and 'private'. He deliberates for a while and then a little reluctantly pushes the one marked 'pop star' ...

> When we started ten years ago what we wanted to do was make records that would be regarded as dance music, probably Hi-NRG dance music as it was then, and we were trying to marry that with traditional songwriting where the lyrics are interesting and make some kind of personal statement.
> Neil Tennant

When they first set out the Pet Shop Boys' dream (soon realized) was to make a record with Bobby O and have it available on the import rack in Record Shack. Since then their music's been evidence of a long love affair with 'gay disco' – a term Neil uses. They make a kind of sophisticated Hi-NRG. Like Jimmy Somerville they've sometimes had to fall back on the cover version to secure hits. They share much the same points of reference, but the Pet Shop Boys have been far more imaginative in their choices, plundering the likes of Sterling Void, Stephen Sondheim, Yvonne Elliman, Village People and Boystown Gang.

> Many of the songs on *Please* are about running away. They're about someone brought up in a middle-class background in Newcastle, who doesn't want to have a normal job, who doesn't want to get pinned down to

bourgeois values, even though he could do that quite
successfully and quite easily.
Neil Tennant

... in quick succession, Jennifer Tennant punches first 'English',
then 'middle class', and 'Northern' ...

Like Morrissey, Neil writes well about the North where he grew up
as a fey, bookish Fotherington-Thomas amidst a sea of Nigel Moles-
worths. Only Neil, unlike Morrissey, has since grown up and
escaped. He once conceded that calling them 'The Smiths you can
dance to' wasn't desperately inaccurate. They make dance music
that's suitable for bedsit listening; you can stay at home and listen to
songs about going out. Though their last album, *Behaviour* – a
collection of sweeping slowies about not going out – augured that
they might be turning into 'The Smiths you can't dance to' (or
something), *Very* sees them walking back to the dance floor once
more.

'English' is a word as often thrown at them as ironic, camp or
post-modern, but is far more fitting. Like The Kinks they have a
love–hate affair with England itself. Their disastrous movie *It
Couldn't Happen Here*, a sort of *Carry On Derek Jarman*, was a
nostalgic yearning for the old England destroyed by that nasty Mrs
Thatcher. But, unlike some, the Pet Shop Boys are still very much in
love with the modern world.

'English' is yet another of those words that has a number of
overlapping meanings. For many, 'Englishness' equals sexual
repression ('It's a, it's a, it's a sin') and reserve – you can hear the
latter in Tennant's delivery, for all his love of Disco he never raises
his voice like the divas do. It's sometimes a euphemism for gay
(particularly in the States), but it's more usually a synonym for fey or
unmanly – which they definitely are. Neil feels that this is the main
reason why they've failed to capitalize on their early success in
America: 'We just can't be a part of it. We're not a macho fantasy.
We're not a heterosexual beach fantasy. Our music isn't macho, it's
barely masculine.'

But when they're called 'English', people mean more than a
machismo deficiency. Above all, the Pet Shop Boys are English in the

sense that you know their records couldn't have been made by someone who'd come from anywhere else. Which is why Neil saying: 'I just don't know why people want to bracket you in one way or another' is bollocks, pure and simple. Pop groups come with brackets.

The music people like, the stuff that moves them most, is that which has sprung from the same mud they have. 'The gay community' may be a myth that only high ranking police officers talk of these days, but gay men do share an identity and a culture. Just like English people, Northern people and middle-class people do; we speak the same language, we like the same things. If Tennant will freely concede that the personal statements in his lyrics have been forged by his other identities – as English, Northern and middle-class – why does he down-play the other differences (and similarities) between people?

Neil knows that even musical taste can be a crucial signifier. 'In "Can You Forgive Her", that line, "you dance to Disco and you don't like rock", gives the idea that the girl sees the guy as a closet queen, and she thinks that if he dances to Disco he's not really a man and he hasn't faced up to this.'

It's one of music's great clichés that it has some universal appeal, but the whole point of rock and roll was that not everyone wanted to listen to records that were aimed at Mr and Mrs Nice White Middle-Class Person. Even that old chestnut 'Gor blimey, everyone falls in love don't they?' is patently piffle – gay men's experience of love is different from heterosexuals'. Which is why so many of us find Tennant's songs so affecting. The three most over-used words in pop's vocabulary 'I love you' are used a lot by Neil but in an unusual way. He always distresses his desire: 'I thought I loved you but I'm not sure now', 'I could leave you, say goodbye, I could love you if I tried', 'I may not always love you, you may not always care', 'If I didn't love you I would look around for someone else', 'I love you, you pay my rent', 'All I wanted to say was that I love you but you tell me now that you don't believe it's true'. The new album queers the pitch rather by containing a love song with no such catches, but the title admits 'I Wouldn't Normally Do This Kind Of Thing'. Tennant writes bitter-sweet love songs – passionate yet worldly, romantic yet realistic, and hampered by insecurity, jealousy and doubt. Love isn't the answer to all your problems, it's just more problems. Not that that stops you from wanting it any the less.

And while gay men used to be able to content themselves with the fact that, though lovers may come and go, our friends would always be with us, even that is no longer a certainty these days. 'Being Boring', 'It Couldn't Happen Here', 'Hit Music' and the new song 'Dreaming Of The Queen' are about how we've coped with AIDS, and how sometimes we can't cope. When singing of AIDS, Tennant sounds bitter, bewildered, desolate but never simply angry. Pet Shop Boys are grace under pressure.

> There are two very distinct ways that people consume pop music. Your laddish music you react to like "isn't it great they're just like us". And then there's what I call aspirational music, which is "oh, I wish I was like that". I think to a certain extent our music is aspirational.
> Neil Tennant

> . . . Jennifer Tennant presses 'aspirational' . . .

This sounds suspiciously like common sense, but doesn't stand up to scrutiny. Most fandom embraces both positions – the joy of the Pet Shop Boys for most queens is that Neil seems 'just like us'. Only a lot of us often wish he was a little more like us.

Christmas 1985. I am 17 going on 18. This girl I know, Tessa, has taken me to Heaven. It's my first time in a gay club, but she's a bit of an old hand. Her big sister's a lesbian you see, and looking back I think the whole thing was probably her sister's idea ('I know what that boy needs'). I spent about six days worrying about what to wear and four hours trying to get my Morrissey quiff just right. I was a bit clueless and a bit disappointed by it all. The men didn't look like what I thought gay men looked like, so I kidded myself it must have been a straight night – even though Tessa was just about the only woman in the place. And I didn't think too much of the music. I didn't like dance music then and only recognized one song all night. That new band that were in the charts. Pet Shop Boys.

October 1991, and I'm in Heaven again, literally and phys-ically. It's six years on and I've been out on the scene for four of them. I'm happy these days. Much happier than I ever thought I could be when I was 17. Pet Shop Boys are my favourite band (I can't remember the last time I played a Smiths' record) and they're playing here tonight. The place is going predictably mad. One queen's holding up a piece of file paper with 'I love Neil' written on it in biro. The rest of us are just screaming our tits off. It's not Christmas this time, but it feels like Santa Claus has finally come to town. Or come home.

After frittering away my adolescence listening to self-pitying guitar groups, the Pet Shop Boys made more sense as I grew older. And I only really fell in love with them after I'd come out on the scene six years ago. Their music seems a far more accurate reflection of the world I move in now – the things that I care about and the things I no longer care about. I don't believe there's anyone who writes so well about the way gay men live their lives now.

By 'now' I mean the late Eighties and early Nineties. The Pet Shop Boys were the archetypal Eighties band. But archetypal *late* Eighties. The first half of that decade gave us Gender Benders and Boy George and Frankie and Bronski Beat. And then? Nothing. The Pet Shop Boys appeared at the end of 1985, just as the party was over. AIDS had hit in a big way and the backlash had begun. The Pet Shop Boys were products of a period as much as of a culture – when the boys who begged to be bracketed gave way to a New Discretion.

... so Jennifer Tennant presses 'Eighties' and quick as a flash Dawn Lowe presses 'Nineties'. One of them presses 'discreet' but it happens too quickly for me to figure out if it was Tennant or Lowe.

The words that they think best describe themselves are 'serious', 'comic', 'light-hearted', 'brittle', 'misunderstood', 'disappointed', 'sincere', 'fun', 'artifice', 'elegance', 'self mocking', 'private', 'pop star', 'English', 'middle-class', 'Northern', 'aspirational', 'Eighties', 'Nineties' and 'discreet'. They rejected 'clever', 'camp', 'post-modern' and 'ironic'.

Then the computer says what she always says at the end of *Star Test*; 'If we think you've been honest we'll play your new video, but if we think you've been dishonest we'll play a video by someone else.'

211: *Seriously: Pet Shop Boys*

As the credits roll we hear the opening strains of 'Go West'. But I can't quite make out if it's the Village People's or the Pet Shop Boys' version ...

Gay Times, October 1993

Chapter thirty-six

This Charming Man: Gene

RIGHT then Martin, I want you to relax and tell me all about your childhood.

'I was brought up in a village eight miles outside Cardiff. And when I was nine I moved to Watford – town of Hell! The whole of suburbia is. Even crossing your legs in public could equate to having your head kicked in.'

Was there more going wrong than just you crossing your legs?

'Well. I, yes, as a really ... my sexuality was developing ...'

Go on ...

'I was at an all boys' school, an ex-grammar school that had recently turned comprehensive. Watford Boys. It was a very "male" school and any degree of homosexuality was unthinkable and I somehow came out. I don't really remember.'

Try ...

'I just sort of started having like just sort of crushes on people and would tell my friends and it spread. I metaphorically stood on a table with a loudhailer at some point and cried it to the world. And I was the only person out of a thousand pupils that did that. It actually gained me a lot of friends – and the odd surprising wandering hand from rugby players. And it gained me a lot of trouble also. I was at a party once – I was far more effeminate than I am now and I became an obvious target and had to literally run for my life. I discovered the following day that a couple of my friends who'd stood up for me were both in hospital – one had a plank of wood which had been yanked from a fence with a nail sticking out of it hit across his back several times. Simply because I was asked by someone if I was gay and I didn't even say "yes" I just didn't deny it.'

Martin Rossiter is twenty-four now. And the one-time small-town boy has grown into a charming man. He's the singer in this year's 'best new band in Britain' – Gene. Things being as they are, by the time you read this, the Gene backlash will already be in full swing. Ignore it. It says more about our times than it does about his band. Gene will be knocked for a number of reasons. One, because 'they sound like The Smiths'. Which they do. A bit. But these days, everything reminds you of something else. It's a sign of rock's exhaustion, not Gene's. And it doesn't seem to have done Blur or Oasis or Suede any harm. Gene reminds me more of the Pet Shop Boys. Both are about the journey from the suburban to the urban, from the mundane to the urbane. And like Neil Tennant, Martin writes in conversational snatches that are every bit as compelling as a crossed line. But I like Gene most because of what they don't remind me of – *lads*.

'We're not afraid of art. We're not afraid of appearing intelligent. We're not a lad's band. A lot of men don't know where to sit themselves – they're unsure of what they should be. I think the heterosexual community is quite scared.'

Do you want to scare people Martin?

'Oh, not at all. I want to take them all to my firm bosom. I'm sure some people are frightened by the fact that I can talk about party politics or gay politics without a single blush. And if that scares people, so be it.'

Sadly, it be so. The queerbashing school of music journalism is after Martin already. You see, if you're not a lad then you must be … Martin gets called 'camp' a lot. For some journalists this is meant as an insult. For others it's politesse.

'I find it quite mysterious because I don't actually consider myself to be camp at all.'

I think you are in one way. You're very mannered, very affected.

'I wouldn't say it's affected. I do consider my words carefully. I like my brain to work before my mouth, but I didn't go to some

Charles Hawtrey-run camp finishing school. But as you say, camp is used because I'm not an out and out lad and I cross my legs and use long words and I've said that I've had gay relationships. Camp is a code word for queer. That's obvious. I see through it and I'm sure I'm not the only one.'

There's another word that's levelled at Gene a lot – 'English'. It throws Martin a bit, what with him being Welsh and everything; 'I know what they're pointing at but I really don't see us as quintessentially English or British. There are references in the songs to London – which is inevitable because I live here.' But just as camp is used as a code – so being branded 'English' lumps Gene in with the tradition of The Kinks, The Smiths and Pet Shop Boys. All of whom revel in those typically 'English' traits of embarrassment, feyness, awkwardness, shyness and not really cutting it as a man. Just like Gene.

'I have very strong opinions on human sexuality. I believe it's nurture not nature – everyone has the propensity for homosexual and heterosexual desire and everyone can *float* both ways. And I do. I've had heterosexual and homosexual relationships but I refuse to give myself a name. I'm not trying to create a mystique. I'm trying to do the opposite. I'm trying to be very clear about my views about sexuality because it's a very important subject – but I refuse to call myself anything because I don't . . . I would like to see the day where the terms homosexual, bisexual, heterosexual become unnecessary . . .'

I'm just about to yawn and do my 'but you must realize how necessary these identities are to people now' spiel when Martin adds: 'But I realize that they are politically very necessary. And I would never dare say that's wrong because it so obviously isn't.'

He's sharp is our Martin. And he's closer to the Buzzcocks' Pete Shelley or Ray Davies than he is to Morrissey – finding that labels really don't fit as opposed to just fleeing from them.

'I understand that some people are going to think "Oh, another guitar pop star trying to create this illusion and this mystique so he can have a little bit of gay kudos" and it's not that at all. I wouldn't dare be that patronizing.'

Let's not start on Suede just yet. Brett may have queered pop's pitch – in a way even he couldn't have schemed – but bisexuality has always occupied a problematic position in pop. It's been *used*. Many will think you're either a lying straight or a lying queen.

'Yes. But I'm not lying. I am often attracted to men, there is no lie there. This is my sexuality. I enjoy women and I enjoy men.'

What do you enjoy about men? Physically?

'Oh, that's far too candid. I wouldn't say what I liked about women so ... '

Oh, go on. Describe your ideal man then people can write in and say, 'Hey, that's me – any chance of a shag, Martin?'

'A man with a brain. Of course. Nice feet and a sense of cleanliness. Umm. I've had girlfriends. There was one person who you could class as a boyfriend – this was around sixteen. And I've had the odd fling since ... '

How odd?

'Not as odd as MPs. But my sexual contacts on both sides are quite few. I've had relationships. Probably a few more with women than with men. But I'm quite self-sufficient. I have a very small group of friends who I love dearly. So I always have someone I can ring at five a.m. and say "tell me I'm not all bad".'

That's odd. Most of your songs are about wanting love. For many gay men that's an obsession and one that's rarely fulfilled.

'Well, it's very hard to fulfil in today's climate. Gay men are often misrepresented as a bunch of screaming queens who go to Kinky Gerlinky, have several relationships a week and like dance music.'

I know. Isn't it fab?

'That's a certain part of the community, the most visible part and it's ... very good fun obviously. But there are still a lot of people who have homosexual urges who would like to be given a chance to fulfil them but don't really have a clue about how to go about it – where to go, who to meet, how ... and never will.'

Martin paraphrased the lyrics to The Smiths' 'The Boy With The Thorn In His Side' just then. Ooh spooky! Did the young Martin Rossiter know where he was going and how to get there?

'Yes, I saw that world; you see the most obvious side, you see gay pop stars, you see a party atmosphere. And it had a certain attraction, as did many other clans that I saw. But I never really wanted to fit in any of them – I wanted to be an occasional visitor . . . with an access-all-areas pass.'

A visitor not a tourist?

'Oh certainly not a tourist. A participator rather than just a voyeur.'

Let's not start on Suede just yet. Martin says he sometimes writes in character. His lyrics are also pretty much a gender free zone – but like Ray Davies, Pete Shelley, Morrissey, Neil Tennant *et al.* he usually expresses the kind of sentiments I can only imagine a man singing to another man. Funny isn't it?

'"Left Handed" is a song about, well, about not being straight. But it also has this line, "I'll find my feet and I'll choose my own name", which is very important to me. That's a very personal, possibly the most personal line that I've written in any song.'

My favourite line of yours is in 'Sick, Sober and Sorry': 'For one taste of a good man I would die.'

'It's actually preceded by the words, "And she said . . . ".'

So? I call lots of my friends 'she' and they're not all women.

'Well, I won't deny you that pleasure but it's actually very close to a conversation that I had with someone at the Tower of London. Sorry to disappoint.'

Bad men taste better, I've found . . .

'I'll take your word for it. I've never come across a bad man . . . '

One all! Hero worship's a constant theme in Gene's songs. In 'Olympian', 'Haunted By You' and 'Be My Light, Be My Guide', is it not?

'Yes, it is. To a taxi driver . . . "So take me home driver and make me more wise".'

I thought that was a sexual metaphor.

'No.'

Say it is . . .

'No.'

Hang on, you're asking a taxi driver to be your light, be your guide . . .

'There was a degree of irony there.'

Why on earth are you singing to a taxi driver???

'Well, taxi drivers are always convinced that they're glowing orbs of knowledge. The character is fairly desperate and the fact that he's talking to a cabbie simply indicates how desperate he is.'

Fine. Martin's also written the 'Smalltown Boy' for the Nineties – 'Sleep Well Tonight'.

'That's one of the few songs that is fairly, no, that is totally autobiographical. It simply is about Watford. The violence that goes with towns – all those signs that people give off – and walking into the wrong pubs! I was in one once with a friend and we both had bomber jackets on – which caused great offence. Without any warning a barstool came hurtling across the pub. We were too worried to leave. We just sat there and this stunted little man came up ten minutes later and said, "Do you want a knife in your guts?" And we both said, "No, thank you very much" in unison, finished our drinks and left.'

Martin, bless him, still manages to bring extreme reactions out in people. ('Love him or hate him, journalists can't stop writing clichés about him.') I myself spent a few months when, to paraphrase Jake La Motta, 'I didn't know if I should fight him or fuck him.' But then I saw the light and decided to worship him in a hero kinda way. If that's alright with you Martin?

'I think it's a strength to admire people and to find allies in this world.'

Thanks. So, err ... do you think there's an element of latent homosexuality in male fans' relations with you?

'I think they all fancy Steve.'

Is that your way of evading the question?

'Yes.'

But why do adolescent boys form these extreme emotional attachments to male stars like yourself?

'I think a degree of empathy certainly does exist, they feel they're part of a gang – but a good gang. The gang that made the Wicked Witch of the West melt.'

Right, let's start on Suede now. It's easy to knock. So I will. Martin has got all the things that Brett lacks – wit, warmth, charm, style, intelligence, handsomeness, a cock the size of a baby's arm (I'll hazard a guess) and the 'best new band in Britain' – yes, really – behind him. You see, pop is all about belief. And pop stars are modern myths. Some we choose to believe in. Others we don't. Back when I was a kid I was – and still am – quite prepared to accept that Ziggy Stardust really had just dropped in from outer space. But when I look at David Bowie these days I can't believe he's anything but a wanker. Same with Brett. Do you know what I mean?

But I believe in Gene. And so should you. They've turned me into a hopeless, fawning fan for the first time since, ooh, the last time. Like so many others I'm desperate for them to succeed.

'I do sense that a lot of people are leaving a lot of hope on our shoulders and . . . *good!* Because I think we will succeed.'

Martin, don't let me down. Please.

'I'll do my best.'

Good.

Gay Times, March 1995

Chapter thirty-seven

Three Little Words:
Pet Shop Boys

'If I had my way this would have happened much sooner,
but until that day,
it was only a rumour.'
'Was It Worth It?'

SINCE they released their fourth album, *Very*, last September the Pet Shop Boys have had a pretty hectic twelve months. They've released four singles. They've worked with Jennifer Saunders and Dawn French on the charity single Absolutely Fabulous (Neil Tennant said they only agreed to do it so they could get to meet the girls). They've contributed a track to Kylie's big comeback album. They've released their third collection of remixes, *Disco 2*. They've already written and recorded four songs for their next album. And – as I write – they're locked away somewhere in London rehearsing for the *Discovery* tour of South America and Australia.

But August was a quiet month. So what was Neil doing on the front cover of that month's issue of the British gay men's lifestyle magazine, *Attitude*?

Coming out, that's what.

'I do think we have contributed to, through our music and through our videos, and the general way we've presented things, rather a lot to what you might call "gay culture",' Neil said. 'I could spend several pages discussing "gay culture", but for the sake of argument we have contributed a lot. And the simplest reason for this is that I have written songs from that point of view. What I'm saying is that I'm gay, and I have written songs from that point of view. So, I mean, I'm being surprisingly honest with you here, but those are the facts of the matter.'

This was news. Big news. But was it *really* news to anyone? I rather excitedly told a (straight) colleague in the music press, gushing to him over the phone, 'Have you heard? Have you heard?' And he just said, 'Oh, you mean he wasn't out already?' Oh well . . .

No, Neil Tennant was never out. But he was never really in the closet, either. You never saw Neil's photo in the papers with his new 'girlfriend' on his arm. In fact he even mocked those gay pop stars who do in the song 'Bet She's Not Your Girlfriend'. We all knew, and Neil, much to his credit, never denied it. It was talking about some accusations that Jimmy Sommerville once made that led to Neil's coming out. 'His view is that the entire point of being a pop star is to be a positive role model. I reject the notion of being a positive role model to anyone. I personally find that an arrogant way to think of oneself.'

Hindsight's a great thing, but I had a feeling this was coming. *Very* was dubbed 'the Pet Shop Boys' coming out album' by many, and the last year can be seen as one big lead up to coming out. In November they headlined a benefit for the British gay lobbying group Stonewall at the Albert Hall. Word has it that Boy George, who was introducing them, wanted to use the line: 'They're here, they're queer, and they're not going shopping . . . It's the Pet Shop Boys!' but was reprimanded by Neil's friend, TV personality Janet Street Porter.

The handful of interviews they did for *Very* saw Neil unusually upfront when talking about AIDS, homosexuality (in general) and the stories behind the songs, and, it seemed, edging ever closer to making some firm kind of statement. When Chris Heath's *Pet Shop Boys Versus America* appeared in February – this was an unauthorized book, remember – Neil was quoted in it as saying, 'I personally think we have a very honest approach to all of this . . . but in the media it's very difficult to discuss. There are plenty of people who live totally deceitful lives, and the Pet Shop Boys could never be accused of living totally deceitful lives . . . I think we are totally honest.' And again – though for the first time – claiming: 'I would never set myself up as a role model ... We are musicians, not politicians.'

I'd been hassling the Boys' press officer for an interview for some time. And then around April, he began saying it was quite likely, and, a little later, began adding, 'But it'll just be Neil on his own.' That's interesting, I thought. That's *very* interesting.

Back in January I met a Pet Shop Boys' fan. Not just any old fan, but one of that hard core of devoted loonies who camp outside pop stars' homes and know the stars' schedules long before they themselves do. She said that they all knew that Neil was gay. They prided themselves on knowing everything about them, and it was one of the reasons they liked him. They were not like other fans. They were mainly female, they were sensitive and intelligent, and they liked to think of themselves as being, you know, different. Me and the girl swapped gossip. She had much better stories than I did. She even told me Neil had got a new boyfriend. This was news to me. And, suddenly, *Very* made sense.

I wasn't too keen on that album at first. But now I've come to see it – and to love it – as a coda to their first three albums. *Please* and *Actually* dealt with being lost – in the big bad city essentially. *Behaviour* was more about loss; be it loss of life ('Being Boring'), loss of innocence ('Nervously') or loss of love ('Jealousy'). And *Very*, their first really upbeat album, was about finding things: about finding yourself ('Can You Forgive Her?'), but more about finding love. 'I Wouldn't Normally Do That Kind of Thing', 'One in a Million' and the gorgeous 'Liberation' were the first straightforward, non-cynical, non-unrequited love songs that the Boys had ever recorded.

'If there is a difference between this album and the albums before,' Neil told *Attitude*, 'it's simply that *Very* was written from the point of view of me being in love. It's a diary of a relationship.' If love be the food of music, play on. Or something. It's not too wild a speculation to suppose that Neil's finding love gave him the strength to finally come out. A decision at once personal and political? *Very* Pet Shop Boys.

Sadly, though, the interview didn't reveal much about how the Pet Shop Boys have contributed to 'gay culture', or tell us which songs or videos or ways of presenting themselves Neil feels have contributed the most. But we did get a little sexual history. 'I didn't want to be gay in any way. I didn't really like what I saw of the gay way of life, and I certainly didn't want to be part of it. Then in the Eighties, I realized that I was probably gay. I mean, by then I knew what I was attracted to. But I didn't really have a proper affair with anyone until about three or four years ago, really. For most of the Eighties I was, well, not exactly celibate, but not far from it.

'I've never wanted to be part of this separate gay world. I know a lot of people will not appreciate hearing me say that. But when people talk about the gay community in London, for instance, what do they really mean by that? There is a community of interests, particularly around the health issue, but beyond that what is there really? There's nightclubs, drugs, shopping, PAs by Bad Boys Inc. Well ... I'm sorry but that isn't really how I define myself. I don't want to belong to some narrow group or ghetto. And I think that if they're really honest a lot of gay people would say that they felt like that as well.'

Neil was apparently not too happy with the interview, and most of all with how the story was fed out to other publications. *Attitude*'s press release asked the hysterically vacuous question: 'How will the Pet Shop Boys' loyal fans react now that Neil Tennant has said those three little words – "I am gay"?' The 'scoop' was leaked to *The Sunday Times*, which effectively broke the story.

A mutual friend told me Neil was furious that *Attitude* had given the story to a Murdoch paper – News International also owns the virulently homophobic papers *The Sun* and *The News of the World*. Just one month before, *The News of the World* had run a particularly callous full-page story headlined 'Pet Shop Boy's Grief as Gay Pal Dies of AIDS.' ('The gay pal that Pet Shop Boys' star Chris Lowe shared a home with for five years has died of AIDS'). In a two-page spread, *The Sunday Times* argued that 'Tennant's admission reflects a growing view that open homosexuality may not now mean the sudden end of a brilliant career. In fact the reverse may be the case: gay artists may even have a commercial advantage. Tennant's admission will give the Pet Shop Boys much free publicity and an ever larger fan club – including more of those wallet heavy pink pounders ... What is there to lose? Nothing. It is now an advantage and Tennant will probably have cause to be gay in both senses of the word.'

Oh *p-lease!*

Despite their disgusting – and laughable – inference that Neil's decision was both financially beneficial and financially motivated, *The Sunday Times* proved exactly the opposite: as an out gay star Neil can now expect a lot of homophobic garbage to start coming his way. The whispers may be over, but now the screams can begin.

For a pop star to do what Neil has now done – to come unequivocally out of their own volition while they're at the peak of both their creative powers and commercial popularity – is still tragically rare. For a man who has built his career on a love of artifice and playfulness, to be so matter of fact was, one could argue, *not* very Pet Shop Boys. What it was, though, was very brave. And it's for this reason that I, for one, am very proud of our Neil.

Outrage (Australia), November 1994.

Chapter thirty-eight

Us Boys Together Clinging: One Night in a Gay Club

IT'S 1991 or 1992. Which seems like a hundred years ago now. Half eleven on Sunday morning and I'm in church with the rest of the sinners. I've been here for eight hours now and I'm beginning to lose it. I haven't danced since they played Zero B's 'The Lock Up'. Everybody danced then. It's one of our favourite records right now. We all go mad for it. Pummel dancing like big, tough men for the fast and furious bits. Then going all gooey, throwing our heads back and tickling the air when the girlie synth lines come in. I'm going to sit down for a bit. The music got really heavy a while back. I'm not too keen on this stuff. It's too brutal, too stark.

Right now I want to rest so I can dance at the end. They always turn the lights on for the last record. It'll be another of those songs we go mad for. Maybe Mombassa's 'Cry Freedom' like last week. Then we'll clap the DJs and clap each other and start screaming for just one more record. All of us looking completely fucked and none of us giving a fuck.

The whole club is one big dance-floor so walking through it takes ages. On I go. Past the serious muscle boys in their corner, all so pumped up all they can do is twitch their hands. Past the bar selling bottles of Spa and soft drinks for £2. Past the heavier dealers, all looking slightly more scary than they did a few hours ago. Make a hopeless attempt to look sexy as I walk past this spoony boy I fancy. When he winks at me I'm so completely thrown I have to keep on walking. Past some friends on the stairs. We kiss and talk in this sign language we've developed. It's not the noise that makes us use it, it's just that sometimes it's difficult for us to put a sentence together. One of them's been really caning it. He's rushing on his fourth E and can't stop his jaw chattering and it's doing my head in. They're still up. I'm a bit knackered. Into the room upstairs where people go to chat or when they feel monged. I sit down on the floor. Take my cigarettes out of the back pocket of my jeans. They're crushed flat and soggy with sweat. Take my bottle of Spa out of the other pocket. Right now there's more water coming off the ceiling. I'll have to go and refill the bottle in the ladies in a bit. They're still turning the cold tap off in the gents. This girl comes in and sits down next to me. A few hours ago I could have talked to anyone but the E's wearing off and now all I feel is fuzzy. 'Alright?' she says with a big grin. I can only manage, 'Mmmm'. 'Good 'ere, innit?' I nod back trying to signal my disinterest. She asks my name and tells me hers. 'I've never been to a gay club before.' I kind of knew she was going to say that. I smile. 'You with your boyfriend?' I say I haven't got one. 'Oh ... you on the pull then?' Not really. There's a big pause. She's staring into my face, just inches away, grinning like a mad thing. She thinks and then she says to me – dead serious question – 'Why are gay people so nice?' I just smile and say 'practice'.

Rewind twenty-four hours. You're all hyper wishing you could be there right now. You pray for Saturdaytime to whizz by, so it does. You might go somewhere first but you're only killing time. In the car on the way here someone's playing a tape of Smokin' Jo's set from a few weeks back. You pull up outside just after three but it still takes ages to get in. Queuing for an hour, then another half an hour for the cloakroom. You only get to show off your new John Richmond top while you're waiting. Most people strip down soon after they get in. It gets too hot to wear anything on top so we all make sure what's on show looks good. Hairless chests, nice tits, great (short) hair. Tattoos, some piercings, a few goatees. The waistband of your Calvins visible above your coloured jeans. Necklaces and pendants, GI dog tags, loads of rings, the right boots.

Get an E down your neck the minute you've got down those stairs. Can't relax till you come up and know you haven't been sold any shit. That stuff you had last time was really snidey. Another one, whenever. Maybe more. Some speed or acid to keep you going. The trip will make things more amusing. The speed will make the sex nice and dirty if you cop off. There's a few optional extras. Some girl's handing out Sudafed like sweets. An air steward friend hands you a miniature bottle of Jack Daniels he nicked from work and laughs. Everyone's told you ketamine's disgusting but you're still dying to try it. You'll have some puff later. It'll just get passed to you. Same as the poppers. When you're on E a good snort can send you spinning right out of it and even if it's a bit too much it'll all be over in a minute. Some boys just do whizz ('you know where you are with speed') and some boys just do acid ('well it's cheap and cheerful, isn't it?'). And some boys you know got into smack, but you don't see them out anymore. This boy who's HIV has been put on Temazepam by his doctor but he doesn't like them so he passes them on – 'Tell the doctor they're not working,' his friend tells him. 'Ask for the ten mil . . . the eggs.' And every month there's some new thing some kid swears will make you rush again or bring your E back up. Nurofen, Diet Pepsi, tequila slammers, Olbas Oil, Vicks Vaporub.

These little secret rituals bond us together. Giving boys Olbas Oil blowbacks or smearing Vicks on their tits. Gently blowing on someone's face or spitting a fountain of water over them to cool them down. Kissing boys' lips or twisting their nipples as you bounce past. Trying to freak out your friends when they're tripping. Trekking off to the toilet and looking in the mirror. You're captivated by your own reflection. You think you look so beautiful with your big eyes and glowing skin. You wait here for ages. Boys come out of the cubicles two by two. Others pour out in gangs, Keystone Kops style. Some have been snorting speed. Others having sex.

We've got more words to describe how we feel than Eskimos have for snow. We can explain the difference between Phase Fours and Snowballs, or New Yorkers and Rhubarb and Custards, 'til you beg for mercy. You get asked, 'Are you alright?' a hundred times tonight. You could go into detail but usually just give the answer, 'Fab . . . I'm off my tits.' Or, if you're really cunted, just 'Fuck'. If you feel bad – which is often – some stranger will always see you through ('You been sick? Ahh, baby . . . '). In so many gay clubs people only talk to their friends or people they fancy. But here we talk to everyone. Maybe because tonight we're everybody's friend and we fancy everyone.

'Have you come up yet?' 'No? Ha! Just you wait'. Here we go. The rush sneaks up on you. You feel like you're going to fall over, like you might puke at any moment, but it's still glorious. You have to sit down or lean against a wall. 'Are you alright?' You raise your eyes, breathe out really loudly and give a twisted, conspiratorial smile. Then you pull your friend to you and cuddle for a bit. So glad you're here.

There's nowhere else anything like this place. The club itself is our star. And like any star it has some great rumours. Someone will always assure you that some boy collapsed here last week or some dealer had his face shot off outside. Or that the police are going to raid it tonight or that this is the last week 'cause the council's withdrawn its licence. There's a constant turnover of people. You can't do this regularly for long. Other people spend the weekend recovering from the week. We spend the week recovering from the weekend. Some keep going until Monday morning, only popping back for a shower and a change of clothes. What will you do when it closes at noon? Up the stairs and out blinking into the real world. You put your sunglasses on and ignore the shouts from the mini-cab drivers lying in wait. Drive out to the Vauxhall Tavern and scare all the clones. Then on to one of those places where – thanks to the buffet meal included in the ticket price (which no one touches) – you can carry on dancing until the next club opens in the evening. Some are going mad after being stuck behind a desk all week. But a lot of us don't have the kind of jobs you have to be up for in the morning. We're waiters or barmen or air stewards. Or we sign on or deal or do rent. And some people, well you just don't ask what they do. It's always more fun when a gang of us pile back to someone's house. Coming down, chain smoking, skinning up, drinking tea and chatting. Noticing who's missing and trying to figure out which boy he slinked off with. This mate who deals gives us all another half. It helps put off that dreadful moment of loss when you realize you feel normal again.

But right now you feel like you've just melted. You're over your rush. You can't really describe what it feels like. The same as you can't describe what it feels like being in love – most of all to someone who's never been in love. You can't stop yourself from dancing. Total joy. Euphoria and empathy. Ecstasy. All the shit disappears and nothing matters but the beauty of being right here, right now. E makes us confident without being arrogant, and it made that scourge of the gay scene, 'attitude', a stranger to this club. Here there's a real sense of belonging, of community. Coming here did me at least as much good as coming out. For a few hours you could glimpse the future – see a different way of doing things – a sort of communism of the emotions. And sometimes you wondered, 'why can't it be like this all the time?' You liked people more – yourself included. Of course we didn't really 'love everybody'. There were some people that, no matter how many drugs we or they had taken, would always be 'vile', 'naff' or 'sad'. But even they couldn't phase us.

I started crying here one time. It was nearly noon and I'm dancing and tripping and looking round at everybody smiling and looking so beautiful and it suddenly hits me that no one in the history of the world could have felt as good as we did right then or could have had this much fun. Or maybe I just knew that my life couldn't get any better.

And we're such drug pigs. All of us running around with more chemicals inside us than your average Boots. Restraint? Repression? The real world? No thank you. Release? Yes please. We're gonna have as much fun with our bodies as we want. And we always want more. Have you got enough for another E? A trip's only three quid. But all you can find are Smileys and they're just *so* pissy. Ask a friend for a line of speed? Some rich queen's bound to start flashing her coke about. You could get something on tick or try and convince your dealer that, even though you've got pupils like saucers, you never came up on that E he sold you.

The place is heaving now. Behind me is a wall of muscle. Sweat dripping off those beautiful bodies, half hidden by the haze of steam and lights. All swaying in time like some gorgeous nelly army marching to trance. So many men, so little *urge*. There's all these cute boys here but you don't feel much like pulling. We're all so touchy with each other, so kind – some boy you've never met before will just come up and start massaging you neck muscles and offering you his drink; you're never sure if he means anything more. When you're at other clubs you can always tell the boys who come here by the way they dance. The dances used to slowly evolve over time. These boys dance with their forearms slicing the air, each hand keeping a different beat, or with that sexy shudder that starts in their arse and then grabs their shoulders and head. Others just throw themselves all over the place. It's not all queens, though. Some complain it's getting too straight, but pretty much anyone's welcome just so long as they've come to have a good time. There's a fortysomething acid casualty spastic dancing between this heavy dyke and a beautiful skinny black boy who's gracefully spinning round and round. And behind them there's some sweet boy who you'll next see breaking young girls' hearts on *Top of the Pops*.

All of us ensnared in the rhythm. The night starts off with bright and breezy Garage and House. Kym Sims' 'Too Blind To See It' and Degrees of Motion's 'Shine On'. But it's the surging, joyous Techno that comes a little later that we really love. Records like Hyper-go-go's 'High', TC 1991's 'Berry', E-Trax's 'Let's Rock', NRG's 'He Never Lost His Hardcore', Bump's 'I'm Rushing', Gat Decor's 'Passion', Glam's 'Hell's Party' and The Age of Love's 'Age Of Love'. They all go 'Bam bam bam BAM!' for a bit, getting harder and faster until 'Whoosh!' A bit like sex really. Gay disco had been sentimental. Ours is just mental. These are songs that speak straight to our bodies. Some, like Felix's 'Don't You Want Me?', let us mouth our desires across the dance floor. But usually if they've got words they're no more than a repeated line telling us what a fab time we're having or how great we are. There's one record, though, that's got lots of words and we all know every one of them. *The* record right now is the big 'fuck you, we're fabulous' of Clivilles and Cole's 'A Deeper Love'. This is our theme tune.

The DJ teases us by mixing Deborah singing 'deeper love, a deeper love, got a deeper love, a deeper love' into the record he's playing. Real quiet at first, then louder and louder and louder 'til we all know what's coming next. Then there's that 'Whoomph!' like a needle dragged right across the record and we're there. Here we go again ...

'Well I got love in my heart, it gives me the strength to make it through the day, pride is love, PRIDE is respect for yourself and that's why I'm not looking for . . . ' BAM! The thing explodes. We all explode. 'Now it ain't easy, but I don't need no help. I've got a strong will to survive and I call it pride, pride, PRI-I-DE . . . ' And by this time everybody's going 'Fuck! Fuck! Fuck!' Lost in one big orgasmic epiphany. You live for moments like this. Only when I'm dancing can I feel this free . . .

All us boys together clinging. Somehow managing to have a good time in these terrible times. We know the world outside is shit and that all there really is is us. Drugs are just part of the glue that joins us together. What we're really rushing off is each other.

Gay Times, September 1994

Chapter thirty-nine

What Do We Want?:
2wo Third3

Let's get the important stuff over with first, shall we? The sexy little bunny rabbit in 2/3s is called Danny. He's twenty. The one with the nice tits is twenty-two and called Victor. Lee, the rough looking but handsome singer, is from Wales. He says he's twenty-two. The boy, the body and the 'pervert' all live in London.

Victor met Lee at Heaven's Fruit Machine. They danced. They chatted. They formed a band with a bloke called Justin. Piece of piss. Last May, 2/3s won a search for a star competition in *Boyz* magazine. The prize was to work with self confessed 'big, fat, gay bastard' Tom Watkins – the man who gave the world the Pet Shop Boys, Bros and East 17. 'We want to find a new Bronski Beat, a new Erasure, a new Pet Shop Boys, a new whatever,' said Tom, 'with the emphasis on youth and being gay.'

Justin left because of 'musical differences'. And in came Danny. He'd previously worked with Tom as a 'talent scout'. There's a fourth third behind the scenes, Biff, who helps with the music. He's the cartoon character you see on all their stuff. 2/3s make breezy synth pop that's as catchy as measles, and a bit early Eighties. I think they're rather good. And you're all gay aren't you boys?

They look at their shoes. Lee smiles. Victor says he's 'very happy'. Danny says 'I'm very jolly at the weekend.'

Oh dear. How boring.

'We don't like to say because . . . ' Victor can't remember his lines. Luckily Lee leaps in. 'If you start talking about being gay and all that, people think you're making it out to be an issue. And as soon as it's an issue then it's made out to be something bad. As soon as you stop talking about it then it's going to be accepted, I find.'

I don't, but anyway, Tom's giving them and their first single 'Hear Me Calling' a big push. They could well be huge, though they might not be. They've been playing gay clubs 'but that's where a lot of people start'. 'There's points we want to get across in our lyrics,' Lee tells me. '"Best Friends" is about someone losing someone. It's about AIDS I guess. We talk about the personal ads in "Prince Albert". Obsession. Everything.'

Victor: You can make of them whatever you want. 'Been this way for years' could be 'been gay for years'. Lee: Could be 'been straight for years'.

None of them have got a Prince Albert but they've all got piercings. At a recent PA at ResErection, Lee wandered on stage wearing a Muir cap and cracking a whip. 'It's just a prop I feel comfortable with. I find it a way to let out my aggression. It gives me confidence. The whip is a dominant symbol. Things like that attract me. I like people who are domineering. Are you domineering?'

I ask the questions.

It reminded me of Soft Cell. A pervier kind of pop group. Is that something you'd like to emulate?

'I'd love it. I'm a pervert. I'm all for masturbation and watching sex. It's educational. I don't think it's a big deal. I don't mind what they say about me. I just love the attention.'

Danny's below the age of consent for gay men. But might not be by the time you read this. 'They should make it the same. You can't stop people doing it. What are they saying? People aren't responsible at sixteen? Bring it down.'

'It should be the same, then people would start thinking it's okay to be gay,' Victor replies. 'That's what I agree with. It's just equality.'

And did you all know what you wanted when you were sixteen?

'I was quite mature for my age,' says Lee, 'but I still made a lot of mistakes with the safer sex thing.'

Victor says: 'It varies. If you ask Tom, he knew what he wanted at six. I still don't know what I want.'

'I still don't get what I want,' says Lee.

'I always get what I want,' pipes Danny.

I ask if they'll tell me what they want now, and get the old 'we don't want to make a big issue of it' chestnut again. I go into one. Don't you think that at a time when the age of consent blah blah blah AIDS blah blah blah you should be making an issue of it? Don't you think it would be cute if we had a pop group with three young gay men in who were quite matter of fact and honest about their sexuality?

Headmaster has spoken. The three naughty schoolboys look at their feet again.

Victor: It's something I'd rather talk to close friends about. Danny: I think there's enough role models out there and I don't think I'm the right person to do it. Lee: The only advice I can give people about sexuality is to express yourself how you want to express yourself. I don't knock anybody for doing anything. So if that's a role model then I'm a role model. Don't get me wrong. We're all for the gay community and I know lots of people are going to disagree with me. Maybe I'll change as we go on. In *Smash Hits* already it says about us having a big gay following.

Mother, I have something to tell you, I am not as other men. I have a big gay following . . .

Lee: Yeah okay, but it says about us going out on the gay club scene. So that's a start. Victor: I think most people will think we're gay anyway. The straight guys. Girls might not. It's like everybody knew Boy George was gay but girls didn't want to believe it. Lee: Just look at us as escorts. We get paid for being a character for the night. Victor: And who knows what will happen further down the line?

Feeling seduced and abandoned once more, it's time for me to go. I say I had some other questions I haven't asked as they rested on my strange presumption that the boys were gay. Little Danny asks what they were. I tell him if they're not going to answer them, I'm not going to ask them. 'Oh please,' he pleads, 'tell me. Tell me. I want to know what's coming . . . '

They're such nice boys, I'd really love to help. But even I don't know what'll happen further down the line.

Gay Times, March 1994

Chapter forty

A Year in the Death of Freddie Mercury: Queen

It's the same old song,
but with a different meaning since you've been gone.

The Four Tops, 'It's The Same Old Song'

November 1991

Though no one's now exactly sure when Freddie Mercury died, the moment his death was announced the battle began to claim him. He'd spent the last weeks of his life being hounded by the press ('What are you trying to hide Freddie?' one tabloid headline had screamed just days before), now they came to bury and to praise him. They curbed their homophobia but heterosexualized his story – homing in on his parents' grief and that of 'the woman in his life', Mary Austin. If he'd been knocked down by a truck perhaps things might have been different but the fact that he'd died from an AIDS-related illness made the fact of his homosexuality – a subject he himself had always been vague about – unavoidable.

After the Elton John debacle five years ago, the tabloids learned that turning a much loved celeb into a hate figure is never easy, and kicking a man when he's down – even if he is a 'poof' – loses sales quicker than you can say 'Hillsborough'. The venom isn't unleashed for a couple of days when the columnists, whose function it is to annoy, have their go. 'Don't cry for killer Freddie,' contended some gobshite on *The Sport*, 'he was a menace to society, a raging poofter who spread his killer virus with characteristic gay abandon. If he were a dog he'd have been put down years ago.' Which, I think, means poofters should be put down because they kill poofters who we'd rather kill ourselves. Or something.

And thus begins his gay-ification. Quotes like this are carefully interwoven into the obituaries in the pink press, painting him as the first man to be martyred *after* his death. BBC2 clears its schedule on the Monday evening to air a special programme about Freddie. There's lots of clips of Queen intercut with a parade of the great and the good from the rock and roll hall of fame saying variations on 'He was a smashing bloke – I'll miss you mate'. At the end they premiere the video for the single, 'These Are The Days Of Our Lives', which is to be rush released with all profits going to the Terrence Higgins Trust. In Queen terms the film is simplicity itself – an emaciated and heavily made-up Freddie singing in the studio. He looks straight into the camera, a rare sight on video, and right at the viewer. Here is a man who knows he probably hasn't long to live singing about how glorious life can be. The pretty, if somewhat slight, song is made painfully moving by recent events and I start crying. Suddenly I like him immensely. He looks proud, defiant, brave, noble. Remember me this way?

December

When 'Days' is released it turns out to be a double A-side with 'Bohemian Rhapsody', effectively relegating the former to the B-side. If the aim is to raise money for the THT, putting this evergreen if execrable 'classic' on top is sensible. Entering the chart at number one, it stays there over Christmas, soon becoming the biggest selling single in the UK ever.

In the interests of variety, TV shows occasionally play the video for 'Days'. But it's been bowdlerized. In place of Freddie's soliloquy there's now a grotesque boy-meets-girl cartoon and some footage of the group 'in their prime'. The song is de-gayed, the new film de-AIDS it. Someone didn't want us to remember Freddie that way.

January 1992

I'm waiting in a gay pub in Soho for a friend who's always late. Last time I was here I swear all they played was Kylie, but tonight all they play is Queen. This has never happened before. Some of the songs are curiously affecting. He's ours now, maybe more because of how he died than how he lived.

February

EMI, Queen's record company, announce record profits for the final quarter of 1991, boosted mainly by Queen sales. They are the biggest selling act in both the album and singles category. The company deny that they'd been gearing up for a Christmas blitz long before Mercury's illness had been officially announced and that they'd sent a memo to record store managers to reserve shelf space in the event of his death. The re-release of 'Bohemian Rhapsody' raised over a million pounds for the THT, helping them out of a major financial crisis.

April

A Freddie Mercury Tribute concert is staged at Wembley Stadium on Easter Monday. It's billed as a night of 'AIDS Awareness' but isn't really. Rank homophobes and heavy metallurgists Guns 'n' Roses make an incongruous appearance. When they play, a threatened protest is inaudible above the deafening cheers. They make no attempt at apology or explanation, and mark themselves out as the only performers who make no mention of Freddie, Queen or AIDS.

At the grand finale all the stars troop back on stage. Elton John puts his arm round Guns 'n' Roses singer A×1 Rose. A gesture caused perhaps less by an uncontrollable groundswell of affection than that this is what one does at such events. Whatever, A×1 looks extremely uncomfortable. It's unlikely that he's the only person in the vast stadium who loved Freddie but hates faggots.

Liza Minnelli is wheeled on as a surprise guest to belt out the penultimate number, 'We Are The Champions'. Queen's inclusion of this song in their set at Live Aid had moved me to vomit, but here it works. Finally a picture of Freddie looking brilliantly batty in ermine and a crown is thrown up on the huge video screens as Brian May plucks away at 'God Save The Queen'. A nice touch. I want to throw my cap in the air and shout 'Hooray!' like happy people used to in *The Beano* – God save that queen.

May

The first of a great batch of books about Freddie start rolling in. I scour them for stuff on Freddie the homo. There were a couple of songs: 'Killer Queen', 'My Fairy King', 'Good Old Fashioned Lover Boy', 'Man On The Prowl', 'The Great Pretender', but only if you squint your eyes and the wind's blowing in the right direction.

The last songs appeared more autobiographical: 'The Show Must Go On', 'These Are The Days Of Our Lives', 'I'm Going Slightly Mad'. They all came from the last Queen album *Innuendo* – which was pretty much all he gave us in his music. He used to open concerts by running through the first few bars of 'Let Me Entertain You' from *Gypsy* – now there's a gay song.

In the Seventies he was all flowing shirts, long hair and painted nails, a look that in the context of Glam wasn't that outrageous. In 1980 he began spending much of his time in big, butch Munich and his style changed accordingly. He cropped his hair, grew a moustache and was often photographed in a Muir cap and a Mineshaft t-shirt. On that year's concert dates fans would bombard the stage with disposable razors. The album *Hot Space* was the first that showed the influence of Disco. It dutifully bombed in the States and their career never really recovered from this nadir over there.

It's an interesting pointer to arguably the first time that a 'butch' look would be read by many as being 'obviously gay'. The razors show the English obsession with wishing gay men weren't quite so obvious about it, but no one seriously objected. Here they were also a pop group, whereas in the States their main fan base was a rock one – they could cope with a bit of silly campery and campish prog rock, but a faggoty look and more faggoty music was box office BO. The British have always been more sensible about such things. 'Everyone in Britain thought the video was just a laugh,'

Brian May said of the one they made for 'I Want To Break Free', in which all four members dragged up, 'but in America they hated it and thought it was an insult.' Damn Yankees ...

June

Gay Pride in London attracts a record-breaking 100,000 people. It closes with a spectacular firework display. The rockets fizz, flash, boom and bang to a soundtrack of Queen numbers. Queen? Gay? Pride? Six months on it would seem so.

July

The simultaneous release of the album and the video *Queen Live at Wembley '86* sees them both going straight in at number one. With hindsight we can be pretty sure Mercury found out that he was HIV-positive around the time this was recorded, and that the Knebworth concert soon after was planned as his undeclared farewell to the stage. On the record you hear him shout between numbers 'We're going to play together until we fucking well die. I'm sure of it.' I increasingly find things he did when alive give me that special chill.

August

'Barcelona', the song he was commissioned to write for the opening ceremony of the Olympics is unceremoniously dropped. They say it's because he can't perform the duet with Montserrat Caballe in person. But the games are all about health and efficiency, joy through strength, so who wants to be reminded of a disease like *that* at a time like *this*?

EMI re-release it all the same and it peaks at number two, six places higher than it reached five years ago.

September

The three remaining members of Queen issue a statement denying that April's Wembley concert lost money. It grossed £2 million in ticket sales but after 'production costs' were deducted a puny

£73,000 is left. Rumours abound that much of the profits that were to go to AIDS charities, were, quite literally, gobbled up by the lavish backstage arrangements.

To mark the silver anniversary of Radio One, listeners are invited to vote for their favourite record of all time. The winner is 'Bohemian Rhapsody'. Queen now look like the biggest and best-loved band in the country. If Freddie's death made him ours, it also made him huge.

October

Brian May puts out his first solo album, trailed by the single 'Too Much Love Will Kill You'. I can't believe it. I can't believe the Mercury-esque vocal intro. I can't believe the title. I can't believe the sentiment. Too much love will kill you? With friends making tributes like this who needs the tabloids?

November

Have you ever been watching the telly with a friend and someone famous comes on and you go 'He's a poof' and your friend scoffs and asks how you know and you realize how puny all your 'evidence' sounds so you end up going 'I just know. I just know'. Freddie Mercury was like that. We just knew. Just.

His death from Aids made an ambiguous star unambiguous. In these cruel times dying was the gayest thing he ever did. It changed everything he ever did and everything he ever said. But he was still a cipher on which we could project the Freddie we want; saint, sinner, martyr or murderer. It made him at once one of us and 'one of them'. Julie Burchill once reviewed a Queen single by saying 'No one can honestly say they've never liked a Queen song. You haven't? What, even when you were drunk?'

Perhaps the world is drunk?

Gay Times, January 1993

Afterwords

Bad?

And then Peter Pan got married ...

Being Boring

Andy Bell liked the interview so much he cancelled his subscription to *Gay Times* and Mute Records stopped advertizing in the magazine. Lots of Erasure fans wrote and told me how evil I was. All of them in felt tip. Good job they never saw the first draft. A week after the piece appeared I got a call from a publisher asking if I'd be interested in writing a biography of a pop group. Can you guess which one? Can you guess what I said?

Blaming it on the Boogie

Jason Donovan: My part in his downfall. No, come to think of it, I daren't.

Cock Rock

One of the photos purporting to be of Marky Mark in his full glory turned up on the Internet (although it could have been a fake). An activist from OutRage! pulled it off the Net and it was used as a placard ('Not just a tiny mind') when the group zapped a signing Mark gave in London to promote his hilarious *Marky Mark Workout* video in January 1994. Marky had said lots of nice gay-friendly things in interviews – telling *The Face* (November 1992); 'Yo! If you're gay, you're in the house, just don't do that shit around me! Don't try to fuck me! Bring your sister though, you can watch!' (How *Faust*!) – but he kept fucking up. Just one month later he appeared on *The Word* with the rapper Shabba Ranks. After a filmed interview with Buju Banton, who'd made the notorious 'Boom By By' single (which advocated shooting lesbians and gay men), Ranks said: 'I'm supportive of what he said. Too many people are doing what they want, living how they want and wanting freedom of speech . . . you deserve crucifixion.' Co-presenter Mark La Marr (a major-league chap) barked back: 'That's absolute crap and you know it!' Marky wouldn't condemn what Ranks had just said and later joined him on stage for a song. In 1993 a number of homophobic comments and actions were attributed to Mark, as well as some youthful misdemeanours. Each was followed by an apology. The idea that he might have been a queerbasher probably caused an extra erotic frisson for some gay men. But when we saw the 'Not just a tiny mind' pictures it was all over.

Yo dear!

Getting Away With It

The public soon tired of the joke. Right Said Fred's comeback single and album, *Sex and Travel*, sunk without a trace.

The God that Failed?

For a reappraisal of how I feel about Morrissey five years on, see 'Jigsaw Puzzle', *Gay Times*, January 1995.

Hope I Get Old Before I Die

Since this piece was written we've also lost Peter Allen, Leigh Bowery, Bruce Carlton, Miles Davis, Eazy E, Kenny Everett, Walter Gibbons, Donna (Peter) Giles, Dan Hartman, Shakespear Kangwena, Kris Kirk, Shepherd Mangama, David Mankaba, Freddie Mercury, Jacques Morali, Tom Morley, Sharon Redd and Vaughan Toulouse.

Little Town Flirt

Brett was to have done a separate interview for *Gay Times*, but after he took part in 'The Maker Great Sex Debate' wasn't so sure. I got a 'phone call from Suede's press officer, Phil Savidge, saying Brett would now do the interview together with Simon Gilbert; 'the only member of the band who's actually gay'. And I thought: 'so why's he only just come out?' After the debate and 'Ambisexuality' appeared in *Melody Maker* (12 December 1992), Brett and Simon decided they didn't want to talk to me at all.

I was wrong though – there weren't more difficult questions to come for Brett. He just got asked time and again for his thoughts about what I'd said. Tony Parsons even asked David Bowie what he thought of my views on Suede in *Arena* (May/June 1993). This gave me such a big kiddy thrill. David also debated it with Brett in *NME* (20 March 1993). They didn't like it much. I'm sure Brett got bored of the question. I certainly started getting bored with Brett. Phil Savidge won *Music Week*'s Press Officer of the Year award in 1993 for his work on Suede.

Murmuring

Michael Stipe gave a number of interviews for REM's next album *Monster*. Asked by *The Guardian* (27 September 1994) how he thought the rumours he was HIV-positive had started Michael said: 'I'm skinny, got bad skin. I've always been a little hard to pin down sexually, I've got funny hair. I write non-gender specific songs. I wore a hat that said "White House Stop AIDS". I wrote a record about death, didn't talk to the press. It all kinda adds up.' By 1995 Stipe was saying he was bisexual.

Pink Vinyl

In 1995 PWL (Pete Waterman Limited) made a move for a slice of the big pink cake by launching a fag-friendly dance subsidiary, Icon. Their first release was Trade DJ Tony De Vit's gorgeously girlie slice of pumpin' Euro, 'Burning Up', which went Top Thirty in March. See my interview with Tony, 'The New Kylie?' in *Capital Gay*, 24 February 1995

Preaching to the Perverted

No they did not. That's why they're not here. I interviewed him in the summer of 1993, told him all about Queercore (I was going to see Sister George straight afterwards) and asked him if he felt part of any movement. He said perhaps Industrial. He just jumped on the bandwagon as he had a new album to promote. I'll send you a copy of the tape if you want. Okay? Just for the record I also tried to sort out a distribution deal for him and tried to get his band featured on Radio One. Considering all the crappy things he later said about me I think that was rather nice of me, don't you? And if you've no idea who I'm talking about, you're not meant to.

What Do We Want?

The band went ballistic after the interview appeared. Manager Tom Watkins 'phoned me up and shouted and swore at me for ten minutes. The band wrote a letter to *Gay Times* (May 1994) which repeated what Tom had told me on the 'phone and said that 'being gay is a fact in our lives'. Somewhat ironically the letter also outed Neil Tennant. 2wo Third3 came out properly in 1995. In a number of interviews Watkins blamed my piece for the band's lack of success – arguing that *Smash Hits* wouldn't go near them after it became known they were gay. I'd really love to think I had that power.

Selected Bibliography

Altman, Dennis. *Homosexual: Oppression and Liberation*, London, Allen
    Lane, 1971
Altman, Dennis. *The Homosexualization of America*, Boston, M.A.,
    Beacon Press, 1983
Attali, Jacques. *Noise: The Political Economy of Music*, Manchester,
    Manchester University Press, 1985
Bartlett, Neil. *Who Was That Man?: A Present for Mr Oscar Wilde*,
    London, Serpent's Tail, 1988
Beadle, Jeremy J. *Will Pop Eat Itself?: Pop Music in the Soundbite Era*,
    London, Faber and Faber, 1993
Berry, B., Buck, Peter, Mills, Mike and Stipe, Michael. *REM: The Lyrics*,
    Bootleg publication, 1995
Boy George, *Take It Like a Man*, London, Sidgwick and Jackson, 1995
Bronski, Michael, *Culture Clash: The Making of Gay Sensibility*, Boston,
    M.A., South End Press, 1984
Cohn, Nik. *Ball the Wall: Nik Cohn in the Age of Rock*, London,
    Picador, 1985
Davenport-Hines, Richard. *Sex, Death and Punishment: Attitudes to Sex
    and Sexuality in Britain Since the Renaissance*, London, Collins,
    1990
Davies, Ray. *X-Ray*, London, Viking, 1994
Dyer, Richard. *Stars*, London, BFI Publishing, 1982
Dyer, Richard. *Only Entertainment*, London, Routledge, 1992
Eliot, Karen and Home, Stewart. *Destroying the Ruins: Essays on Culture
    and Anarchy*, London, Nonesuch Press, 1992
Frank, Lisa and Smith, Paul. (eds) *Madonnarama: Essays on Sex and
    Popular Culture*, Pittsburgh, P.A., Cleis Press, 1993
Frith, Simon. *Sound Effects: Youth, Leisure and the Politics of Rock 'n'
    Roll*, London, Constable, 1983
Frith, Simon. *Music for Pleasure: Essays in the Sociology of Pop*,
    Cambridge, Polity Press, 1988

Frith, Simon. (ed.) *Facing the Music: Essays on Pop, Rock and Culture,* London, Mandarin, 1990

Frith, Simon and Goodwin, Andrew. (eds) *On Record: Rock, Pop and the Written Word,* London, Routledge, 1990

Gallaher,Bob. and Wilson, Andrew. 'Sex and the Politics of Identity: An Interview with Michel Foucault' in M. Thompson (ed.) *Gay Spirit: Myth and Meaning,* New York, N.Y., St Martin's Press, 1987

Garber, Marjorie. *Vested Interests: Cross Dressing and Cultural Anxiety,* London, Penguin, 1993

Garfield, Simon. *The End of Innocence: Britain in the Time of AIDS,* London, Faber and Faber, 1994

George, Nelson. *The Death of Rhythm and Blues,* London, Omnibus Press, 1989

Goss, Luke. *I Owe You Nothing: My Story,* London, Grafton, 1993

Heath, Chris. (ed.) *Pet Shop Boys, Annually,* Manchester, World International Publishing, 1988

Heath, Chris. *Pet Shop Boys, Literally,* London, Viking, 1990

Heath, Chris. *Pet Shop Boys Versus America,* London, Viking, 1993

Hocquenghem, Guy. *Homosexual Desire,* London, Allison & Busby, 1978

Holleran, Andrew. *Ground Zero,* New York, N.Y., William Morrow and Company, 1988

Holleran, Andrew. *Dancer from the Dance,* London, Penguin, 1990

Jackson, Michael. *Moon Walk,* London, Mandarin, 1988

Johnson, Holly. *A Bone in My Flute,* London, Century, 1994

Kadis, Alex and Ollerenshaw, Philip. *Take That in Private,* London, Virgin, 1994

Kirk, Kris. 'What a Difference a Gay Makes', *Collusion 4,* 1983

Kirk, Kris and Heath, Ed. *Men in Frocks,* London, GMP, 1984

Kureishi, Hanif and Savage, Jon (ed) *The Faber Book of Pop,* London, Faber and Faber, 1995

Lahr, John. *Automatic Vaudeville: Essays on Star Turns.* London, Methuen, 1985

Laing, Dave. *The Sound of our Time,* London, Sheed and Ward, 1969

Laing, Dave and Taylor, Jenny. 'Disco-pleasure-discourse: on "rock and sexuality"', *Screen Education,* 30 (1979), pp. 43–48

Lewis, Lisa A. *The Adoring Audience: Fan Culture and Popular Media,* London, Routledge, 1992

Liberace. *Liberace: An Autobiography,* London, W. H. Allen, 1973

McLaren, Jay. *Out Loud! The Encyclopaedia of Gay and Lesbian Recordings*, Amsterdam, Outloud Press (PO Box 11950, 1001 GZ Amsterdam, The Netherlands), 1994

McRobbie, Angela (ed.) *Zoot Suits and Second Hand Dresses: An Anthology of Fashion and Music*, Basingstoke, Macmillan, 1989

McRobbie, Angela. *Feminism and Youth Culture: From Jackie to Just Seventeen*, Basingstoke, Macmillan, 1991

Marcus, Greil. *Mystery Train: Images of America in Rock 'n' Roll Music*, London, Omnibus Press, 1977

Marcus, Greil. *Lipstick Traces: A Secret History of the Twentieth Century*, London, Secker & Warburg, 1990

Marky Mark and Goldsmith, Lynn. *Marky Mark*, London, Boxtree, 1992

Martin, Linda and Segrave, Kerry. *Anti-Rock: The Opposition to Rock 'n' Roll*, New York, N.Y., Da Capo Press, 1993

Medhurst, Andy. 'Pitching Camp', *City Limits*, 3 May 1990

Medhurst, Andy. 'That Special Thrill: Brief Encounter. Homosexuality and Authorship', *Screen*, 32:2 (1991), pp. 197–208

Peelaert, Guy and Cohn, Nik. *Rock Dreams*, London, Pan Books, 1974

Reynolds, Simon and Press, Joy. *The Sex Revolts: Gender, Rebellion and Rock 'n' Roll*, London, Serpent's Tail, 1995

Rimmer, Dave. *Like Punk Never Happened: Culture Club and the New Pop*, London, Faber and Faber, 1985

Rogan, Johnny. *The Kinks: The Sound and the Fury*, London, Elm Tree Books, 1984

Rogan, Johnny. *Starmakers and Svengalis: The History of British Pop Management*, London, Futura, 1989

Rogan, Johnny. *Morrissey & Marr: The Severed Alliance*, London, Omnibus Press, 1993

Ross, Andrew and Rose, Tricia (ed). *Microphone Fiends: Youth Music & Youth Culture*, London, Routledge, 1994

Savage, Jon. 'Androgyny', *The Face*, June 1983

Savage, Jon. *The Kinks: The Official Biography*, London, Faber and Faber, 1984

Savage, Jon. 'Tainted Love: The Influence of Male Homosexuality and Sexual Divergence on Pop Music and Culture Since the War' in Tomlinson, Alan. (ed.), *Consumption, Identity & Style: Marketing, Meanings and the Packaging of Pleasure*, London, Routledge, 1990

Shapiro, Harry. *Waiting for the Man: The Story of Drugs and Popular Music*, London, Mandarin, 1990

Sinfield, Alan. *Literature, Politics and Culture in Postwar Britain,* Oxford, Basil Blackwell, 1989

Sky, Rick. *The Take That Fact File,* London, Grafton, 1993

Slee, Jo. *Peepholism: Into the Art of Morrissey,* London, Sidgwick and Jackson, 1994

Smith, Richard. 'Frock Tactics' in Baker, Roger, *Drag: A History of Female Impersonation in the Performing Arts,* London, Cassell, 1994

Sontag, Susan. 'Notes on Camp'. In Sontag, Susan, *A Susan Sontag Reader,* London, Penguin, 1983

Steward, Sue and Garrat, Sheryl. *Signed, Sealed and Delivered: True Life Stories of Women in Pop,* London, Pluto Press, 1984

Street, John. *Rebel Rock: The Politics of Popular Music,* Oxford, Basil Blackwell, 1986

Taraborelli, J. Randy. *Michael Jackson: The Magic and the Madness,* London, Headline, 1992

Tennant, Neil (ed). *The Best of Smash Hits,* London, Emap Books, 1985

Thomas, Bob. *Liberace: The True Story,* London, New English Library, 1989

Thomson, Elizabeth and Gutman, David (ed). *The Bowie Companion,* London, Macmillan, 1993

Vaneigem, Raoul. *The Revolution of Everyday Life,* London, Rebel Press, 1983

Vermorel, Fred and Vermorel, Judy. *Starlust: The Secret Fantasies of Fans,* London, Comet, 1985

Vermorel, Judy and Vermorel, Fred. *Fandemonium!: The Book of Fan Cults and Dance Crazes,* London, Omnibus Press, 1989

Young, Jock. *The Drugtakers: The Social Meaning of Drug Use,* London, Paladin, 1971

Index